Civil Liberties
in Conflict

Civil Liberties in Conflict

E D I T E D   B Y
Larry Gostin

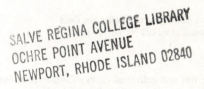

Routledge
London and New York

First published in 1988 by
Routledge
11 New Fetter Lane, London EC4P 4EE

Published in the USA
in association with
Routledge, Chapman and Hall, Inc.
29 West 35th Street, New York NY 10001

Set in 10/11pt Plantin Compugraphic by Mayhew Typesetting, Bristol
Printed and bound in Great Britain by Biddles Ltd,
Guildford and King's Lynn

British Library Cataloguing in Publication Data
Civil liberties in conflict.
   1. Civil rights
   I. Gostin, Larry O.
   323.4   JC571

   ISBN 0-415-00679-1
   ISBN 0-415-00680-5 Pbk

Library of Congress Cataloging in Publication Data
Civil liberties in conflict/edited by Larry Gostin.
     p.   cm.
   Bibliography: p.
   Includes index.
   Contents: Collective and individual rights: Towards resolving the conflict /
Larry Gostin – Rights and political conflict / John Dunn – Preserving public
protest / Denis Galligan – Trade unions and their members / Clyde
Summers – Affirmative action / Drew Days – Politics, socialism, and civil
liberties / Bernard Crick – Is there a right to stop offensive speech? /
Norman Dorsen – The spider and the fly / Stephen Sedley – Pornography, sex
discrimination, and free speech / Cass Sunstein – Pornography and free speech :
the civil rights approach / Barry Lynn – National security and freedom of
information / Sarah McCabe.
   ISBN 0-415-00679-1   ISBN 0-415-00680-5 (pbk.)
   1. Civil rights – Great Britain. 2. Civil rights – United States.
3. Civil rights – France. I. Gostin, Larry O. (Larry Ogalthorpe)
K3240.6.C58 1988
342'.085–dc19
[342.285]

Contents

Foreword by The Honorable William J. Brennan, Justice of the Supreme Court of the United States

It is an honor to share with Lord Scarman the privilege of writing a Foreword to this series of essays highlighting the conflicts of civil rights and liberties that often mark the scene in both Great Britain and the United States. Lord Scarman is the acknowledged leader among the valiants in the English-speaking world who strive most ardently for the defense of civil liberties.

Principles of liberty and justice, even of equality and fraternity, are traced by both countries to Magna Carta, "the starting point of the constitutional history of the English race;"[1] "its signing was the most important event in English history. To have produced it, to have preserved it, to have matured it, constitute the immortal claim of England upon the esteem of mankind."[2] Magna Carta, said Lord Coke, was called "the Charter of the Liberties of the Kingdom, upon great reason – because . . . it makes the people free."[3]

Magna Carta is, however, hardly a complete catalogue of the civil rights and liberties we know today. Notably, nothing in it concerned the freedom of religion, of speech, or of the press. Yet even these liberties, taken for granted today, find their root in the spirit of Magna Carta. Once it was recognized that an individual had rights against the government and that there was a domain of personal autonomy and dignity in which the government had no right to intrude, it was only a matter of time before the full range of civil rights and liberties was called forth in service of the same ideal.

There is substantial overlap in the rights and liberties protected by Great Britain and the United States. But there is one important difference between the two countries. When the Colonists formed the United States they entrenched the safeguards in a written Constitution and Bill of Rights. England has not chosen similarly to entrench them. The degree of loyalty to the great principles is nevertheless very much the same for both of us, with one notable exception. In England, the provisions of Magna Carta were originally intended, and have since been regarded, as a limitation upon the Crown and the courts, not upon Parliament. For the United States, the safeguards of the Constitution and the Bill of Rights delimit the powers of all departments of government – the legislative, as well as the executive and judicial. And in the United States, the people's chosen agent for testing actions of the legislative and executive branches against the commands of the Constitution is, ultimately, the Supreme Court. Ever since Chief Justice Marshall's holding in *Marbury* v. *Madison* that "It is emphatically the province and duty of the Judicial Department to say what the law is,"[4] the court and the country have accepted judicial review as a permanent and indispensable feature of our constitutional system. That is because judicial review has proved in the United States to be vital and indispensable for the protection of the individual's liberty in our democratic society – a society imbued with a desire to guarantee the individual's liberty under the law and his freedom from governmental oppression. When constitutionally protected rights and liberties collide, the arbiter of the conflict is thus, ultimately, the Supreme Court. In the United States, controversies over constitutional limits upon governmental powers have been with us from our national beginnings; we settle one only to have another emerge of different mien. If the form of the challenges of the future cannot be predicted with any assurance, we know it is inevitable that such challenges will emerge, and that, as in the past, the issues they create will take the form of cases and controversies. Certainly we may expect not less but greater implication of the various constitutional guarantees designed to protect individual freedom from repressive governmental action, federal and state. Of course, the federal system's diffusion of governmental power has the purpose of securing individual freedom. But this is not all the Constitution provides to secure that end. There are also explicit provisions to prevent government, state and federal, from frustrating the great design. I don't think there can be any challenge to the proposition that the ultimate protection of individual freedom is found in court enforcement of these constitutional guarantees.

But how does the Supreme Court go about adjudging conflicts between contending constitutional rights and liberties? We must keep in mind that while the words of the Constitution and the Bill of Rights are binding, their application to specific problems is not often easy. For the Founding Fathers knew better than to pin down their descendants too closely. Enduring principles rather than petty details were what they sought to write down. Thus it is that the Constitution does not take the form of a litany of specifics. There are, therefore, very few cases where the constitutional answers are clear, all one way or all the other. Particularly difficult in this regard are the cases raising conflicts between the individual and governmental power – the area increasingly requiring the court's attention. Ultimately, of course, the Supreme Court must resolve the conflicts of competing interests in these cases, but, as the essays of this volume demonstrate, all should keep in mind how intense and troubling these conflicts can be. Where one man claims a right to speak and the other man claims the right to be protected from abusive or dangerously provocative remarks, the conflict is inescapable. Where the police have ample external evidence of a man's guilt, but to be sure of their case put into evidence a confession obtained through coercion, the conflict arises between his right to a fair prosecution and society's right to protection against his depravity. Where the orthodox Jew wishes to open his shop and do business on the day which non-Jews have chosen, and the legislature has sanctioned, as a day of rest, the court cannot escape a difficult problem of reconciling opposed interests. Finally, the coming of age of the Negro citizen, politically and economically, presents a conflict between the ideal of liberty and equality expressed in the Declaration of Independence and, on the other hand, a way of life rooted in the customs of many of our people. If all can be made to appreciate that there are such conflicts, and that they require difficult choices, which in many cases mean between contending constitutional rights – if this alone is accomplished – we will have immeasurably enriched our common understanding of the meaning and significance of our freedoms, as well as having a better appreciation of the Supreme Court's function and its difficulties.

Our decisions in the racial discrimination cases have applied the Equal Protection Clause to prevent states from discriminating against citizens because of the color of their skin. Equal protection of the laws means equal protection today, whatever else the phrase may have meant in other times. In the same area of responsibility falls, I think, the series of decisions extending some of the guarantees of the first eight amendments to the states. The Bill of Rights is the primary source of expressed information as to what is meant by constitutional liberty. Its safeguards secure the climate which the law of freedom needs in order to exist. It is true that they were added to the Constitution to operate solely against federal power. But the Fourteenth Amendment was added in 1868 in response to a demand for national protection against abuses of state power. That amendment extended the protections of most of the first eight amendments against state power.

It is true, as Justice Brandeis said, that "It is one of the happy incidents of the federal system that a state may serve as a laboratory, and try novel social and economic experiments," but the Supreme

Court has concluded that this does not include the power to experiment with the fundamental liberties of citizens safeguarded by the Bill of Rights. Further, the court has concluded that to deny the states the power to impair a fundamental constitutional right is not to increase federal power, but rather to limit the power of both federal and state governments in favor of safeguarding the fundamental rights and liberties of the individual. This, I think, promotes rather than undermines the basic policy of avoiding excess concentration of power in government, federal or state, which underlies our concepts of federalism.

How conflicts such as these ought to be resolved is a question which constantly troubles our whole society. There should be no surprise, then, that how properly to resolve them often produces sharp division within the Supreme Court itself. When problems are so fundamental, the claims of the competing interests are often nicely balanced, and close divisions are almost inevitable.

The essays in this book brilliantly shape the kinds of collisions between rights and liberties of which all should be aware. Their resolution in the United States by judges one way or another almost always triggers complaint that the Supreme Court is reshaping the Constitution, is innovating, is injecting uncertainty in place of stability. But judges, unlike legislators or the executive, must explain how and why they resolve a particular conflict. That is because Americans demand of their Supreme Court what they do not ask of the executive or Congress, namely an explication of the grounds of decision, a reasoned demonstration in writing to support a result. This explication is addressed not just to judges and lawyers but also to all Americans; for when the Supreme Court has decided an important social, economic, or political issue, the grounds upon which the decision rests are important to all of us. Because of this, the American tradition has been general acceptance of the judicial role and of the decisions handed down. The most fundamental explanation of the Supreme Court's survival and prestige is that they rest on public understanding of the role and mission of the court.

I have been a participant in judicial review for more than thirty years now. This public encounter with the text of the Constitution and its amendments has been a profound source of personal inspiration. The vision of human dignity embraced there is deeply moving. It is tireless. It has inspired us for two centuries and it will continue to inspire as it continues to evolve. The Constitution with its amendments has a bright future, as well as a glorious past, for its spirit is inherent in the aspirations of all Americans.

NOTES

1 Lord Denning, *American Bar Association Journal* 51 (October 1964): 922.
2 *Hurtado* v. *California*, 110 US 516, 542 (1884).
3 Id., at 542.
4 1 Cranch 137, 177 (1803).

Foreword by The Right Honourable
The Lord Scarman OBE,
House of Lords

It is an honour overwhelming in character to join with Mr Justice Brennan in introducing this book. Human rights are built into American life by the Constitution, and protected by a court, the Supreme Court of the USA. Not so in my country. 'Human rights' is not a term of art in English law. Civil liberties – yes, our courts understand and protect them. We rely on the common law: but the common law has no constitutional protection against the inroads of the legislature. Judges are, in terms of power, subordinate to parliament. Mr Justice Brennan's approach to human rights is the pearl of great price that we have lost in the rough seas that prevail outside the world of a written constitution.

Larry Gostin and his colleagues have produced a work of real worth. They tackle a subject which lies, and will always lie, at the very heart of free societies. Put in mundane, practical terms, a free society has to find answers to two questions. In what circumstances can the citizen be required to refrain from exercising or enjoying the civil liberties guaranteed to him by law? In what circumstances may the state, through its legislative, executive, and judicial organs, restrain the citizen from the exercise of his 'inalienable' rights or the enjoyment of his civil liberties?

Different societies have differing legal mechanisms for answering these questions. The American answer is a written constitution defining the powers of the state and embodying the basic civil rights and liberties of the people. The price paid for constitutional protection is that the constitution formulates the rights it protects. In other words, the constitution sets limits to the exercise of the rights which it protects so that their exercise does not conflict with other people's rights or with the national interest.

The Fourth Amendment illustrates the point. It recognizes the citizen's right of privacy but protects it only to a limited extent: its protection is only against 'unreasonable' searches and seizures.

Some constitutional liberties, are, however, unconditional in their formulation, e.g. the First Amendment. I doubt, however, whether the courts would ever accept that freedom of the press is truly unlimited and unconditional. Liberty, like other rights, is open to abuse: and the courts of the United States are themselves, and are seen as, the mechanism established by law to relieve the citizen from abuse of power.

The French have their own legislative way of answering my two questions. The Declaration of the Rights of Man and the Citizen (1789) declares the principles of their polity. Article 4 declares that:

> Liberty consists in the power of doing whatever does not injure another. Accordingly the exercise of the natural rights of every man has not other limits than those which are necessary to secure to every other man the free exercise of the same rights: and these limits are determinable only by the law.

Article 5 declares that the law ought to prohibit any actions hurtful to society. These declarations are not mandatory in the way that American and British statutes are, but they are part of the principled basis of French law. And they keep the law responsive to the need for setting limits to the freedoms recognized by law.

It may be truly said, therefore, that the Americans and the French approach the conflict between competing rights and interests upon the basis of a constitutional definition of the extent of each competing right or liberty. And both systems leave it to the legislature and the courts to adjust limits within the principle constitutionally established.

The British have no constitutional guidance to the solution of the problem. They leave the courts to resolve the conflict unless the legislature has by statute set limits. The common law has, of course, its own inbuilt flexibility and possesses a concept, that of reasonableness, which is well suited to the task. It also recognizes the principle that no one may use his rights so as to injure another.

This glance at the American, French, and British approaches to the conflict of rights and interests in society suffices to emphasize the need for such studies as are contained in this book. The value of these essays is that they expose new sources and areas of conflict in our complex world. The reader is shown how freedom of speech and of action needs to be limited to protect the rights of minorities: he sees the developing problem of adjusting public protest to the requirement of public order: and he can reflect upon the conflict not yet settled, or perhaps even understood in the United Kingdom (see the 'Spycatcher' litigation) between freedom of information and national security.

There is a general consensus that the conflict must be settled by law. But should it be settled in the constitution, by the legislature, or by the courts? The answer is not scientific. For the proper balance between rights and liberties will vary from one generation to another: and it may differ in war and peace. It will vary according to the shifting kaleidoscope of social patterns, notably in line of population structure, of wealth and poverty, of commercial, industrial, and cultural activity. There has to be a continuing public debate on social values, revealing what is good, exposing what is dangerous, or what is rotten in contemporary society. Given such continuing debate, a constitution can provide a platform upon which the legislature and the courts can adjust rights and interests.

The role of the legislature is, without derogating from the constitutional or, in the United Kingdom, the common law protection of civil liberties and human rights, to enact the major adjustments that are required to meet changing social needs. The race relations and equal opportunities legislation of the United Kingdom are good examples, setting, as they do, such limits to common law rights and freedoms as are deemed necessary to protect the interests of ethnic minorities and of women.

The role of the courts will be to apply the law to particular cases. This, their traditional role, provides ample scope for the exercise of judgment, fine-tuning the law to meet the justice of the case. American and British courts are adept at creating law by judicial decision without infringing statute law. They can adjust limits to the exercise of rights within the common law tradition of developing law by judicial precedent.

I welcome the publication of this collection of essays as a valuable contribution to the continuous public debate without which neither legislatures nor courts can take the decisions or make the judgments necessary to protect our liberties and the values of our society. Liberty is itself a social value, and must itself be subject to such restraint as is necessary for the survival of the society which cherishes it.

Notes on contributors

BERNARD CRICK is Professor Emeritus of Politics of Birkbeck College, University of London and Honorary Fellow of the University of Edinburgh. He is author of *The American Science of Politics* (London, 1959); *In Defence of Politics* (London, 1964); *The Reform of Parliament* (London, 1964); *Political Theory and Practice* (London, 1972); *Crime, Rape and Gin* (London, 1974); *Orwell: a Life* (London, 1980); and, most recently, *Socialism* (Milton Keynes, 1987). He is also a frequent broadcaster and freelance journalist. He was chairman of the Hansard Society's working party on political education, and received an honorary degree in 1986 for services to political education in Northern Ireland. He is currently working on a trilogy on the nations of the British Isles.

NORMAN DORSEN is Stokes Professor of Law, New York University, and the President of the American Civil Liberties Union. He served as a law clerk to US Appeals Judge Calvert Magruder and to Justice John Marshall Harlan of the US Supreme Court. He has been Visiting Professor at Harvard Law School, the University of California at Berkeley, San Diego Law School (Oxford and Paris programs), and the London School of Economics. He served as president of The Society of American Law Teachers 1973–5. He has lectured at many other universities and he has written or edited several books on constitutional law and civil liberties, including *Frontiers of Civil Liberties* (New York, 1968); *The Rights of Americans* (New York, 1971); *Disorder in the Court* (New York, 1974); *Our Endangered Rights* (New York, 1984); and *The Evolving Constitution* (Middletown, 1987).

JOHN DUNN is Fellow of Kings College, Cambridge and Professor of Political Theory, Cambridge University. He has been Visiting Professor at the University of Ghana, the University of Bombay, and at the Faculty of Law, Tokyo Metropolitan University; he was Murphy Distinguished Professor, Tulane University, in 1986. He is the author of nine books, including *The Political Thought of John Locke* (Cambridge, 1969); *Modern Revolutions* (Cambridge, 1972); *Western Political Theory in the Face of the Future* (Cambridge, 1979); *Political Obligation in its Historical Context* (Cambridge, 1980); *The Politics of Socialism* (Cambridge, 1984); *Rethinking Modern Political Theory* (Cambridge, 1985).

D. J. GALLIGAN is Professor of Law at the University of Southampton and Co-Director of the Institute of Criminal Justice within the University. Professor Galligan was a Rhodes Scholar at Magdalen College, Oxford. He later became a Fellow of Jesus College and was a lecturer in the University of Oxford. He also taught at University College London and at Melbourne University before taking a chair at Southampton in 1985. Professor Galligan's main interests are in jurisprudence, public law, and criminal justice. His main publication is *Discretionary Powers: A Legal Study of Official Discretion* (Oxford, 1986); he has also edited *Essays in Legal Theory* (Melbourne, 1984), and *Law, Rights and the Welfare State* (with C. J. Sampford) (London, 1986).

LARRY GOSTIN is Associate Professor of Health Law, Harvard University School of Public Health and Executive Director of the American Society of Law and Medicine. He is on the Board of Directors of the American Civil Liberties Union and was previously General Secretary of the National Council for Civil Liberties/Legal Director of MIND and Fellow at the Oxford University Centre for Criminological Research. His previous publications include *Secure Provision* (London, 1985); *Mental Health Services: Law and Practice* (London, 1986); *Mental Health Tribunal Procedure* (London, 1984).

SARAH McCABE was a founder member of the Oxford University Penal Research Unit which later became the Centre for Criminological Research. She worked there for many years. Her publications include studies of detention centres, the operations of the jury system, and police activities together with a major study of the working of the Mental Health Act in relation to mentally abnormal offenders. She was a member of the Parole Board for England and Wales from 1981 to 1984. In 1984 she was awarded an Emeritus Fellowship by the Leverhulme Trust for the completion of a long-term project on concepts of crime.

BARRY LYNN serves as a legislative counsel to the American Civil Liberties Union in Washington, DC. He is also an ordained minister in the United Church of Christ. Mr Lynn is the author of many articles on First Amendment issues and is a frequent guest on national television shows. He is also the co-host of the syndicated radio program "Battleline". He monitored the activities of the 1986 Attorney General's Commission on Pornography and wrote a critique entitled *Polluting the Censorship Debate*.

STEPHEN SEDLEY QC practises principally in public law and civil rights law at the English bar. He was called to the bar in 1964 and took silk in 1983. He served as a member of the International Commission on Mercenaries in Angola in 1976, and is currently a president of the National Reference Tribunals for the coalmining industry and sits as an assistant recorder. He is an active member of the National Council for Civil Liberties, and a vice-president and former secretary of the Haldane Society of Socialist Lawyers. He has published articles and contributed to books on the politics of law, and has been a visiting professorial fellow at Warwick University and a visiting fellow at Osgoode Hall Law School.

CLYDE SUMMERS is Jefferson B. Fordham Professor of Law, University of Pennsylvania. He has been Visiting Professor at Yale University Law School, The University of Puerto Rico and The University of Minnesota. He acts as a consultant to The Department of Labor, The Department of Housing and Urban Development, The Equal Opportunities Commission, and various other governmental agencies or commissions. Besides many articles on employment rights, he has written *Rights of Union Members* (with R. Rabin) (New York, 1979) and *Cases and Materials on Labor Laws* (with A. Hyde) (New York, 1982).

CASS R. SUNSTEIN is Professor of Law, Law School and Department of Political Science, University of Chicago. He has served as law clerk to Justice Thurgood Marshall; as Visiting Professor of Law at Columbia and Harvard; as attorney-advisor in the United States Department of Justice; as vice-chair of the American Bar Association Committee on Separation of Powers and Governmental Organization; as expert witness before numerous congressional committees; and as a member of the Council of the administrative law section of the American Bar Association. He has published over forty articles and is co-author, with Stone, Seidman, and Tushnet, of *Constitutional Law* (Boston, 1986).

Acknowledgements

Civil liberties principles, as the title of this book suggests, are often born of conflict. The conflicts of principle are debated in the boardrooms of great civil liberties organizations. My first acknowledgement is to the National Council for Civil Liberties of England and Wales (NCCL), to the American Civil Liberties Union (ACLU), and to the authors in this book who in good humour and friendship vigorously argued their side of the ideological divide. All of the proponents have put their case well.

I owe a great debt to my warm friends on NCCL's independent inquiry into the miners' dispute: John Alderson, Sarah McCabe, and Peter Wallington (chair). Ian Martin withdrew from the inquiry team when he was appointed General Secretary of Amnesty International. I have had many eloquent friends on NCCL's Executive Committee who have provided guidance and rigorous thought on civil liberties principles – Ian Martin and, leaders in the groups movement, Roger Cornwell, Brian Richardson, and Jean Rogers. On the other side of the Atlantic I would like to thank Norman Dorsen, President of the ACLU, who offered guidance as to the most respected civil liberties authors in the United States.

I completed much of this book with the support of two of the fine universities on both sides of the Atlantic: Oxford University, Centre for Criminological Research, and Harvard University, School of Public Health.

The support of Justice Brennan and Lord Scarman in reading an advance copy of the manuscript and writing Forewords makes this book special, from a public policy and a personal perspective.

Taking a viable position on charged civil liberties issues requires help from a loving family, and my final and most important acknowledgement is to Jean, Bryn, and Kieran.

Larry Gostin, 15 April 1987

Editor's introduction

This collection of essays addresses genuine conflicts among cherished civil liberties: freedom of expression and the rights of minorities and women; anti-discrimination and affirmative action; freedom of assembly and association and public order; freedom of information and protection of national security.

There could be no more charged issues for civil libertarians than those examined here. The issues are also real. Legislatures, courts and law-enforcement officials make decisions in these areas with regularity. Should individuals or groups expressing opinions which are offensive or degrading to ethnic groups or women be permitted to do so? Governments are under pressure to prohibit or seriously limit fascist views or hard pornography by electorates which thoroughly disapprove of such expressions. Should blacks and women be treated more favourably than white males for jobs and promotions? Governments and courts face wrenching decisions on whether to approve or require 'race-conscious' affirmative action designed to reverse a pattern of past discrimination. Should peace groups, environmental groups, anti-nuclear groups, and other collective entities have the freedom to assemble and demonstrate in ways that interfere with public order, passers-by, or the rights of their members? Governments and police have to make the difficult decision of restricting marches or demonstrations in order to safeguard individual rights and keep the peace. Should dissenting members of trade unions have the 'right to go to work' during an industrial dispute? Governments and police must decide whether to enforce the right of a few to enter the workplace even at great expense or public turmoil. These decisions are not cost-free or theoretical. The consequence of defending one right is to devalue another. By enforcing one set of rights the government can abrogate the rights of others. The decision, whichever way it is made, is open to the criticism that it is politically partisan.

The two oldest and largest national organisations devoted to civil liberties are the American Civil Liberties Union (ACLU) and the National Council for Civil Liberties (NCCL). These organizations are faced with publicly stating a preference for one set of rights over another; and to give reasoned answers as to why one right is more important than another. There are, moreover, conflicts inherent in these decisions which go beyond substance. To choose one set of rights over another is implicitly to recognize one interest or constituency more than another.

Tactically, should civil liberties organizations align themselves with their 'natural' constituency of minority groups, or should they seek a broader appeal? However much such organizations claim that their policy is value-free or non-party-political, will it be seen that way? At stake is not merely which side will be embraced or estranged but, more importantly, the public credibility of the organization.

This book offers a unique perspective. It makes a comparative analysis of these competing principles and interests within two robust democracies – the United Kingdom and the United States. The ACLU and NCCL take different positions on many of these issues. I have been privileged to be closely associated both with NCCL, as its General Secretary, and with ACLU, as a member of the National Board of Directors. This book is written and edited from a position of admiration for both of these organizations, and respect for their differences. The intention is to provide a forum for debate of 'civil liberties in conflict' among highly respected scholars and civil libertarians on both sides of the Atlantic.

The book is based on a 'point–counterpoint' style. Editorially, I have sought to interject a series of observations and questions, trying to sharpen the focus of the conflict. I confess not to be neutral on these conflicts, and my preferences are made clear. During my tenure as General Secretary of NCCL I sought to bring NCCL towards a non-partisan position by forming an all-party parliamentary civil liberties group co-chaired by John Wheeler MP (Conservative) and Alf Dubs MP (Labour).

The arguments made by distinguished authors in this book do not purport to be 'correct' or the best way to resolve each conflict. Ultimately, there are no 'right' answers, but only honest processes of seeking a principled balancing of interests.

The importance of these questions and the common bonds between Britain and America are evidenced by the fact that William Brennan, Justice of the Supreme Court of the United States of America, and Leslie Scarman, Lord Justice in the House of Lords, have both written Forewords. Lord Scarman and Justice Brennan have earned reputations as the finest civil libertarians and constitutional scholars on the highest court in their respective countries.

Their guidance over decades has inspired and guided civil libertarians on both sides of the Atlantic.

PART I

Collective and individual rights

1

Towards resolving the conflict

Larry Gostin

Anglo-American society has a strong individualistic concept of civil liberties, influenced by the philosophy of John Locke and J. S. Mill. Under this libertarian view, rights belong to individuals, not groups. Our most cherished rights to liberty, free expression, and the practice of religion and conscience were essentially conceived as applicable to individuals.

This individualistic conception of civil liberties has served us well. It gives individuals a freedom to speak, believe, and act without governmental restraint, provided they do not harm others. It also allows individuals to participate actively in the political process, thereby strengthening democracy.

The rights of groups in Anglo-American society are largely dependent upon the exercise of the rights of individuals in those groups. Each individual has the right to associate with whom he or she pleases. Seen in this way, the rights of the group are derived solely from the sum of its parts. We respect the rights of individuals which comprise the group but give little formal recognition to the right of the collective.

While this atomistic conception of civil liberties has seemed to work well in the past, it is beginning to look ill suited to meet the challenges of modern society. Individual expression today has little impact on political decision-making; a single voice has little sway. The pluralistic democracies of the west are heavily influenced by major groups and associations.

Increasingly, individuals are making their voices heard by joining together to march, demonstrate, and attend public meetings. Individuals join associations, unions, and organizations which represent their political, social, or economic philosophies. This includes trade unions, peace groups, environmental organizations, and political parties. On almost every issue of moment there exists one or more large national or regional group representing the views of its members. These organizations clearly do not reflect the views of each one of their members. The dynamics of collective organizations take on a significance of their own. The conception that groups should have only those rights possessed by their constituent members is a fiction.

Indeed, new legal rules doubtless apply when individuals exercise their rights in concert. When several individuals join together in association there are laws which have special application. Obstruction of a public way, riot, and affray are all offences essentially of the collective (see Chapter 3).

Groups of people acting together have special strengths to influence political decisions. Men and women increasingly choose to exercise their rights together as part of a coherent organization of people. The gravest modern dangers to civil liberties involve government decisions to restrict the political or trade union activity of groups of people. We need to devise a theory of collective rights which is not reliant upon the exercise of individual liberties. The first task of this essay, therefore, is to assert the importance of collective rights against unreasonable government interference. If Anglo-American society placed the same emphasis on collective rights that is already placed upon individual rights, this would increase political freedoms.

Groups of people acting together also pose special dangers to public order, and to the rights of individuals outside of the group. A group by its sheer presence and mass can obstruct, intimidate, and cause injury to others. The power of the group both to promote political dissent and to threaten public order often provokes repression and reduction of its activities by governments. The second task of this essay is to balance the rights of the collective with those of others who may be harmed.

The third task is to explore the conflict of rights between the group and its dissenting members. A group can also pose a danger to the security and freedom of individuals within the group. Members of a group who choose not to follow a collective decision can impede the effectiveness of the group. Does the collective have a right to curtail the liberties of its members by forcing compliance with its decisions? For example, can a trade union force its members not to go to work?

The goals of this essay, then, are to assert the importance of collective rights; and to suggest a formula for balancing collective rights against those outside and within the group.

THE RIGHT TO COLLECTIVE EXPRESSION

'Collective civil liberties' is used in this essay to refer to the right of a group of people to join together for some commonality of purpose. Freedom of expression has increasingly been exercised in modern times in a collective fashion. It is a major civil liberties challenge to defend the right of people to organise and to speak with a unity of purpose. A union of ideas is a necessary civil liberties conception in modern democracies, because it has become one of the few effective ways to enter the political debate.

The exercise of collective civil liberties should be based upon the same standards as individual liberties. Individual rights in the west are widely respected. For the most part, governments, under scrutiny of the courts, abridge the individual right to liberty or expression only where its exercise poses a clear and immediate danger to others. Even pornographic or racist statements which undermine the dignity of groups, and perhaps indirectly cause them harm, are often tolerated. Governments often refuse to intervene in the private realm because of an appreciation of individual rights deeply ingrained in Anglo-American culture. Where the individual is concerned, intellectually, we are better able to put the danger in perspective. The threat to others, while worrisome, is merely speculative or indirect. When an indirect harm is balanced against the high value placed upon individual liberty, we choose liberty. Clearly, there are many illustrations where individual liberty will bend in the face of the most speculative harm. But under the US Constitution or the European Convention on Human Rights, individual rights command respect and will often prevail.

Anglo-American society does not have a similar respect for collective rights, which bend and sway at the slightest hint of a danger to security or the public order. In Great Britain, there is no positive right to march, demonstrate, picket, or attend a public meeting. These collective freedoms are tolerated only so long as they are exercised in a way which does not violate any law. A group of people can demonstrate. But they may do so only if they do not obstruct the highway, trespass on private property, create a nuisance, breach the peace, or fail to comply with the order of a law-enforcement officer to leave the area. The law places no special premium on the collective right. The rights of groups hold no special place of importance in the law; when balanced against the slightest interest in public order or convenience, collective rights often yield.

The negative framework for the protection of collective expression is highly unsatisfactory, for it posits that the rights of groups must defer to any statutory right, however insignificant in social importance. Since the exercise of collective rights by way of public assembly, mass picket, or procession is bound to infringe upon some individual right, there is really no right to collective expression at all. Collective rights are exercisable only when they are 'cost free'. Few rights in the real world can be exercised without some conflict with the rights of others.

It can immediately be seen how collective freedoms are under-valued when weighed against public order and convenience. The policies of the British and American governments have been attacked by major organizations such as those concerned with nuclear disarmament, the environment, freedom of information, animal rights, and unfair industrial or labour practices. The consistent response of government has been to limit the freedom to assemble whenever it interferes with other, more specific, legally protected rights of passers-by, shopkeepers, or those wishing to travel to work.

American nuclear missiles are based at Greenham Common in the south of England. For several years women concerned with nuclear disarmament have set up a camp around the base in protest. The government has repeatedly sought to disband the women's peace camp despite the fact that during the years of its presence it has caused little personal harm to others. The government based its attempts to restrict this collective protest on the most flimsy of social justifications. These ranged from the profanity used by some of the women, to littering the Common, to the complaints made by some local residents. Finally, the government claimed that the land was needed to build a new road. Government officials never acknowledged that the value of free collective expression could outweigh these relatively minor social disturbances.

In 1984–5 the British government faced one of the most bitter industrial actions of the twentieth century. The National Union of Mineworkers (NUM) went on strike without a ballot among its members. The issue concerned the closure of what the National Coal Board referred to as 'uneconomic pits'. The strike was in defence of jobs for union members. During the year-long dispute the NUM organized mass picketing of major pits across the country. In particular, pickets were dispatched from the south of England to the north in order to assemble in mass at the gates of collieries where some of the work-force wished to work. The government made it clear that the right of individuals to go to work was an absolute priority. Pursuant to that policy, the police restricted the right to picket whenever it was perceived to interfere with the individual right to travel to work. Road-blocks were set up to prevent miners from travelling from one part of the country to another for the purposes of picketing. Road-blocks were set up in Kent, hundreds of miles from the locus of the mass picket in Yorkshire. Nearer to the site of the picket there were large numbers of arrests for non-violent offences such as obstruction of the highway or obstruction of a police officer in carrying out his duties. Other charges were vague, such as for old common-law offences like riot or affray. When individuals were charged they were frequently given highly restrictive bail conditions, even for non-violent offences. These conditions included a prohibition on being in the area of NUM property. The cumulative impact of government and police action was the certain knowledge that individuals' right to go to work would always prevail over the right to picket.

A similar scenario took place at Wapping in East London in 1986, where newspaper unions were picketing against the introduction of new technology without union agreement. The use of road-blocks and the dispersion of picketers in the manner described above have developed into a clear pattern. Where collective rights come into conflict with individual rights, the latter prevail.

The police intervention to disperse travellers ('gypsies' or people who like to travel in caravans) shows the preference for private over collective rights. Travellers have camped on the land of private farmers for days or weeks before moving on, and usually no significant danger to property or interference with livelihood has occurred. Yet in the summer of 1986 in the west country, for a large group of travellers, the temporary inconvenience of a private landlord was used as the justification for a constant police presence and for interference with the freedom to assemble peacefully and travel to areas of choice. Thus, at the focal point of civil liberties tension, the proprietary rights of landlords prevailed over those of travellers seeking to live their lives the way they wished, and to be free from interference. Since most land in England is owned, it would be virtually impossible for travellers to maintain their life-style without some small interference with a private right.

Thus the state has assumed powers which, as clearly and unambiguously as possible, restrict collective freedoms of association, assembly, demonstration, and picketing. These collective freedoms have been shown very little respect within Britain's constitutional framework. The potential for the state to make it difficult to express political and/or industrial ideas it disapproves of is now real and substantial.

It may be argued that no democratic government would restrict the right to express political ideas which it did not favour. The answer is that it would not censor those ideas blatantly and with declared intention. It would claim that its purpose was private safety and public order, and it would act upon the most flimsy evidence and prejudicial assumptions about the demonstrators.

That is what the British government has systematically done when seeking to justify restrictions on the right to picket or demonstrate.

The government has made no secret of its support for the employer's position in each major industrial dispute, or of its opposition to groups such as the Campaign for Nuclear Disarmament. Based upon its pure political preference, there is nothing surprising, nor necessarily improper, about a Conservative government taking a view on the merits of economic or armament issues. But the government has allowed its political dislike for a viewpoint to spill over into a justification for the restriction of the right of groups to express their view. The government's tacit use of the police to restrict picketing, marching, or public gatherings is not necessary for public safety, but is a certain diminution of the political freedom of groups of people.

The overwhelming majority of picket lines and demonstrations (even during impassioned conflicts like Wapping or the miners' dispute) have been non-violent, and almost all men and women joining these assemblies have done so for the purpose of peaceful persuasion. To restrict the freedom of all such people because a few may be disruptive thoroughly undermines the principles of collective freedom.

If the government truly valued political freedom, it would not trade off the certain denial of freedom for much more speculative assumptions about the intention of demonstrators. It would ensure that the only justification for the deprivation of collective liberties is where the harm caused is clear and substantial. The right of men and women to join together for the purposes of expressing a common point of view cannot be so fragile that it can be swept aside at a mere suggestion of tension or inconvenience.

TRADE UNIONS: THE RIGHT TO PICKET VERSUS THE 'RIGHT TO WORK'

In the previous section I attempted to demonstrate that collective rights such as the right to picket too often yield whenever they appear to impinge on the rights of others. In this section I will examine the tension between the rights of the collective and those of its dissenting members. The best illustration is provided within the trade union context.

There has been a marked tendency in Britain to restrict the collective rights of the trade union to strike and picket when the exercise of those rights interferes with those of individual members of the union. This reinforces the notion stated earlier that the rights of the group are perceived only as the sum of the individual rights of its members.

In Britain, the 'right to work' has been used by the government and the press, often with confused meanings. There is no 'right to work' in the sense of there being an entitlement to a job or a livelihood. The 'right to work' during an industrial dispute can be understood only as the right not to take part in the strike and the right to travel to one's place of employment for the purpose of working.

The political Right sees the primary role of the police in an industrial dispute as ensuring the 'right to work', which always takes priority over the collective right to strike. Conservatives' concern for the civil liberties of strike-breakers is, in part, based upon their philosophical belief in the rights and autonomy of individuals. Where the freedom (economic or political) of a single person may be interfered with by a collective entity such as a trade union, the interests of the individual are to take precedence. This pure philosophical bent is usually mixed with the pragmatic policy of the necessity of 'defeating' the trade union action. Taken together, philosophy and pragmatism have led conservatives straight to the defence of individuals' 'right to work'.

A characteristic dilemma during the miners' dispute of 1984–5, shows how conservative philosophy operated: the case where a single miner wished to travel to work. The pit in such a case often could not be made operational, and it would serve no practical purpose for the miner to travel to the colliery gate. The miner was allowed into work solely for the purpose of publicly showing his defiance of the strike. He would sit idly without any productive work to do.

Conservative philosophy nevertheless required the miner to be escorted to work, by force if necessary, to effectuate his civil liberty. This might cause more public disorder than if he were not permitted to cross the picket line. However, his fictitious interest in 'working' would outweigh both the union's collective right to picket and the community's interest in public order.

The overall sense one has of the policing of industrial disputes is that this essentially conservative philosophy is now adhered to by the police and the government. Thus, whenever there is a conflict of rights – as inevitably there will be in a charged industrial dispute – it is almost always resolved in favour of the individual's right to work. The police are used by government, not primarily to keep the peace, but for the purpose of ensuring that people who choose to do so can get to work. From the conservative perspective, this is mere enforcement of a civil right; but from the trade union's perspective, it is strike-breaking. The consequence, then, of the police's near exclusive concentration on enforcement of one set of rights, at the cost of another, results in a strong and lasting feeling on the part of trade unions that it is the proprietary interests of the employers that are being defended.

Conservatives have come to see the right to work as a political symbol, to be enforced regardless of the cost. One can understand the force of political symbolism in examining law enforcement. Many of us, for example, would share the conviction that the police's duty to enforce a black person's entry to a public institution (as occurred during the civil rights campaign in the United States) is essential. Yet we do not think that it is as important to enforce an individual's right to work. Why? In the case of breaking a colour-bar, the civil right in question is clear and powerful. Even here, however, reasonable men and women might believe it would not be essential to enforce this right at a particular moment if the certain result was the loss of dozens of lives. Yet there is no benefit achieved by using force to ensure the right of one person to work where the pit is not, in many cases, operational. The right to work, unlike breaking a colour-bar, cannot be seen as some moral imperative that requires invariable conflict and hostility to enforce on every occasion.

THE CIVIL LIBERTIES OF 'SCABS'

There are those on the political Left who see industrial action, and other forms of mass demonstration, primarily as political and economic struggles to be won or lost. In this context they are not unduly concerned about the civil liberties of the other side. In the opinion of many, as John Dunn says in Chapter 2 (p. 34),

> there is no serious question that the passion on which union leaders must rely to keep a fraying strike solid is the passion of fear. Mass picketing is a ritual of self-righteous solidarity . . .; but its instrumental purpose is the intimidation of those at whom it is directed. The most effective means of intimidation . . . is the threat to life and limb.

There is little doubt that this intolerance towards individual freedom of the political Left has been fuelled by the intolerance of Mrs Thatcher's government towards collective freedom. The major inequality in the formulation, of course, is that the state has enormous power, while just about all the power on the Left is based upon its political freedom to persuade.

The Left is understandably in no mood for reasoned argument when the rights of trade unions are under attack. But if it does not listen, this intolerance will rebound, and it will be unable to extricate itself from an overall restrictive and intolerant society in which it is the chief victim.

In the following section I will maintain that a trade unionist has the right not to participate in a trade dispute. This is not an absolute right and should yield if it significantly interferes with the civil liberties of the group. Moreover, I encourage trade unionists to join in collective action, for failure to do so destroys the fabric of the trade union. But I defend the right of the person to dissent as a matter of conscience, and to be free from threats or coercion if he or she chooses this course of action. To this extent I disagree with the position taken by the National Council for Civil Liberties.

THE NCCL INDEPENDENT INQUIRY INTO THE MINERS' DISPUTE

NCCL established an independent inquiry into the civil liberties implications of the miners' dispute at its Annual General Meeting in April 1984. The inquiry's terms of reference were:

> To inquire into and thereby establish the fullest possible account and the civil liberties implications of the role of the police, the police authorities and the events arising from and relating to the NUM dispute, which began in March 1984.

The terms of reference were criticized by Conservative members of parliament as 'one-sided' for referring only to the police and the courts, and not to what they regarded as the threat to the civil liberties of working miners. The members of the miners' inquiry rejected these criticisms because they considered it proper to focus on the actions of public agencies, not private individuals in organizations.

The opposite criticism, made by the NCCL Executive Committee on 28 February 1985, was that NCCL 'regretted' that the independent inquiry 'exceeded its terms of reference in commenting on the conduct of striking and working miners and in setting out civil liberties principles which did not directly relate to the role of the police, police authorities and criminal courts'.

The independent inquiry's position was that 'any sensible examination of the policing of the strike must take fully into account the circumstances which have shaped the context of police actions and their objectives'.* It is simply not possible to assess the policing of an industrial dispute without taking a view as to whether and when there has been a policing function essential to the protection of civil liberties. In the absence of policing, would mass pickets have physically prevented miners from going to work rather than peacefully trying to dissuade them? What were the nature and extent

---

* *NCCL Independent Inquiry into the Policing of the Miners' Strike*, Interim Report (1984), NCCL: London.

of violence or threats in mining communities? Does picketing of the private home of a working miner infringe upon the civil liberties of his family?

The decision of NCCL's Executive Committee to define its interests so narrowly that it would not permit an examination of the 'conduct of striking or working miners' suggests an inappropriately selective analysis of civil liberties.

NCCL's Executive Committee on 28 February 1985 also passed a motion 'regretting' the presentation of the interim inquiry report as 'unnecessarily damaging to the miners' cause'. The Executive Committee specifically rejected the inquiry's first conclusion that all sides to the dispute should 'refrain from violence, intimidation or other actions likely to cause injury or public disorder or provide unnecessary ill-feeling'.

The appropriate role of a civil liberties organization is not to take a substantive position on which side of an industrial dispute is correct. If its conclusions on civil liberties principles are damaging to a particular side of the dispute, that does not provide a justification for failing to come to those conclusions. In the particular case, a plea for all sides to refrain from violence was not particularly damaging to any side, and it stated a basic civil liberties principle of freedom from harm. Indeed, the vast majority of the inquiry report was highly critical of police behaviour, and supportive of the collective right to picket.

NCCL's Annual General Meeting in April 1985 endorsed the Executive Committee's views. (1) It defeated a motion by Professor Peter Wallington, chairman of the inquiry, that the inquiry 'exceeded its terms of reference in commenting on the conduct of striking and working miners'. (2) It defeated a motion by Brian Richardson, a representative of NCCL groups movement, that 'only considerations of civil liberty are relevant to NCCL and that it is improper for it to take sides in an industrial dispute'. And (3) it passed a motion rejecting the principle stated by the inquiry that there is a right not to take part in an industrial dispute, because that principle 'undermines the collective rights of others, and cannot be supported as a fundamental freedom'.

What is the appropriate civil liberties framework for resolving the tension between the union's right to take industrial action and a member's right not to take part? Trade unions have the basic freedom to act as a collective entity and democratically to make their own rules. This means that, subject to complying with their own democratically made rules, trade unions can call an industrial action and organize their members to take part in all those necessary con-stituent parts of that action – not to go to work, to picket, to distribute literature, to march, and so on. These rights all need to be preserved in a free society, for they are part of the right of groups of people to express their political and industrial opinions and to take an active part in the democracy of which they form a part. Ardent protection of these rights is one of the most important tasks for government, courts, and the police.

In the report of the independent inquiry into the miners' dispute originally established by NCCL, the right not to take part in a strike was defended as an important civil liberty. That right is derived from the individual's freedom to follow his or her conscience in dissenting from the majority's decision; and the freedom to refuse to take part in actions based upon a majority decision. The right not to take part in an industrial dispute, therefore, is grounded upon the freedom of thought, conscience, and action. The individual in going to work also exercises a freedom to travel for a lawful purpose. He or she has the right to be free from threats of harm or actual violence. A person does not join a trade union with the expectation that he or she forfeits the right conscientiously to object to the decisions taken by the union. Trade unionists would expect to be disciplined or expelled for not joining in collective action, but they would reserve their right to make a choice.

While it may be conceded that strike-breakers have some abstract rights to dissent, should this be at the cost of the exercise of the rights of the collective? The trade union represents the rights of many, while dissenters are numerically few. The union, moreover, has many liberties at stake – freedom of association, of speech, and to withdraw their labour. When trade unions are deprived of their civil liberties they lose their ability to counterbalance the substantial economic power of the employer. When the consequence of enforcing the right of the individual will necessarily be to prevent the exercise of the liberties of the collective, the union's rights should prevail. Thus, if the only way to enable one person to go to work is to prevent five hundred people from exercising their rights to free expression and association, then the worker's rights should yield. For example, if the cost of giving a small group of people the 'right to work' is to set up road-blocks to prevent hundreds of trade unionists from picketing, the conflict should be resolved in favour of the union.

Yet it is perfectly possible in many cases for both parties peaceably to exercise their rights. The worker who crosses the picket line should do so without fear, but he or she must hear the attempts of trade unionists to persuade him or her. If the police steadfastly defend the right of trade unionists to picket, the union should, in turn, respect the right of dissenters to enter the workplace without obstruction or harm. I am not blind to the real tensions in this situation involving three angry parties – trade unionists, workers, and police. But a democratic tradition of respect for the liberty of all calls for some peaceful coexistence and tolerance on all sides.

It is argued that respecting the right of a person not to take part in an industrial dispute wholly undermines the economic purpose of strike action. Social, economic, and political arguments against strike-breakers are powerful. The union's ultimate strength in defending the wages and jobs of its members lies in the collective withdrawal of labour. It is the ability of the union to halt production which counterbalances the economic strength of the employer. But if a union cannot persuade each of its members to strike, it should not be empowered to use compulsion. Strike-breakers do undermine the *effectiveness* of strike action, which may be deplorable. But dissent from the trade union decision does not interfere with the *civil liberties* of the collective to withdraw their labour, to peacefully persuade and to picket.

It is further suggested that there is no right to 'work', because 'scabs' or strike-breakers are seeking a 'free ride'. The economic gains of strike-breakers are obtained at the expense of loyal trade union members. The moral force of this argument becomes clearer when it is realized that strikers during the miners' dispute received little or no strike pay from the union or social security from the state. The fact that strike-breakers would gain on the backs of those who suffered is galling.

The response to this argument is familiar to civil libertarians, who sometimes must support liberties exercised for a repugnant purpose. Our judgment of the immorality of the workers' position does not endow us with the authority to compel them to change their mind and follow the strike action. The content of the exercise of freedoms in many contexts is objectionable – for example, the defence of those who write pornography or those who express racist views. But it is the essence of a civil liberties position that it does not pick and choose among liberties based upon agreement with the content of the argument or the morality of the person.

Perhaps the image of self-effacing civil libertarians determined to defend the rights of those they disagree with is outdated. After all, we are in a pragmatic, political age where power reigns. But there is also an argument based upon self-interest here. During a strike there are individuals and groups each asserting their freedoms. Government will have its own view of the moral correctness of the position of each of the parties to an industrial dispute. To allow the government or any other body to favour the exercise of liberty by the 'morally correct' party is a dangerous precedent. Many governments, as previously explained, will instinctively prefer the rights of 'workers' against those of strikers. It is in the interest of the trade unionist to defend civil liberties for all parties, particularly when the government's preference for employers' rights is so obvious.

The final argument often stated is that aberrant individuals must comply with a democratic decision of the majority of trade union members, just as all of us must respect the majority view in Parliament or Congress. The right of the majority to decide was central to the judgments of many observers during the miners' strike. But on closer reflection, most observers used this 'majoritarian' notion to support their own substantive view of the strike. To the National Union of Mineworkers, the men had 'voted with their feet', and therefore the union had the moral authority to insist upon the solidarity of all union members. To the National Coal Board and the government, the miners had no such moral authority because the union had never called a ballot. I take the view that, as a civil liberties proposition, it does not matter which side was in the majority. Civil liberties are not so fragile that they can be abrogated by majority vote.

The analogy between Parliament's power to exact binding requirements on the public and the power of a private union or group of individuals to bind its own members is a false one. Any society must respect the legislature's right to restrict certain freedoms for the greater social good, recognizing that there are constitutional boundaries which society should not allow even Parliament or Congress to transgress. But we could not, and do not, allow private groups to have the same powers over their members. The union's legitimate authority is limited to setting and enforcing rules within its membership. If a member flouts these rules, the union has the right to fine the person or even expel him or her. But the union's power cannot properly extend to coercion, intimidation, or obstruction. Only the organs of government have the right to use force to obtain compliance with their majority decisions.

The robust 'majoritarianism' exhibited by many in society is in many ways the antithesis of a true civil libertarian position, which is to defend the right of the isolated and powerless not to have to conform to what a majority of people may want.

The 'majoritarian' view means that as a pre-condition to exercising the right – for example, to withdraw labour, assemble, and picket – there must be more workers in favour of the strike than against. Many others argue, particularly on the political Right, that this exercise of civil liberties is conditional upon the outcome of a democratic ballot. There are many good reasons, both social and strategic, for a trade union to have a secret ballot. But whether or not there is a ballot, and irrespective of who is in the majority, it should not prevent the exercise of the right to withdraw labour, to picket, or to travel for a lawful purpose.

Failure to accept this argument would have meant that once 51 per cent of miners during the 1984–5 dispute returned to work, all the others would have been robbed of the right to continue their strike action and to picket. Such collective and individual rights cannot be so tenuous that they can be overridden by the majority.

CONCLUSION

I have robustly defended collective rights as necessary to the fulfilment of human beings in fully participating in their social and political life. Collective rights should yield only in the face of a strong and immediate danger. Mere interference with passers-by and shopkeepers or obstruction of the highway is insufficient to justify interference with collective rights. Why then give such credence to the rights of individuals within the union who refuse to participate in collective action?

The tension between collective and individual rights in this context has been overstated. If the necessary consequence of defending the right of individuals 'to work' is that union members would be impeded in the exercise of their rights to picket and demonstrate, I would not support such individuals' right. But in most cases an individual who chooses to walk through a picket line does not interfere with the civil liberties of trade unionists to assemble and picket.

Civil liberties – even of hostile antagonists – can peacefully coexist. For that to happen each party must exhibit a tolerance for the freedoms of others. It also requires a government and police which will not pick and choose among liberties but will have a true respect for civil liberties as a high democratic value, whether exercised by individuals or by groups.

2
Rights and political conflict
John Dunn

In the course of the last three decades the concept of rights has come
to play an increasingly prominent role in Anglo-Saxon moral
philosophy. Over much the same period of time it has also come to
play a increasingly prominent role in the domestic political conflicts
of the United States of America and in the litany of (all too well-
founded) political complaint at the governmental practices of
communist states and of military and civil dictatorships throughout
the world. There are clearly numerous connections between these
three trajectories of discourse and understanding. In the case of
some of the major recent contributions to Anglo-Saxon moral and
legal theory these connections have often been made highly specific
(Hart 1968 and 1983, Dworkin 1977 and 1985). But despite the
political energy and the high intelligence which have often gone into
these discussions it cannot be said that our current understanding of
the status and scope of claims of right in political controversy is as
yet especially clear. I shall try to show why this is so. I shall also try
to suggest how far it is reasonable to look to an analysis of the
concept of individual and collective rights to help us to resolve
political conflicts in modern capitalist democracies, and how far any
such recourse is necessarily the pursuit of a forlorn hope.

Rights are standardly analysed by philosophers and jurists as
bundles of distinct forms of entitlements: liberties, claim-rights
(discretionary or otherwise on the part of an agent), powers, and
immunities (Hohfeld 1919, Waldron 1984: 5–8). Civil rights or civil
liberties (such as the right to freedom of expression, of movement,
and of religious practice, to physical security, and to the ownership
of personal property) are bundles of rights which either are or, in the
judgment of the speaker, ought to be recognized by the public law
of a political community and protected by the courts and law-
enforcement agencies of that community. It is important in modern
political dispute that civil liberties should be in this way ambiguous

between rights which citizens ought to possess and rights which under existing law they uncontentiously do enjoy. It is one of the least controversial features of modern conceptions of political justice that any substantial and historically continuing body of persons living within a particular territorial state is entitled to the citizenship of that state (Dunn 1979). The distinctive odium attached to the politics of the Republic of South Africa has been a direct product of its refusal to acknowledge the black majority of its own population as citizens at all, a choice the normative anomaly of which was in effect acknowledged by the brazen invention of the Bantustans as ersatz states in which the subjugated majority could find themselves as citizens of at least somewhere in particular.

There is therefore no contradiction in affirming that the civil liberties of the black population of South Africa are regularly and systematically violated, even where such liberties are in fact ascribed to them by the existing public law of the Republic. What marks South Africa out from other massively right-violating states in the modern world (Uganda, Afghanistan, Iraq, and – in the Lebanon if not on the west bank of the Jordan – the state of Israel) is not the comparative scale on which human rights are violated in practice but the explicitness with which political rights are withheld in principle. Perhaps unsurprisingly, most right-violation in the modern world is more a matter of practice than of principle. The use of obviously brutal techniques of interrogation in the course of criminal investigation is well nigh universal in modern states; and the routine practice of protracted and technically sophisticated physical and mental torture is a commonplace of the domestic politics of a wide miscellany of modern states. But no state today (as far as I am aware) explicitly claims in the constitutive documents that define its sovereignty or in its formal public law the entitlement to treat its citizens (or any other human beings) in such loathsome ways. (The legal prescription of brutal punishments is not at all the same as the instrumental infliction of extreme pain without legal sanction by state functionaries in pursuit of what they take to be state interests, let alone for their personal amusement.)

Civil liberties which are formally recognized by the public law of a particular society can reasonably be spoken of as civil rights. All modern states acknowledge a wide range of civil rights on the part of those whom they acknowledge as their citizens. (Indeed all except the exuberantly barbaric overtly extend these rights to such aliens as they legally permit to enter or reside within their territories.) Some modern states (the United States being the most conspicuous and historically imposing example) secure such rights in a particularly robust and thorough manner by entrenching them within the set of constitutive texts that defines their sovereignty. In the United States the civil rights of its citizens are defined in the first instance by the Bill of Rights, a series of amendments to the US Constitution, and redefined in accordance with this Bill and with the requirements of the original Constitution itself through the decisions of the full range of domestic courts under the final jurisdiction of the Supreme Court. As a first approximation, what the disputed civil rights of American citizens at a given time really are is what the Supreme Court has tacitly or explicitly determined them to be. In the very different legal and political structure of the United Kingdom civil rights have a decidedly less crisp texture. Here they derive from the complex amalgam of prescription and judicial precedent characteristic of the common law and from the statutory provisions of the presumptively sovereign Crown-in-Parliament. Whereas American civil rights are a historically emergent (and perhaps also in some instances a potentially historically recessive) feature of American public law, the terminology of civil rights does not apply very happily to English political debate and conflict. In Britain, consequently, the language of civil liberties has more the flavour of moral criticism of the workings of society, economy, and state than of a confident appeal to existing positive or constitutional law. The fact that in a given instance there may well be no relevant positive law to which to make appeal is itself often part of the ground of the complaint, while the sense that there is seldom or never a relevant provision of constitutional law to appeal to serves to render the complaints markedly shriller and correspondingly less disciplined. In addition, and quite distinctly from this contrast between the legal terrain on which conflicts over civil liberties arise in the two countries, the far greater ideological salience of conflicts of class interest in British politics greatly accentuates the externality and conceptual instability of political defences of beleaguered civil liberties. The view that moral prescriptions are essentially to be analysed in terms of the emotional force for their proponents that they seek to convey and the emotional impact upon their auditors that they are intended to achieve is less fashionable than it used to be amongst moral philosophers (compare Mackie 1977 and 1984 and Blackburn 1981 with McDowell 1981 and Raz 1984). But it is wise to be alert to how much better fitted such an analysis is likely to prove for capturing the character of British disputes over civil liberties in the United Kingdom than it is for doing justice to American arguments over civil rights within the United States.

To see why civil liberties that are not anchored in any determinate constitutional protection are open to such limitless and disorderly contestation, it is helpful to consider one key transition in the modern understanding of rights. When Thomas Jefferson came to draft the American Declaration of Independence, he began his defence of the menaced interests of the American colonies by taking his stand on a set of truths which he claimed (optimistically) to be self-evident (Malone 1975, Wills 1978). All men – he meant all human beings – are created equal, and all are endowed by their Creator with certain inalienable rights, the rights to life, to liberty, and to the pursuit of happiness. Modern philosophers disagree vigorously over whether any human rights can reasonably be said to be inalienable (Gewirth 1984, Simmons 1983). Even those who in effect concede human beings all to be in some sense born equal disagree extravagantly over the implications of such equality for their subsequent legitimate entitlements (compare Nozick 1974 with Cohen 1979, Dworkin 1981, Vlastos 1984). Some modern philosophers still believe all men to have been created; and a few, even writing outside the rubric of Catholic or Protestant dogmatics, do presume that the more fundamental rights which human beings enjoy are rights with which they have been endowed by their Creator (Finnis 1980). But many citizens in all civilized states in the modern world doubt that there ever was a Creator. Even more citizens of these states doubt their capacity to infer the purposes of a Creator from the properties of the created universe; and more citizens still doubt the practical good sense of grounding their own political claims in the last instance on premises which, as they well know, many or even most of their fellow citizens confidently reject.

Most modern theorists of human rights, accordingly, whatever their personal religious predilections, ground such rights in what they take to be the relevant properties of human nature. Some, indeed, acknowledge frankly that 'rights are not plausible candidates for objective existence', though they naturally proceed to add with greater or less elaboration that neither are goods, or goals, or duties, or any other organizing categories of human evaluative discourse (Mackie 1984: 170). But many, understandably, seek to blur the harsh line of division between essentially capricious human invention (Raz 1984: 182, Putnam 1981: 127–216) and theocentric credulity by elaborating some more or less ingenious or evasive variety of ethical naturalism: the thesis that human goods, whatever their historical origins, are now firmly part of the furniture of the historical world that human beings inhabit (compare MacIntyre 1981, Putnam 1981, Raz 1984, and Scanlon 1984, with Williams 1981: 101–13 and 1985). If human goods are genuinely part of the furniture of the human world, why not human rights?

There can be no doubt that the view of human goods or rights as historical inventions of the human species is metaphysically more relaxed and parsimonious than any view which grounds such goods or rights in the purposes of a Divine Creator. To believe that human goods are cultural inventions could hardly strain the credulity of even the most sceptical. It certainly does not entail the view that such goods or rights are arbitrary or whimsical in their specification (Blackburn 1981, Putnam 1981, Waldron 1984, Williams 1985). But what it does do is to limit severely their externality and in particular their recalcitrance to the ebbs and flows of individual sentiment. This may seem to us admirably unsuperstitious in itself. But it does have some consequences that we might reasonably regret. John Locke, for example, constructed his entire moral and political theory – and arguably his entire philosophy (Dunn 1984a) – around the commands and threats of a concerned Creator precisely because he judged that without such an extra-terrestrial focus of authority and source of sanctions there could not be a secure rational basis on which human beings could live with one another in peace and amity (Dunn 1985: 13–67). It is possible, of course, that he was simply in error in so doing. But it is also possible (and in my view more likely) that he showed a sounder strategic judgment at this point than the more optimistic liberal and socialist thinkers of the past two centuries. The externality of divine authority in Locke's theory (like the putative objectivity of the Forms in Plato's *Republic*) gave to every human being the most pressing and decisive reasons for subjecting their own idiosyncratic tastes and preferences to a wholly independent range of requirements.[1] It fused together the demands of rationality and those of morality.[2] It converted the severely external reasons of the divine law of nature into reasons genuinely internal to each human agent's grounds for action (compare Williams 1981: 101–13).

Without a comparable externality and independence of the contingent preferences of individuals or cultural communities, no human value, good, or right can enjoy any greater authority than the individuals or cultural communities concerned feel inclined to accord to it.

> A belief in moral prescriptivity has flourished within the tradition of moral thinking, but it cannot in the end be defended. So we are not looking for objective truth or reality in a moral system. Moral entities – values or standards or whatever they may be – belong within human thinking and practice: they are either explicitly or implicitly posited, adopted, or laid down.   (Mackie 1984: 170–1)

This is a natural enough perspective for a moral philosopher whose most urgent preoccupation in relation to morality may often (and even appropriately) be with the design of a moral system.[3] But it is a profoundly discouraging perspective for anyone who hopes that claims of right may serve not merely to capture more compellingly their own sense of their moral intuitions, but also to direct political choice and political power towards ends that these would not otherwise have pursued.

In recent Anglo-Saxon moral philosophy the most important disagreement over the standing of rights has been a disagreement about their centrality to the design of an adequate moral and political theory. It is a disagreement between philosophers who suspect or hope that it may prove possible to explain the force of rights ultimately in terms of consequences (Scanlon 1984), philosophers who see the two concepts as possessing an essentially independent weight (Scheffler 1982, Dworkin 1977 and 1981), and philosophers who either tacitly presume the priority of rights over goods (Nozick 1974) or even hope that rights may serve to ground a comprehensive moral theory (Mackie 1984). This last view draws its attractions from the extreme deference shown by many recent philosophers to the value of autonomy. But it may well be the case that it impairs the intelligibility of autonomy as a value (Raz 1984, Dunn 1985: 139–89) and it certainly involves an unacceptable separation between a narrow conception of morality as a political system of uniform self-protection and a more expanded conception of morality as a theory of how to live well.

With the exception of Robert Nozick's (1974) arbitrarily specified and practically inapplicable theory of rights, none of these theories strays much beyond the bounds of a fairly confined liberalism (except perhaps Raz 1984). They are therefore, after their respective fashions, well enough equipped to speak to contemporary political sentiment wherever (but only wherever) this already happens to be fairly resolutely liberal in character. No doubt there are (or at any rate could be) some important conflicts of putative rights in which both sets of rights in question can be readily identified in purely liberal terms. (Abortion seems a plausible candidate.) But there can be no doubt that most major political conflicts which involve the affirmation and denial of claims of right, most cases where claims of right are keenly felt but plainly conflict with one another, stray beyond the confines of liberal values. In these instances – and especially where a liberal theory openly sanctions one set of claims and repudiates the force of the other – such a theory can add nothing but intellectual embellishment to the claims which it sponsors. All it can do is to express more elaborately a historically given political interest. Indeed, if it were to do any more than this – and to do so by any other means than the rational conversion to its own tenets[4] of the exponents of the rights that it denies – it would precisely secure that constitutional over-representation or double-counting which Dworkin (1984: 158) regards as the major moral blemish of unrestricted utilitarian preferences.

If moral tenets are merely posited, adopted, and laid down, then conflicts between the moral tenets of two or more persons or social groups or political communities are fundamentally clashes of will.

True, one person, group, or community may be more confused or ignorant than its opponent; and one may also (and perhaps even consequently) be worse or better placed to commend to others the values that it has posited, laid down, or adopted than its less coherent or more benighted opponent can hope to prove. But even after a relatively intense process of mutual persuasion or mutual abuse the clashes of will are seldom likely simply to dissipate. Behind conflicts of will – individual, social, or political – there stand conflicts of (at least imagined) interest. Between the conflicting wills and interests of individuals, at least in many instances, a wider community or even, *in extremis*, a legitimate state can reasonably claim to mediate. Between the conflicting wills and interests of communities or social groups, even not especially legitimate states are apt to find themselves compelled sooner or later to mediate. Between states in serious conflict the only appeal is still today, as Locke put it, the appeal to Heaven: a bleaker thought for most of us than it was for him (Dunn 1985: 34–54, Kenny 1985).

I have insisted that in modern political conflicts of right there are always clashes of will and interest, and that modern philosophical analysts of rights have no satisfactory basis on which to override such clashes. In many instances, indeed, they do not really possess any satisfactory basis on which to adjudicate between claims of right even from the viewpoint of their own preferred moral theory. To round out our understanding of the significance of such conflicts of right we need two further elements: a somewhat richer conception of how best to represent the character of such clashes of will and interest, and a more definite view of the similarities and discrepancies between the right-claiming units that come into conflict in these clashes. The first of these is rather less challenging than the second. The conflicting claims of right represent clashes of wills, and the clashes of will in turn derive from perceived interests. But here the perception is at least as important as the interest. What comes into conflict is not just particular persons in externally specifiable social or economic locations (miners, police officers, students, blacks) but conceptions of how the social, economic, or political relations of these persons or groups ought to be. Speaking only a little fancifully, what comes into conflict is the moral or political theories or systems held by individuals or groups (MacIntyre 1983, Taylor 1983, Dunn 1985: 119–38). In the uncomfortable (and not always terribly authentic) moral and political pluralism of capitalist democracies today we are all amateur moral and political theorists. To abandon our claims to be so is in effect voluntarily to disfranchise ourselves (one vote, one amateur moral and political theory).

Hence the overwhelming contemporary political importance of the issue of just which units really are the legitimate bearers of rights

and responsibilities. In the societies which first seriously attempted
to set out the rights of man it was still a central cultural assumption
for the great majority of their inhabitants that individual human
beings possess immortal souls. For this reason (and no doubt also for
others) human rights were first articulated in a highly individualist
form. This form plainly has its analytical advantages. Human beings
all evidently are individuals. The principal point of affirming the
rights of man was to make such rights more systematically and
dependably available to their legitimate beneficiaries. There is
nothing puzzling in the idea that every beneficiary of a human right
will turn out to be either an individual or a set of individuals. Some
rights, most notably the right to life, are individual or they are
nothing. But with the disappearance of a determinate external locus
of authority conceptually impervious to human whim and the
concomitant evanescence of the individual soul, claims of purely
individual right become markedly less imposing. It is one thing to
affirm that the will of a common Creator denies to another person
or group or state the right to take one's life. It is a very different
matter to insist that one's own amateur moral theory disputes the
same entitlement. (The notably absolutist political theory of Thomas
Hobbes, for example, begins precisely from the fact that all human
beings are strongly inclined to value their own opinions and
judgments – Hobbes 1983: 46, 75, 84, 95, 137–8, 196, 229.) The
more numerous and the less externally restricted the potential
sources of rights, the more imperative the need to constrain them in
practice: to render them compatible with peace, security, and the
wide range of contingently or inherently public goods – Raz 1984:
187 – that a society of any merit must hope to offer to its members.)

Where claims of right conflict systematically, recurrently, and on
a large scale in a society, they reflect the collision of wills, of
perceived interests, and of moral and political theories. Liberal
political theory, in so far as it centres on the value of autonomy,
naturally attaches great weight to encroachments upon the liberties
of individuals: liberties of thought, expression, religious practice,
physical security. To attach great weight to the rights of individuals
is an effective prophylactic against paternalist moralism (Dworkin
1977 and 1984). But, as Joseph Raz (1984) has insisted, it does not
necessarily enable one to give a very compelling account of the point
(or, indeed, even the character) of many individual liberties. Perhaps
more importantly, it is also poorly endowed to do justice to the
significance of claims of right which cannot be clearly formulated in
terms of rights of individuals to act as they happen to choose.

Modern political theory is inclined to recognize only two conceptual locations for genuine rights: the individual and the state. Even
this degree of plurality is often somewhat unstable – liberal theories

being inclined to collapse state rights without residue into individual entitlements (Dunn 1980: 249–99),[5] while socialist theorists, notoriously, find acute difficulties in rationalizing the subsistence of any individual rights at all where these rights have plainly become rights against a socialist state (Lukes 1985).[6] It is clear why both individuals and states should be generally recognized as at least claimants of rights, however disputed their respective titles may be. What is not clear is why anyone should suppose that states and individuals are the sole legitimate bearers of rights. The view that many other human groupings intermediate between individual and state have an equally good claim to bear rights has had important defenders in European politics from the days of Althusius to those of Gierke, Maitland, and G. D. H. Cole (Gierke 1934). It registers much of the practical political consciousness and action of the pluralist and neocorporatist politics of capitalist democracies today (Goldthorpe 1984). Where human moral and political discourse is seen to be merely a field of cultural invention it is difficult to see how it can be justified to ignore coherently and realistically formulated claims of right that emanate from any definite human source.

What is disturbing about the plethora of groupings that advance such claims is not their ontological insubstantiality or (at least in many cases) their lack of moral dignity; it is simply their number and diversity. Theories of human rights were at first elaborated to prune drastically the sorts of valid claims that human beings can levy upon one another (Tuck 1979). But once the relativity of human values to 'forms of life' has become widely acknowledged, it is no longer clear that the concept of rights retains the theoretical force to prune anything at all. True, the constraints of consistency and compatibility with fact place some restrictions upon the range of right claims that possess any rational cogency. But, given consistency and compatibility with fact, it is hard to see how any authentically presented claim of right offered on behalf of a determinate human grouping can properly be simply discounted. It is not the cacophony of actually presented claims of right but the residual chaos of conflicting claims that survives, even after these have been filtered for consistency, authenticity, and compatibility with fact, which suggests that there cannot really be a rights-based theory of modern politics that possesses any great intellectual force (Dunn 1985, Raz 1984).

I have argued that it is appropriate to see, encapsulated within any claim of right presented by a human individual or group, a tacit moral and political theory espoused by that group. A natural response for modern intellectuals to the chaos of conflicting claims of right is to identify, independently of such tacitly espoused theories, a set of 'objectively existing' social and political groupings, and to interpret the theories in question as psychological mechanisms of defence instrumentally deployed by their proponents in the course of social conflict.[7] To this strategy of understanding there is one simple but fundamental objection. What constitutes a right-claiming human grouping in the course of social and political conflict is not an externally specifiable social location. Rather, it is precisely the espousal of a moral and political theory about its own identity and social extension (Dunn 1984b, Przeworski 1985, more equivocally Elster 1985). What the interests of a given individual, group, community, or even state truly are depends partially on how they conceive themselves and on what, consequently, they deem their own interests to be. (It does not, of course, depend exclusively upon such considerations. Interests are not just individual or collective fantasies – Geuss 1981.)

There is no Archimedean cognitive vantage-point outside the space of human social and political conflict from which the latter can be validly apprehended and appraised. When it comes to the understanding of modern politics, we are all ideologues whether we like it or not (though some of us are certainly crasser and less self-aware ideologues than others). In the case of reasonably extensive conflicts of rights, accordingly, whether these rights be individual or collective, natural or cultural, there will seldom be any decisive means of intellectual adjudication on just how far any particular set of claims must be taken as valid. Even to describe a reasonably extensive conflict of rights adequately is a formidable intellectual task; and in many instances an adequate description of such a conflict would be as much of an adjudication as it is sensible to hope for.

There certainly are such things as inherently public goods: goods which if they are provided for any members of a group must be made equally available to all. The massive importance of such goods in social and political life has been strongly emphasized in recent decades (Olson 1965 and 1982, Elster 1985). The practical problems of free-riding (of drawing the benefits of a public good while actively seeking to avoid contributing to the costs of its provision) have become a central theme in the understanding of modern politics. What makes a good a public good is not that it is in fact provided by the public or that it is not enjoyed by an individual. It is simply that once it has been provided at all to the members of a given group it cannot be withheld from any of them. It is not, by analogy, clear that there really are any such entities as inherently collective rights. (If there appear verbally to be such rights this is simply because they can be generated, trivially, by adding the formula of 'a right to' to some favoured collective goods.) What certainly exist, however, are rights of agency or protection claimed by particular collectivities. These rights are valued and demanded, like the most classic of the rights of human beings, as rights for the individual members of the collectivity. It is these individual members (if anyone) who would enjoy them. What makes them appear to be collective rights is not the *nature* of their prospective beneficiaries but, rather, their identity. Such rights are collective in the sense (and only in the sense) that their scope and distribution explicitly mention the collectivity of members on whose behalf they are claimed. On the beneficiary theory of rights, if not on the liberty theory (Waldron 1984), there is no contradiction in insisting that the rights to act claimed by a collectivity are simply the rights of its individual members even where the actions in question are unwelcome to some of these members. As Rousseau insisted, membership in a benign political community is a peculiarly strong example of an inherent public good. It is possible, if seldom agreeable, to be forced to be free (Skinner 1983 and 1986).

In the case of a lengthy and anomalous industrial dispute such as the 1984–5 British miners' strike, many different conceptions of right customarily come into collision. It is absurd to think of some particular subset of these as transparently valid and the remainder as evidently misplaced. An adequate description of these collisions of right would have to take the form of an adequate history of modern Britain (and perhaps not just of *modern* Britain either; and perhaps not just of *Britain* either; and so on). There are, of course, always complicated questions of positive law involved in such disputes: what state officials are obliged and permitted to do, what forms of picketing are or are not legitimate, under what conditions the leadership of a union possesses the authority to instruct its members to take strike action, and to what degree its existing legal immunities depend upon its respecting these conditions. The analysis of what the law is in relation to such questions is a matter for lawyers. But neither lawyers, union officials, industrial managers, nor professional politicians have any privileged standing in determining what the law should be. There, we are all of us simply amateur moral and political theorists strictly on a par with one another.

The most important disagreement in the case of the miners' strike – as in the case of most other major industrial disputes – was over the question of whether the law ought to be designed to favour or obstruct, to facilitate or to impede, strike action. In this instance only the very callow could hope to resolve the dispute (perhaps indeed even to express it) with anything less elaborate than a complete moral and political theory. For those who own only their power to labour – in an economy founded upon public as well as in one founded upon private ownership – the right to withdraw their labour is of overwhelming importance. (How could it not be so?) The wages won by a powerful union from a monopoly employer are a clear instance of a public good for the union's own members. (They may well have a more disputable status from other points of view.)

To choose to draw the benefits of union membership while refusing to incur the costs of co-operating in the threats which secure these benefits is to choose to ride freely. On the other hand, a union closed shop in a monopoly employer is rather less evidently a public good from any definite point of view. It can be defended as an instrumental pre-condition for effective self-defence on the part of the workforce; and the occupational community to which it applies can be celebrated for its social merits. But the closed shop as such can hardly be celebrated in itself. Under full communism – as a moral ideal (Elster 1985) – there would most certainly not be closed shops.

Egalitarian socialists naturally regret the obstruction of strike action within a capitalist economy. Liberal economists, by contrast, are still inclined to hanker after the Loi Le Chapelier and to regret that any combinations of employers or workers should be legally permitted (let alone protected). Both have quite important arguments for their point of view. Both, that is, can point to real and substantial costs, often costs which fall as much on others as they do on the principals, of disregarding their convictions. The present position of those inhabitants of Britain who lack market advantages is not an enviable one. But in an economy which is going to remain capitalist, virtually all members of the community (including the entire working class) share with entrepreneurs and even with many *rentiers* a clear common interest in the continuing profitability of capitalist enterprise (Przeworski 1985). Hence the drastic importance of the strategic judgment, whether or not a given economy is going to remain capitalist. Hence, too, the equally drastic importance of the probable short- and long-term welfare consequences of its ceasing to remain capitalist. On no possible understanding was the miners' strike a direct positive contribution to the profitability of British capitalist enterprise. But nor, for that matter, was it plausibly much of a contribution to enhancing the competing political charms of socialist enterprise.

Conflicts between classes that own the means of production and classes that are obliged to sell their labour, however they may be best described and whether or not they are ineradicable in principle, remain central to the politics of capitalist societies. (At least in imagination they also stretch far beyond these at present into the potentially eschatological conflicts between societies.) Because they are still so central, the moral and political theories to which they give rise are exceedingly complex in structure. They certainly eventuate in sharply contrasting conceptions of right; but these conceptions themselves rest upon extremely elaborate causal beliefs. At least in the case of the causal beliefs, issues of validity or error arise not just contingently and from time to time but permanently and by necessity. (Here, again, it is plainly inadequate to see the clash of wills, interests, and moral and political theories simply as the collision of fantasies.)

Let us take a highly simplified interpretation of the claims of right that came into collision in the course of the miners' strike. Is it or is it not convincing to insist that the remaining members of a trade union, the majority of whose fellows have (however grudgingly or irregularly) come to take strike action, have a right to be protected by the agents of the government in continuing to work as they choose? Is it or is it not convincing to insist that in a major industrial dispute those with only their labour to sell are fully justified in systematically menacing their reluctant fellow workers into withdrawing their labour, even if this policy of systematic menace results in extensive injury and even occasional loss of life?

The first of these questions, understood as a question of moral and political entitlement and not as a question of positive law, is relatively easy to answer with confidence. There definitely are some doubts about the constitutional merit of the process through which the National Union of Mineworkers came out on strike in 1984. There are separate and at least equally pressing doubts, simply from the viewpoint of the interest of its own members, as to whether it was well advised to do so. (This is a complicated question, not resolvable simply by pointing out that the strike failed. At the point at which the strike began no one could in principle have *known* that the strike would fail.) There are further – and perhaps even more pressing – doubts as to whether the success of the strike would have been in the interest of the British working class at large. (To ignore the price-competitivity of a nationally subsidized energy industry within a national economy massively committed to international trade is to impose a substantial and indefinitely extensible rent on all other national producers. On any coherent economic theory, much of this rent will fall sooner or later upon the rewards of labour.) But what there cannot be, waiving all these doubts, is a right on the part of members of a trade union to be assisted by the force of the state in subverting the properly arrived-at decisions of their union. (The issue of the legitimacy of a closed shop is a distinct question. But here too the case against is scarcely overwhelming. It may be very difficult to become a coal-miner without becoming a member of the NUM. But no one in Great Britain is *obliged* to become a coal-miner.) The legal definition of picketing is a proper (and, in any society in which strike action is not simply outlawed, an inevitable) focus of public policy. But a public policy explicitly aimed at weakening the capacity of unions to impose their collective authority upon their own members is in intention a partisan intervention against the institution of trade unions as such. To assist free-riding on the part of union members *is* to impair the capacity of unions to secure public goods for their membership (Olson 1965 and 1982). It is not an appealing view that union membership should deprive a person of their major civil rights. But the 'right' of a union member to break a properly declared strike is not a civil right at all. Indeed it is a clear violation of the duties incumbent on any member of such an association. There is no *right* on the part of union members to break strikes properly declared by their own unions. It is pure hypocrisy to pretend that the use of massive police or military power to control mass picketing within a single union has anything to do with the protection of the right of other members of that union to work as they choose. The justification of its use must rest, if it is to rest anywhere at all, on the public policy grounds which motivated the legislation that made mass picketing illegal.

On the other hand, even if membership of a union implies the incurring of duties and the forgoing of liberties corresponding with these duties, it plainly does not imply the abrogation of all the civil, let alone all the human, rights of the member. The immediacy and intensity of some forms of class conflict have a somewhat corrosive impact upon even such central liberal values as freedom of expression or autonomy. (The autonomous breach of a duty is not really any more beguiling than the heteronymous breach of one.) It calls into question their relevance, where it does not impair their intrinsic appeal. But it has decidedly less impact on rights to physical security.

The view that mass picketing is merely a legitimate means of expressing the sentiments of fellow workers (an impeccably liberal view as far as it goes – and one much emphasized in public by union leaders in the course of strikes) can hardly be held altogether in good faith. The contempt of others does have some motivational force, though it is as apt to arouse anger as it is to evoke shame. But there is no serious question that the passion on which union leaders must rely to keep a fraying strike solid is the passion of fear. Mass picketing is a ritual of self-righteous solidarity for the pickets; but its instrumental purpose is the intimidation of those at whom it is directed. The most effective means of intimidation, both for those seeking to enforce a strike and for those seeking to break it, is the threat to life and limb. Dissident union members do not have a right to try to break a properly declared strike of their own union. But if they choose to flout their union duties in this way, they certainly do retain a legal entitlement to the civil (and, if necessary, military) protection of their rights to life and to physical security. For a trade union or a political leader to claim the entitlement to entrench on these rights is implicitly (or explicitly) to challenge the legitimacy of the state. A moral and political theory sufficient to back such a challenge is an elaborate and ambitious venture and requires the support of a great deal of well-justified belief about economic, social, and political causality. So too, of course, does a moral and political theory sufficient to demonstrate the legitimacy of the state (Dunn 1980: 249–99 and 1984b).

This may well seem too sceptical a note on which to close. But it is, I think, worth insisting upon it with some vehemence. The intellectual and political appeal of claims of right is that of powerful and authoritative simplification. To *claim* a right which is not simply a contingent right under positive law is to seek to cut through the tangle of conflicting sentiment and belief that prevails in any modern capitalist society[8] to something solid and unchallengeable that lies beyond it. But there is no reason to believe that anything solid and unchallengeable does lie *beyond* the heterogeneity of belief and sentiment that makes up a human society (Lear 1982, Putnam 1981, Rorty 1979). All that lies behind all human judgments of truth and falsity are forms of human life.

We can see how important such a conclusion is wherever we ourselves are inclined to reject the legitimacy of a state. Throwing petrol bombs at policemen is as natural an expression of prevailing popular sentiment on occasion in Catholic or Protestant districts of Belfast or Londonderry, or even in black areas of Toxteth or Brixton or Handsworth, as it is in Chile or Poland or South Africa. But since the majority of the population of the state in question takes a very different attitude towards the legitimacy of its government in the former cases than it does in the latter ones, it is natural for it to feel that the cases differ decisively from one another. (From the point of view of the majority, they *do* differ decisively.) But if anyone has human rights, individual soldiers and police officers possess them also. The right deliberately to kill simply in order to intimidate seems a bold claim in the face of riot, even in what is otherwise a state of impeccable legitimacy. (Could riots actually occur in a state that truly was of *impeccable* legitimacy?) But the right to kill simply in individual self-defence in the face of riot is hard to deny, even to the forces of coercion of the most repressive state. Riot is a form of temporary or local civil war. Only moral imbeciles welcome the onset of civil war for its own sake. But in a state which is profoundly unjust the choice which its inhabitants face is a choice between submitting to tyranny and injustice or unleashing civil war. In those circumstances, as Locke long ago insisted, the responsibility for the exercise of force and for the harm that follows from it rests on the unjust authorities (Locke 1960). The blood is on their hands.

Today, as in the late seventeenth century, the most important question about any political community is always the question of how far it has contrived to make itself a true civil society, and how far it remains (for many or even most of its members) just a state of suppressed war. The degree to which particular claims of right are acknowledged and secured is one important criterion of where a particular society should be placed along this continuum. But this very assessment requires the tacit elaboration of an entire moral and political theory. Conflicting claims of right must be adjudicated within the theory as a whole. (Particular claims, of course, may themselves be best expressed by constructing an alternative theory of equivalent scope and then confronting the two theories systematically with one another.) What we cannot rationally hope today is that such claims should possess the power to validate themselves one by one and out of their own superior authority.

We may choose to regard human beings as equal (Vlastos 1984, Dworkin 1981 and 1984). We may build and believe and defend moral and political theories that deny that any power on earth possesses the moral authority to deprive a human being of some particular rights. We may even claim that some human rights are absolute or inalienable (Gewirth 1984) – though it is unlikely that our claim will be entirely convincing (Simmons 1983). But only the grossly ignorant or confused can any longer suppose that any human rights at all truly are self-evident.

NOTES

1   If therefore Men in this Life only have hope; if in this Life they can only enjoy, 'tis not strange, nor unreasonable, that they should seek their Happiness by avoiding all things, that disease them here, and by pursuing all that delight them. . . . For if there be no Prospect beyond the Grave, the inference is certainly right, *Let us eat and drink*, let us enjoy what we delight in, *for tomorrow we shall die*. . . . Men may chuse different things, and yet all chuse right, supposing them only like a Company of poor insects, whereof some are Bees, delighted with Flowers, and their sweetness; others, Beetles, delighted with other kind of Viands; which having enjoyed for a season, they should cease to be, and exist no more for ever.   (Locke 1975: 269–70)

    For the impact on Locke's understanding of rights, see Simmons (1983: esp. 204).
2   For the cultural and political importance of their subsequent divergence, see Dunn (1980: 243–99) and Putnam (1981).
3   Compare virtually all the contributions to Waldron (1984). On a common contemporary philosophical understanding, the design of moral theories is in effect their profession. But compare Williams (1985) and Rorty (1979).
4   It is conceptually more than a little obscure how such a process is to be understood on a modern liberal theory. But compare Geuss (1981).
5   For the analogous pressure in social explanation, see James (1984) and Dunn (1985: 119–38).
6   I do not wish to defend the view that this failure is compatible with the fundamental principles of socialism (compare Elster 1985, Dunn 1984b). I merely note the historical and conceptual pressures involved.
7   This is not in my view an intellectually defensible conception of what an ideology really is (Dunn 1980: 81–111 and 1985, Elster 1985). But it is a conception that

social scientists are apt to find particularly compelling.
8 And no doubt, more surreptitiously, in every modern socialist society. And perhaps, functionalist social anthropology notwithstanding, in every geographically extended human society there has ever been.

REFERENCES

Blackburn, S. (1981) 'Reply: rule-following and moral realism', in Steven Holtzman and Christopher Leich (eds.) *Wittgenstein: To Follow a Rule*, London: Routledge & Kegan Paul.
Cohen, G.A. (1979) 'Capitalism, freedom and the proletariat', in Alan Ryan (ed.) *The Idea of Freedom*, Oxford: Oxford University Press.
Dunn, J. (1979) *Western Political Theory in the Face of the Future*, Cambridge: Cambridge University Press.
—— (1980) *Political Obligation in its Historical Context*, Cambridge: Cambridge University Press.
—— (1984a) *Locke*, Oxford: Oxford University Press.
—— (1984b) *The Politics of Socialism*, Cambridge: Cambridge University Press.
—— (1985) *Rethinking Modern Political Theory*, Cambridge: Cambridge University Press.
Dworkin, R. (1977) *Taking Rights Seriously*, London: Duckworth.
—— (1981) 'What is equality? Pt 1: Equality of welfare; Pt 2: Equality of resources', *Philosophy and Public Affairs* 10 (3, 4): 185–246, 283–345.
—— (1984) 'Rights as trumps', in J. Waldron (ed.) *Theories of Rights*, Oxford: Oxford University Press.
—— (1985) *A Matter of Principle*, Cambridge, Mass.: Harvard University Press.
Elster, J. (1985) *Making Sense of Marx*, Cambridge: Cambridge University Press.
Finnis, J. (1980) *Natural Law and Natural Rights*, Oxford: Clarendon Press.
Geuss, R. (1981) *The Idea of a Critical Theory*, Cambridge: Cambridge University Press.
Gewirth, A. (1984) 'Are there any absolute rights?', in J. Waldron (ed.) *Theories of Rights*, Oxford: Oxford University Press.
Gierke, O. (1934) *Natural Law and the Theory of Society 1500 to 1800*, tr. Ernest Barker, 2 vols., Cambridge: Cambridge University Press.
Goldthorpe, J.H. (ed.) (1984) *Order and Conflict in Contemporary Capitalism*, Oxford: Clarendon Press.
Hart, H.L.A. (1968) *Punishment and Responsibility*, Oxford: Clarendon Press.
—— (1983) *Essays on Jurisprudence and Philosophy*, Oxford: Clarendon Press.
Hobbes, T. (1983) *De Cive: The English Version*, ed. Howard Warrender, Oxford: Clarendon Press.
Hohfeld, W.N. (1919) *Fundamental Legal Conceptions as Applied in Judicial Reasoning*, New Haven: Yale University Press.
James, S. (1984) *The Content of Social Explanation*, Cambridge: Cambridge University Press.
Kenny, A. (1985) *The Logic of Deterrence*, London: Firethorn Press.
Lear, J. (1982) 'Leaving the world alone', *Journal of Philosophy* 79 (7): 382–403.
Locke, J. (1960) *Two Treatises of Government*, ed. Peter Laslett, Cambridge: Cambridge University Press.
—— (1975) *An Essay Concerning Human Understanding*, ed. Peter H. Nidditch, Oxford: Clarendon Press.
Lukes, S. (1985) *Marxism and Morality*, Oxford: Clarendon Press.
McDowell, J. (1981) 'Non-cognitivism and rule-following', in Steven Holtzman and Christopher Leich (eds.) *Wittgenstein: To Follow a Rule*, London: Routledge & Kegan Paul.

MacIntyre, A. (1981) *After Virtue: A Study in Moral Theory*, London: Duckworth.
—— (1983) 'The indispensability of political theory', in David Miller and Larry Siedentop (eds.) *The Nature of Political Theory*, Oxford: Clarendon Press.
Mackie, J. (1977) *Ethics: Inventing Right and Wrong*, Harmondsworth: Penguin Books.
—— (1984) 'Can there be a right-based moral theory?', in J. Waldron (ed.) *Theories of Rights*, Oxford: Oxford University Press.
Malone, D. (1975) *The Story of the Declaration of Independence*, Oxford: Oxford University Press.
Nozick, R. (1974) *Anarchy, State and Utopia*, Oxford: Blackwell.
Olson, M. (1965) *The Logic of Collective Action*, Cambridge, Mass.: Harvard University Press.
—— (1982) *The Rise and Decline of Nations*, New Haven: Yale University Press.
Przeworski, A. (1985) *Capitalism and Social Democracy*, Cambridge: Cambridge University Press.
Putnam, H. (1981) *Reason, Truth and History*, Cambridge: Cambridge University Press.
Raz, J. (1984) 'Right-based moralities', in J. Waldron (ed.) *Theories of Rights*, Oxford: Oxford University Press.
Rorty, R. (1979) *Philosophy and the Mirror of Nature*, Princeton: Princeton University Press.
Scanlon, T. (1984) 'Rights, goals, and fairness', in J. Waldron (ed.) *Theories of Rights*, Oxford: Oxford University Press.
Scheffler, S. (1982) *The Rejection of Consequentialism*, Oxford: Clarendon Press.
Simmons, A.J. (1983) 'Inalienable rights and Locke's treatises', *Philosophy and Public Affairs* 12 (3): 175–204.
Skinner, Q. (1983) 'The idea of negative liberty: philosophical and historical perspectives', in Richard Rorty, J.B. Schneewind, and Quentin Skinner (eds.) *Philosophy in History*, Cambridge: Cambridge University Press.
—— (1986) 'The paradoxes of political liberty', in *The Tanner Lectures on Human Values. Vol. VII*, Salt Lake City: University of Utah Press.
Taylor, C. (1983) 'Political theory and practice', in Christopher Lloyd (ed.) *Social Theory and Political Practice*, Oxford: Clarendon Press.
Tuck, R. (1979) *Natural Rights Theories: Their Origin and Development*, Cambridge: Cambridge University Press.
Vlastos, G. (1984) 'Justice and Equality', in J. Waldron (ed.) *Theories of Rights*, Oxford: Oxford University Press.
Waldron, J. (ed.) (1984) *Theories of Rights*, Oxford: Oxford University Press.
Williams, B. (1981) *Moral Luck*, Cambridge: Cambridge University Press.
—— (1985) *Ethics and the Limits of Philosophy*, London: Fontana/Collins.
Wills, G. (1978) *Inventing America: Jefferson's Declaration of Independence*, New York: Doubleday.

3
Preserving public protest: the legal approach
Denis Galligan

According to Machiavelli, 'good examples proceed from good education, good education from good laws and good laws . . . from those
very tumults which many so inconsiderately condemn' (Machiavelli
1970: 114). He went on to argue that in the republic of Rome where
apparently such tumults were a common occurrence, far from
leading to banishments or acts of violence inimical to the common
good, they 'led to laws and institutions whereby the liberties of the
republic benefited' (Machiavelli 1970: 114). Public tumults or acts
of public protest are a common feature of British history, and
whether or not they have had the beneficial consequences claimed
for them in Rome, there is some recognition that they are not just
the dangerous outbursts of unruly mobs but may be a legitimate
form of political action. But there are difficulties in handling public
protest. At the theoretical level, there is little common ground as to
how the liberties involved – assembly, speech, and movement – are
to be reconciled with each other, with conflicting rights and liberties, or with notions of public order. At the practical level, these
conflicts become real and immediate; decisions have to be made and
actions taken which directly or indirectly define the scope of public
protest. Sometimes the problems of clashing values and interests are
solved by legislative enactment; the disturbances of the 1930s, for
example, led to the passing of the Public Order Act 1936 and so
settled for the time being a number of issues. More typically,
however, matters are left to be determined in a piecemeal way by the
police, the courts, the Home Secretary, and a variety of other
officials. And even where there are statutes, they are unlikely to
provide more than a broad framework of guidance within which
specific decisions are to be made.

The result is that the scope of personal liberties, and in particular
the liberties involved in public protest, depends on a patchwork of
legal regulation and in practice on the case-by-case decisions of

disparate officials. The object of this essay is to examine that patchwork, in order not so much to define the precise scope of the freedom to protest, but to identify some of the general characteristics of the way that issues about that freedom are resolved, and to point out the directions in which the law is moving, particularly in the light of the Public Order Act 1986. The essay divides broadly into two parts. In the first part, three background factors are considered: (1) the residual legal nature of civil liberties; (2) the idea that liberties are to be balanced against other values and against notions of the public interest; and (3) the pervasiveness of discretion in the decisions of the police, the courts, and other officials in fixing the boundaries of public protest. In the second part of the essay, I consider a number of the specific issues that arise in fixing these boundaries: (1) the clash between public protest and the everyday activities of the community; (2) public protest and the hostile audience; (3) public protest and the conflict with other rights and liberties; and (4) public protest aimed at harming specific vulnerable groups.

BACKGROUND FACTORS

The forms of public protest are various but usually involve meetings, marches, demonstrations, or processions in one guise or another. A main element is communication whether through speech, writing, or symbols of some other kind. Protest may be the action of a lone demonstrator, but more often depends on a combination of people massing together, sometimes statically, but typically where free movement is an important feature. And while communication of an idea or position is a basic component, acts of public protest often portray a shared intensity of feeling and commitment to a cause, which adds to the impact. It may be possible to think of public protest as a distinct, generic activity, but I am not able to develop that idea in this essay, nor to consider the place of public protest in political life; for ease of reference, however, I shall refer rather loosely to public protest as a mixture and combination of these various elements.[1]

The legal status of public protest

The first task then is to examine the legal status of public protest. Americans and most western Europeans can point to a constitutional statement of civil rights which, although expressed in abstract terms, gives rights a secure position in political life and provides a foundation for their application as specific, concrete rights. Such statement of rights is a source of guidance to legislators and administrators; it is also a yardstick against which the legality of their actions can be tested in the courts. The position in Britain is less straightforward. There is no constitutional declaration of rights, and so the legal status of public protest is less certain. One can point to a political commitment to personal liberty and to a network of laws, both statutory and common law, which give effect to that commitment, not by specifying positive rights but by limiting the powers of officials and others to interfere. Since there are no legal constraints on Parliament, it may legislate as it chooses on matters affecting civil liberties, the only real restraint being the force of its own commitment to liberty. Similarly, there is no judicial review of legislation and only limited review of administrative actions, but in practice many areas of civil liberties are left to the common law and so to the courts. Some claim that this combination of the political and the legal has provided a firm foundation for civil rights and that the absence of a bill of rights is irrelevant. Indeed, it is often said that these arrangements might properly be analysed in terms of rights. According to Dicey, the general principle of English law is that 'individual rights are the basis, not the result, of the law of the constitution' (Dicey 1961: 207). Judges sometimes talk in terms of rights to freedom of speech, movement, and assembly;[2] Lord Scarman in one of the important social documents of the times has written of the right to protest (Scarman 1975); and the White Paper on public order reaffirms the existence and importance of rights to peaceful protest and assembly.[3] Moreover, Britain's subscription to the European Convention on Human Rights might be taken as positive affirmation of rights already existing in English law.[4]

Talk of rights in this context can serve useful political ends, but we must be clear about the sense with which the concept may be used if it is to be an accurate representation of English law.[5] In the first place there is no direct support for a right to public protest in so far as that carries the suggestion of public protest as a discrete activity. As Dicey argued in relation to the right to assembly, it is 'nothing more than a result of the view taken by the courts as to individual liberty of the person and individual liberty of speech' (Dicey 1961: 271); A, B, C, D, and 'a thousand or ten thousand other persons' may meet anywhere that each otherwise has a right to be and may say what each otherwise has a right to say. This analysis holds true for the even broader idea of a right to protest; it consists in whatever scope the law allows for personal liberty to move about, to assemble, and to speak. Indeed, it might be added to Dicey's account that the very act of assembling together with a view to protest may provide the basis for restricting those personal liberties of movement and speech that one otherwise would have. Whereas A may lawfully walk up and down a public road, the moment he is joined for a common purpose by B, C, D, and a thousand others there is a risk of obstruction, conflict with other interests, and a greater threat of disorder.

The second point is that any putative legal right to public protest is negative rather than positive, negative in the sense that the right is primarily to forbearance by state officials and private individuals from restricting public protest. In terms of Hohfeld's analysis of legal concepts, it is an immunity-right, the correlative being no power on the part of an official or citizen to interfere. A case could be made for positive rights to the resources and facilities necessary to ensure the worth and effectiveness of public protest, but there is little support in English law for even the most modest claims. All that the law typically recognizes is a liberty to enter certain public places, such as streets, parks, and halls, for a range of possible activities which may include acts of protest. That liberty may, according to the circumstances, be protected by a range of immunities from interference by persons acting in an official or private capacity. But everything does indeed depend on the circumstances, and, when the object is public protest, the liberties in issue are likely to be subject to a host of restrictions, some flowing from the general law, for example the legal restrictions on the use of roads and streets, others depending on the discretion of officials, for example the powers conferred under local authority by-laws to restrict access to public places or the powers of the police to maintain order.

The third characteristic of public protest under English law is that in so far as there are rights, they are not specified as such but have to be inferred from the surrounding laws; rarely do those laws confer rights directly or indeed make any reference to rights. In other words, the existence of rights to protest is established and their content is defined by considering what scope for personal action is left after taking account of (a) positive restrictions on those seeking to assemble, communicate, and move about in a public place, and (b) the powers conferred on others to restrict actions including acts of protest. This idea is often expressed in the maxim that in English law one is free to do whatever is not prohibited, a freedom which includes public protest; it is also presumably what Dicey (1961: 207) meant by his claim that individual rights are the basis, not the result, of the law of the constitution. For him, the residual nature of civil rights was one of the strengths of the English constitution, since it meant that liberties were not dependent on positive constitutional statements, but were in a fundamental sense to be taken for granted, subject only to explicit legal restrictions, and were protected by legal remedies such as habeas corpus. This approach has clear attractions, but there are two qualifications to bear in mind. First, the rider might be added that whether or not the approach of English law is preferable to some alternative depends on how extensive the legal restrictions are; if they are highly restrictive, leaving little residual scope for civil liberties, then the abstract virtues of the approach count for little in practice. Secondly, the other side of the presumption-of-liberty coin is that actions done in pursuance of civil liberties have no special status, and so for legal purposes are no different from other actions which might cause disorder or inconvenience to the community. Whereas the specification of rights would be evidence of a commitment that certain actions have a protected status and carry a special loading against conflicting factors.

The fourth characteristic of the legal approach to public protest, consistent with its negative and residual nature, is that it is protected, to the extent that it is, indirectly. It is in Hart's terminology a liberty-right rather than a right correlative to duty (Hart 1973). This means that A's liberty to march down the street with a banner is protected not by precisely matching duties on others to abstain from interference with his protest, but by a range of general duties under the criminal and civil law which restrict interference with an indeterminate range of actions, normally including public protest. The laws relating to assault, obstruction, false imprisonment, and licence to pass and re-pass are examples of the many laws which serve in that way to protect public protest.

The next question is whether this view of rights to protest as reductivist, negative, residuary, and indirect has any significance in terms of the level of personal liberties. The differences between such a system and one where rights are proclaimed and entrenched may be more appearance than substance. Where civil rights do have express, constitutional status they are cast in abstract terms, leaving open their meaning and scope for settlement in specific cases. On the English approach, on the other hand, the general commitment to civil liberties should manifest itself in the decisions of legislatures, administrators, and courts. The same hard questions arise about the relative strength and importance of conflicting values and interests, and the net content of, for example, free speech as extrapolated from the residue of restrictions may be similar to the net content of a constitutional right to free speech after all exceptions and qualifications have been taken into account. And while there are obvious advantages for the protection of rights in a system of judicial review based on entrenched rights, so much depends finally on the political culture, and it is a complex empirical question as to whether one set of institutional arrangements is likely to produce greater overall regard for civil liberties than another.

It might still be urged, however, that the positive enactment of a right to protest would have two clear advantages: it would give public protest a more secure legal basis, and it would give courts a greater role in its protection. As to the first, to have a general right to public protest would mean that the community has recognized that activity to be sufficiently important to warrant special protection against competing factors. To have a right is to have a protected interest, protected in the sense that it carries a certain weight against competing goals.[6] The precise content of the right would need to be worked out in different contexts, depending on what other rights or important values might be in conflict. The importance of the general, abstract right would be that, in those calculations, the claims of free protest would have a guaranteed position, guaranteed in the sense that the decision-maker, whether Parliament, administrator, or court, would have to show through its reasoning that a serious attempt had been made to give free protest an appropriate weighting against conflicting considerations. The result might but would not necessarily ensure greater net protection of free protest; however, it would ensure the acceptance of free protest as a positive, enduring value providing guidance in novel and contentious cases.

Judicial review would be a natural companion to such a system; it would mean that final decisions as to the scope and content of civil rights were left to the courts. This has advantages and disadvantages. It would signify a shift of power from Parliament to the courts, but this may not be so significant, since, with notable exceptions like the Public Order Act, the law of civil liberties has anyhow in the main been left to the courts. Indeed, one of the puzzling questions is why the English courts have done so little to develop common law concepts of civil rights clearly defined and settled in status. Ample opportunities have been available, but, in a line of cases, some of which are considered later in this essay, virtually nothing has been done to develop concepts of rights.[7] It is rare to find judicial discussion of civil rights, particularly anything approaching a right to protest, even in cases where the very issue is about the extent of civil rights. The same point could be made about judicial attitudes to a whole range of areas involving issues of civil rights – for example, the rights of suspects, rights to confidentiality, and rights of prisoners.[8] Whatever judicial commitment there may be to civil rights in these various contexts, it remains at a high level of abstraction and generality and offers little guidance in practical decisions. Admittedly, few cases have gone to the higher courts, and perhaps a legislative or constitutional enactment of civil rights is precisely the catalyst that now is needed to initiate a jurisprudence of rights.

Balancing interests and values

The second characteristic of the legal regulation of public protest is the idea that values and interests are likely to be in competition, and so must be balanced against each other. Balancing is the popular metaphor. Lord Scarman, in his report on the disorders of Red Lion Square, wrote of the balance to be struck between the exercise of the right to protest and public order in the sense that ordinary people may go about their business and pleasure without obstruction or inconvenience (Scarman 1975: 2). Lord Widgery invoked a similar idea in describing the duties of the police to regulate the use of the highway by competing groups and to make sure all got a fair share.[9] The same approach lies behind the White Paper on public order and the Public Order Act 1986 which followed; the right to protest is to be balanced against public order and the rights of non-protesters.[10]

The metaphor of balancing is a way of recognizing that freedom to protest is important but not absolute. Other interests must be given their place, and this may mean restricting protest. Those other interests can be substantial: one's interest in not being libelled; in being able to carry out the daily activities of social and commercial life; the interests of individuals and groups in not being denigrated and vilified in the eyes of the community; and the common interest in public order. If balancing means that decisions have to be made about the importance of different interests and as to mutual accommodation when conflicts occur, then balancing is unavoidable and lies at the heart of any system of legal regulation. All laws represent a view about the relative importance of different, conflicting interests, and we shall see later in this essay how the balance has been struck in four key areas. Moreover, no matter how clear the policies and principles within which decisions are made, it may be very difficult in a given case to provide a fully reasoned account of how the lines have been drawn and the balance settled. There is finally an irreducible element of personal judgment and assessment. However, the main point of present interest is the difficulty of finding any objective, generally accepted, or even rational basis for ranking interests in such an inherently contentious matter as public protest in a society which is deeply divided over many fundamental issues.

One step towards making the process of balancing more critical and objective is to ensure that there are real interests in conflict. A minority group has a real interest in not being subjected to violence or intolerable provocation by the protests of others; those seeking access to their workplace have a real interest in not being prevented or intimidated by pickets. Similarly, serious outbursts of disorder are easy enough to identify, and there is both an individual and collective interest in their prevention; the riots of Brixton and Toxteth are clear cases of serious disorder against which preventive action must be taken. Often, however, the disturbances created by public protest fall far short of that, and it is then necessary to look behind the claim of public disorder or disruption of the community and identify the specific interests that are affected. Only then is it possible to consider their importance in relation to the interest in free protest. What, for example, is at stake in the claim to a right to continuous calm on the streets, or a right to go about one's business and pleasure without obstruction or inconvenience?[11] Either the claim is too abstract and subject to too many qualifications to carry any argumentative weight, or it is a pretext for interests less meritorious.

The more fundamental difficulty with the idea of balancing is in finding principles and policies to measure the relative importance of competing values and interests. When a judge decides that protest must be restricted in favour of order, he is relying on some view of the relative importance of each.[12] Similarly, when the Home Secretary defends the added restrictions of the Public Order Act 1986, he is claiming that order and the smooth running of society justify an alteration in the scope of free protest.[13] Judgments of this kind are made at many points in the system not only openly by senior officials, but also by lesser officials in circumstances of low visibility. It is noticeable, even in decisions open to public scrutiny, that efforts are made only rarely to provide a reasoned account of how the balance is reached. The White Paper on public order, for example, appears merely to assert that added restrictions are necessary to prevent serious disorder, that being a goal which is accepted already. Little attention is paid to the fact that while such powers may help to prevent disorder, they also restrict free protest. The two goals do not occupy separate territories; they are in competition. Similarly, from decisions where balancing is supposed to have occurred – between free speech and the protection of minorities, between the freedom to picket and the freedom to go to work or to conduct a business, between public meetings and public order – it is difficult to extrapolate principles and policies of a general kind; and in the less accessible, discretionary decisions, these problems are compounded. One is left with the suspicion that balancing too readily becomes an empty metaphor, a device for avoiding clear and vigorous reasons of explanation and justification, so that the limits of protest come to depend on the loose and impressionistic judgments of diverse officials.

It is hardly reasonable to expect that there can be any set of social principles, clear in terms and widespread in acceptance, about the importance of free protest relative to other values and interests. The divisions within British society over such matters as the legal enforcement of morality, the rights and wrongs of abortion, surrogate motherhood, and any number of other matters, are deep and unbridgeable. These same divisions apply to questions about civil liberties. But if there is little by way of agreed principles for balancing competing values, how is it to be done? One approach would be to look beyond the diversity of views popularly held and try to reconstruct from the basic institutions, practices, and beliefs of the society a set of deep political principles. Some guidance might be derived in this way, but it is bound to be limited, since, even at this critical level, it is not clear that society is based on any set of coherent and consistent principles sufficiently clear and specific to assist in practical decisions.[14]

In the absence of objective principles, issues of balancing depend to a significant degree on the views of the decision-makers. The strategy then is to ensure that such decisions are made subject to acceptable principles of accountability. This is the general thrust of modern constitutionalism: since there is no overriding yardstick against which the decisions of officials can be tested, the emphasis falls on the *process* of decision-making. Good processes may help to produce good results; but, quite apart from results, processes are themselves important to the legitimacy of decisions. In the present context, process requires at least the following: (a) that in the allocation of powers and responsibilities, important issues of policy and principle are left to be decided by authorities suitably accountable to the democratic process; and (b) that every effort is made by decision-makers – whether legislators, judges, or senior police – to explain and justify the principles and policies on which their decisions are based. This opens the way for public scrutiny and is the first step towards a pattern of principles.

The discretionary character of legal regulation

Talk of balancing leads to the third matter pertinent to the legal regulations of public protest: its discretionary character. Decisions about public protest are made by the police, local officials, the Home Secretary, and the courts, and are to a substantial degree discretionary. By 'discretion' is meant that decisions are made in the relative absence of reasonably specific and binding standards, and depend to a significant degree on the views and assessments of those making the decisions.[15] Typically the exercise of discretion is not subject to appeal or review on the merits. The extent of discretion can be seen at each level of control: at the level of prior restraint in relation to processions, for example, in refusing permission for, imposing conditions on, or banning altogether; at the level of preventive intervention in dispersing or controlling protest; and at the level of punitive action in deciding whether to prosecute or pursue some other course in respect of offences committed in protesting.

The high level of discretion depends on a number of factors. One is that the law is expressed in general terms which leave open matters of interpretation and application. The concept of breach of the peace, for example, is of basic importance, and yet there is still dispute as to its elements.[16] A more important point is that so many decisions, such as whether to impose prior restraints or whether to intervene once protest has begun, depend on the express or implied discretion of the police or other officials, usually with inadequate guidance from the law. Moreover, the question for the police is more likely to be not whether the conditions for intervention have been made out, but assuming they have been, whether or not action should be taken. That decision may depend on the evaluation of the single officer at the scene, or it may reflect a whole set of policing policies made at various levels of authority. And while some discretion in regulating public protest within a legal framework may be inevitable, there is another more fundamental way in which discretion occurs. Lord Scarman has made explicit that the primary duty of the police is to maintain the Queen's Peace, a duty which is more fundamental than upholding the law (Scarman 1981: 62–3). This means that where there is conflict between the requirements of the law and public order, the latter must prevail. Lord Scarman goes on to say that 'the successful solution of the conflict lies first in the priority to be given in the last resort to the maintenance of public order, and secondly in the constant and common-sense exercise of police discretion' (Scarman 1981: 63). In exercising their 'common-sense discretion' the police, presumably, have no authority to break the law, but they do have authority to enforce it only partially and selectively. The existence of an overriding duty to maintain order reinforces the point that the scope and enjoyment of personal liberties depend in so many ways not on the even-handed application of clear legal standards, but on the discretion of the police and other officials, discretion against which there is seldom recourse.

The pervasiveness of discretion in regulating public protest brings with it obvious disadvantages. The very fact that the liberties at stake in public protest depend to a large degree on discretionary judgments is one. Reasonable certainty and stability in the law are not the only values, but they are important, particularly in matters relating to personal freedom. Secondly, the breadth and extent of discretion allow decisions to be made by officials about the importance of public protest relative to other social goals. The process of weighing and balancing, of drawing lines between legitimate protest, the interests of others, and public order, often depends on the judgment of officials who have neither the training to make what is a complex assessment, not the commitment to ensure that the liberty to protest gets a proper weighting. Moreover, questions of common sense become questions of policy and politics. Legislative guidance has been sketchy, and judicial scrutiny tends to avoid a close examination either of the policies being pursued or of the acceptability of individualized decisions. Also, there is evidence to show that policing proceeds to an extent according to its own momentum, with norms and strategies shaped by its own organizational and ideological factors.[17] These are especially influential where the legal standards are loose and incomplete. The law may have little impact, being more in the nature of a resource to be used as a last resort in ensuring compliance with the police's conceptions of good order; how the law can be made effective in such circumstances is a vexed issue upon which a body of empirical research is starting to be gathered.

There is no easy solution to the issues raised by widespread discretionary powers in regulating protest. Some discretion is inevitable in individualized decision-making; it is also unavoidable in decisions that more clearly involve matters of policy. However, the same issues of accountability occur in these areas as in other contexts of official discretion, and much can be done by applying the principles that have been developed in public law. Steps along the following lines would mark the modest beginnings of effective accountability: (a) the channelling of policy issues, like the policies of policing major demonstrations, through democratic processes;[18] (b) greater efforts to specify clear legislative standards; (c) the formulation and publication by those exercising discretion of the policies and strategies applied; (d) more vigorous application of the principles of judicial review regarding unreasonableness, lack of evidence, irrelevant considerations, the statement of reasons, and the requirements of procedural fairness. These strategies do not eliminate discretion, but they help to bring it within an acceptable framework of regulation.[19]

SPECIFIC ISSUES

Public protest in conflict with other activities

Turning now to public protest in practical cases, the first concerns the clash between public protest and ordinary daily activities. Leaving aside the quiet and solitary demonstrator, the impact of acts of protest depends on numbers assembled together in a public place so that the community is forced to take notice. For this reason, virtually any act of public protest will disrupt daily life to some degree. How then are lines to be drawn? A major theme running through discussion of this issue is that protest is to be tolerated provided it is peaceful. Legitimacy depends on peacefulness and non-violence; from J. S. Mill's famous example of the agitated crowd outside the corn-dealer's house (Mill 1962), to Lord Chief Justice Lane's recent strictures against miners who were said to be picketing by intimidation and threat,[20] the idea of peaceful protest has exerted a powerful influence. Provided that protest is peaceful, the consequential disruption of everyday activities will be tolerated. Once it crosses that line and degenerates into violence or the threat of violence, whether deliberately, unavoidably, or even because of the actions of others, protest loses its immunity and is liable to regulation.

These ideas can be seen at work in the law. Where there is serious public disorder, which usually means a high level of confrontation between opposing groups with violence to persons or property the likely outcome, there are ample powers of prevention. These may take, in the case of marches or processions, the character of prior restraints; that is, conditions may be imposed, or, as a last resort, a banning order may be obtained. These methods are not available for forms of public protest that are static in character, such as meetings, demonstrations, and picketing. In respect of those, the police may call on a bevy of powers which are aimed primarily at intervention, but which may on occasions have the effect of prior restraint; those powers range from the quelling of riots and affrays to the prevention of breaches or threatened breaches of the peace. In clear cases of serious disorder the police are bound to intervene, whatever the initial causes, in order to restore order. It is in the more borderline cases, where the basis for intervention is a threatened breach of the peace, that the line between legitimate protest and public order opens up controversy. Breach of the peace has never been defined with precision, but it is a legal concept of antiquity, having been used for different purposes at different times. It certainly covers actions which constitute a threat of violence to the person; it may also extend to acts which produce alarm that 'what is being done causes or will cause real disturbance to the community and the breaking-up of the peace of the neighbourhood' (Brownlie and Supperstone 1981: 2). On the other hand, it appears not to extend to disturbances which might result from disorderly conduct, abusive language, excessive noise, and so on, unless there is reasonable cause for apprehending a threat or use of force (Brownlie and Supperstone 1981: 3).

Whatever the difficulties of definition and application, keeping the peace, in the sense of preventing breaches of the peace, lies at the heart of the powers of the police to intervene in acts of public protest. Whenever the police have reasonable grounds (a matter likely to be left largely to their judgment) for believing that a breach of the peace is occurring or threatened, they have the power and probably the duty to take preventive steps.[21] Failure by a person to comply with any order directed to that end constitutes obstruction of a police officer in the execution of his duty, for which that person may be arrested and prosecuted for a criminal offence, or bound over to keep the peace.[22] This view of the law, which has been established in a chain of judicial decisions, means, first, that the police have extremely wide powers to intervene in acts of public protest and, secondly, that the decision to do so turns to a large degree on the exercise of judgment and discretion both as to whether the conditions have been made out and, if so, whether there should be intervention. The power has been used in a wide variety of situations, including preventing a person addressing a public meeting which might have led others to create a disturbance;[23] controlling the manner of picketing, and limiting the number of pickets;[24] entering and remaining on private premises where a public meeting was being held;[25] and preventing miners from travelling to the pitheads in order to picket.[26]

The common element running through these powers of restraint and intervention is the prevention of violence. However, where the life of the community is disrupted in some other way, the powers of regulation are sparse and fragmented. There may be some scope to prevent non-violent forms of disruption where the permission of an official body, such as a local authority, is needed for the use of a park or other public place. One example is public protest around the Houses of Parliament, where specially restrictive conditions apply.[27] Also it appears that any form of static demonstration (other than in the course of a trade dispute) on a public road or footpath, may be dispersed as an unlawful user quite apart from any threat of violence or other serious disruption.[28] Similarly, a march or procession, initially lawful, may be subject to intervention if it becomes an unreasonable obstruction to other users.[29] These are clear exceptions to the general requirement that intervention is based on violence or the threat of violence, but they do not appear to be used widely, and the legal foundation for the most important – the unlawfulness of static demonstrations on roads and footpaths – is shaky.[30]

Capacious though they may be, the powers of restraint and intervention, whether based on the criterion of violence or on one of the exceptions, do not extend to various forms of disruption no matter how unpleasant, inconvenient, or annoying. It is here, however, that opinions begin to divide. A case can be made for making violence or the threat of violence the touchstone for restrictions, with departure from that principle only in exceptional circumstances. This so far has been the main thrust of English law. However, according to the contrary view, which appears to be the view of the British government, public protest has taken on novel forms which, although untouchable under existing law, are sufficiently obnoxious to require regulation. Indeed, the law does seem more suited to the acts of protest which are of short duration and confined locality, rather than of indefinite duration, like the women's protest at Greenham Common, the miners' picketing of pitheads, or the actions at Wapping by former employees of *The Times*: nor, on this view, is the law able to control mass protest, such as an attempt to bring The City of London to a halt (Stop-the-City), over a wide area. There may be powers to deal with specific incidents occurring in the course of such protests, but not to prevent or control the overall enterprise.

The response of the government to these limitations is major reform of the law. The Public Order Act 1986 proposes three changes of special significance in drawing the line between protest and order: (1) the power to impose limiting conditions on marches and processions based on preventing not only serious public disorder but also serious disruption of the life of the community, serious damage to property, or the intimidation of others with a view to compelling them to act in a particular manner; (2) forms of static protest – that is, meetings, demonstrations, and picketing – will for the first time be subject explicitly to limitations as to numbers, place, and duration where these are considered necessary to prevent serious public disorder, serious disruption of the life of the community, serious damage to property, or the intimidation of others with a view to compelling them to act in a particular manner; (3) the creation of a criminal offence based on certain kinds of conduct in a public place which causes substantial alarm, harassment, or distress. The government tries in its White Paper to justify these changes. It is declared that 'it does not seem right that the police should have no power to re-route a procession in order to limit traffic congestion, or to prevent a bridge from being blocked, or to reduce the severe disruption sometimes suffered by pedestrians, business and commerce'.[31] Nor is it right that the National Front should be able to march through Asian districts, avoiding disorder only because the members of the local community are intimidated enough to board-up their shops and stay at home.[32] If processions are to be subject to such limitations, then so should static forms of protest, since in most respects there is no difference between them in either logic or policy. So the power to set conditions could be used to prevent Stop-the-City-type demonstrations, to restrict those occurring outside foreign embassies, to reduce the disturbance resulting to local residents from prolonged picketing, or to stop interference by pickets with those wanting to go to work. The new offence dealing with harassment, alarm, or distress caused by a variety of acts, including disorderly conduct, will prove useful, according to the White Paper, in dealing with 'minor acts of hooliganism' such as 'groups of youths persistently shouting abuse and obscenities', regardless, presumably, of whether those acts of hooliganism constitute in the eyes of the actors a form of protest.

These provisions signal a rebalancing of the interests in free protest against the interests of the community, resulting in a substantial reduction of the scope for free public protest. The general principle that protest is legitimate provided it is non-violent remains the basic yardstick, but one now to be supplemented by broader notions of community disruption and individual intimidation. Whether the changes are justifiable is arguable. There clearly are cases where the disruption from mass protest, whether static or mobile, is so severe that the power to impose conditions may justifiably be employed: a mass march or demonstration might bring the City of London to a halt; prolonged mass picketing in a residential area might make life for local residents intolerable. In favour of the proposed new powers it can be said that in such cases they enable a reasonable balance to be drawn between conflicting interests: the protest can still go on since there is no power to ban, but conditions can be set which recognize the importance of other clear and serious interests.

There are, however, two major objections. First, while the new powers may be welcome in extreme cases, they might also be invoked in a wide range of cases which are much more borderline. Any assembly for purposes of protest disrupts the life of the community, often substantially, so that the question is where the line is to be drawn. There is a severe risk that the protests at Greenham Common and Molesworth, outside foreign embassies, and in countless other cases will be liable to new and exacting conditions, which will mean either dispersal or that the impact of the protest is lost. Secondly, there are problems in applying the tests of serious disruption, intimidation, and coercion. These are loose ideas which depend in practical application on the discretionary judgments and policies of the police. Since most acts of public protest will cause disruption capable of being judged to be serious, the real question will be whether or not to intervene. This increases the extent to which free protest depends on police discretion, and thus on the factors and policies that influence that discretion. The possibility that conditions may be challenged in the courts provides some safeguards, but this is bound to be of limited effectiveness. The main possible advantage of the increased powers to set conditions on public protest is that this encourages more open and public discussion and negotiation, and may result in sets of guidelines which will constitute an acceptable code for public protest. There is no strong basis, however, for being optimistic that these advantages will eventuate.

Public protest and hostile opposition

The relatively simple principle that public protest is lawful provided that it proceeds without a breach of the peace needs to be re-examined to take account of the problems that are created by hostile opposition.[33] The spectacle of an otherwise peaceful and orderly protest being opposed and disrupted by hostile people or groups is not uncommon. The major source of disorder in the 1930s was the clash between Mosley and his supporters on the one side and opposing groups on the other; similarly, the Red Lion Square affair was due partly to the fact that the same hall had been booked by the National Front and leftist groups on the same day, making a clash inevitable. Less spectacular conflicts are a regular feature of meetings, marches, and demonstrations.

If the general principle of allowing protest provided that the peace is kept were absolute, then it would not matter where the source of disorder lay, nor how responsibility for it should be allocated. Where public protest resulted or was likely to result in a breach of the peace, the usual powers of restraint and prevention would apply in order for the peace to be restored. There are strands of the law indicating that this is the case; the intervention in *Duncan* v. *Jones*[34] which prevented Mrs Duncan from addressing a meeting, and resulted in her arrest and prosecution, was upheld even though the evidence was clear that any threatened disturbance would come from hostile groups in the audience. The court did not directly address the issue of the scope of preventive powers, since, according to the obtuse views of its members, the case did not raise matters of civil liberties; however, the court's affirmation of wide powers of intervention to prevent a breach of the peace has become a mainstay of the law. Moreover, resort to the more drastic powers allowing conditions to be put on processions, or even providing for them to be banned, is based on preventing serious disorder regardless of its origins or the rights and wrongs of participants.

The trouble with this approach is that it gives insufficient importance to the freedom to protest; if it is vulnerable to the disruptive tactics of opposing groups, that freedom is of slight weight. It means that any protest, no matter how peaceful and orderly itself, may be the subject of intervention by the police merely because those hostile to its aims are able to create disruption amounting to a threat to the peace. The threat of disruption leading to serious disorder may even be the basis for prior restraint. Oswald Mosley is not the first authority one would look to on civil rights, but it is interesting to note that, at the time he and his followers were provoking opposition, he persistently argued that they were merely exercising rights to free speech, and that the disorder which accompanied his activities was the result of disruption by opposing groups. The long delay in enacting the first Public Order Act is partly attributable to this argument (Benewick 1967). Considering the extent to which his tactics were aggressive and inciting, the principle of Mosley's argument could not fairly apply to his own case, but there is an important point at stake, for which there is some legal support in *Beatty* v. *Gillbanks*.[35] There the Salvation Army was held not to be guilty of the criminal offence of unlawful assembly arising from disturbances the immediate cause of which were the disruptive tactics of the Skeleton Army. There is some dispute as to what was decided, but the Divisional Court appears to have held that the police had no power to require the Salvation Army to disperse in order to prevent breaches of the peace, since their only purpose was to hold a peaceful procession, even though they knew from past experience that their actions would be opposed with violence. If action is to be taken, it should be against the hostile opponents not the Salvationists, thus protecting the freedom of the latter to march. Dicey took this case to be an example of the general principle that a 'meeting otherwise in every respect lawful and peaceable' is not made unlawful nor should it be dispersed simply because there may be a breach of the peace provoked by opposing wrongdoers (Dicey 1961: 276).

Now while the problem of hostile opposition to otherwise peaceful protest has no easy solution, the law has been particularly inept in offering guidance. Two different and conflicting approaches are at work, one more protective of public protest than the other, but neither developed adequately. There are a number of matters to consider in devising a more satisfactory approach. First, in forming some view of the relative importance of freedom to protest, the traditional principle that protest is legitimate provided it is non-violent is a reasonable starting-point. Secondly, acceptance of that principle carries a commitment to protect forms of protest which fall within it. This may mean adopting methods of policing which ensure that peaceful protests can proceed without disruption. The emphasis then would be to maintain order by preventing disruption rather than the often easier alternative of dispersing the protest. The new powers requiring advance notice of processions, and the greater scope for limiting the size, place, and duration of marches and demonstrations, may assist the police in preventing disruption. Thirdly, it is necessary to develop limitations on what constitutes peaceful protest. One of Dicey's limiting principles was that the assembly should be lawful; if its objects are unlawful, or unlawful acts are committed in conducting it, and the unlawfulness provokes opposition, then the claim to be protected against disruption is lost (Dicey 1961: 277–8). The difficulty with this is to know what constitutes unlawfulness. It is not clear that the actions of Mosley and his followers in wearing fascist uniforms and marching through areas inhabited by immigrant groups were unlawful (at the time) and yet those actions were highly provocative and the catalyst for severe disorder. Similarly, it might not have been strictly illegal for Mrs Humphries to parade through a Roman Catholic community at the time of the troubles with an orange lily attached to her person.[36] The wearing of uniforms in such circumstances is now prohibited, and in the second case the police were held to be justified in forcibly removing the offending flower. The actions of one group may be within the bounds of legality and yet so highly provocative to others that serious disorder is likely to result. In many such cases, it is difficult to see why the public demonstration should be protected, and yet in this context it is particularly difficult to define the limits of legitimate protest, to draw the line between protecting the expression of unpopular views, on the one hand, and unacceptable provocation, on the other. One line of development is to be found in the Public Order Act (1986), which prohibits words which are threatening, abusive, or insulting and are likely to create a breach of the peace. Similarly prohibited are words or actions likely to stir up racial hatred.[37] Further scope for development may also be available in the new powers of the Public Order Act, which allows conditions to be imposed in order to avoid conflicts between groups, or the intimidatory actions of a particular group. In exercising these powers, however, the relevant authorities will have to decide in the exercise of their discretion how that line is to be drawn.

There are two other points to note. One is that the clash between opposing groups is not necessarily the result of one being innocent, the other wrongdoing. It may be that each is trying to express a view in such a way that conflict is almost inevitable. When the National Front marches, it is to be expected that other groups will want to contest the views expressed. It is not obvious in such cases that one group should have special protection just because it is first on the scene. The final point is that there may be occasions on which, because of the nature and history of the issue, protective policing is impossible. In such extreme cases, the power to ban processions or to impose stringent conditions on static demonstrations may be a justifiable last resort.

Public protest in conflict with other rights and liberties

The use of public places for the purposes of protest is likely by its nature to cause conflict with the enjoyment of the rights and liberties of others. Meetings, processions, and demonstrations are bound to lead to inconvenience, delay, and obstruction to others whether they be users of the road or other public place, or people going to or coming from work or carrying out business or other commercial activities. In considering the legal approach to such conflicts, a number of different situations can be identified. The first general point is that the law recognizes the inevitable degree of give-and-take in the enjoyment of any rights and liberties, and that many occasions of public protest can be accommodated without special legal provision or intervention. The user of a road knows that there is a range of activities which may occur on thoroughfares and which can cause inconvenience and delay; he or she can have no just complaint when forms of protest are included within that range. Secondly, where the conflicts between competing liberties are not accommodated within the normal give-and-take, but are likely to create disorder, ranging from a breach of the peace to more serious disturbances, the law may intervene according to the conditions considered earlier. To take an example, it is common enough to have serious conflicts between pickets acting in the course of a trade dispute and workers trying to enter and leave their place of work. The police may intervene in such conflicts under their normal powers to control and prevent breaches of the peace or more serious disorders, and to take whatever measures are necessary to that end. This might mean imposing conditions aimed at securing a peaceful compromise or, where that fails, it may mean dispersal, arrest, and prosecution.

The situation in *Kavanagh* v. *Hiscock*[38] is not untypical: the police knew from past experience that pickets would attempt to stop a coach carrying non-strikers to work in order to dissuade the latter from continuing; that the coach driver would resist such attempts; and that disorder was likely to result. To prevent that from happening, the police formed cordons to make a path for the coach; when a picket attempted to push through and to approach the driver, he was arrested for obstructing a police officer in the execution of his duty. In situations of this kind, once disorder occurs or is threatened, the law is likely to take against the protesters whatever steps are necessary to allow non-strikers access to their work. When serious disorder is threatened, this may be necessary and defensible, but it should be noted that, in such cases, the line between the conflicting liberties – protest on the one hand, access to work on the other – is left to be drawn according to the discretionary policies and on-the-spot judgments of the police. Whether these policies and judgments show sufficient concern by the police to hold a justifiable balance between different activities, and to adopt methods of policing which maintain that balance while trying to avoid serious disorder, is a question requiring further examination. The experience of the miners' strike and numerous other lesser cases suggests that this question has now become one of urgency (Fine and Millar 1985).

Not all conflicts between public protest and other rights and liberties pose a threat of serious disorder. Accordingly, a third situation where legal intervention may be sought is where there are such conflicts but an absence of disorder. Many of these situations are regulated simply on the basis that public protest violates another's legal rights; for example, the liberty to protest provides no basis for a violation of property rights through trespass, nuisance, or otherwise. In such cases, private legal rights prevail, and any abstract right to protest must appropriately be confined. However, the position is more complex and contentious when the conflict is with activities which are themselves in the nature of liberties or at best abstract rights. The circumstances of *Hubbard* v. *Pitt*[39] provide a good example: there the point of the demonstration was to call attention to the alleged malpractices of the estate agents. But it occurred on a public road outside the offices of the estate agents and might have had the effect of deterring their potential customers. It certainly did little for their commercial reputation. The estate agents sought an injunction prohibiting the demonstration and damages for the losses they claimed to have suffered.

The question for the courts was then whether the demonstration could be banned on the grounds that it interfered with commercial activities. It is perhaps typical that such issues are approached through an obstacle course of legal doctrine, which allows a decision to be made without ever really confronting the issue of principle. It is not possible here to examine the legal background, except to note the important fact that the balance of law, at least in the view taken by the trial judge, does not recognize static demonstrations, as opposed to a march or processions, as lawful use of the highway. The contrary view is that it is lawful to hold a meeting, protest, or demonstration on a public road, provided that it is not an unreasonable obstruction and does not create a breach of the peace. The trial judge took the first of these views, and the estate agents were able to take advantage of the unauthorised nature of the protest by obtaining an interlocutory injunction against it until the trial could be held on the substantive issues. The judgments given on appeal do little to clarify the law or to address the issue of principle, namely, the conflict between two apparently legitimate activities. In the absence of a more authoritative ruling, the longer-term implications are uncertain; but it is hard to resist the conclusion that, while freedom to protest remains of unclear residual status, conflicts with more familiar and established private activities are likely to be resolved in favour of the latter.

The powers granted under the new Public Order Act, allowing conditions to be put on public protest in order to prevent the intimidation of individuals or groups, open up another aspect of the conflict with other rights, liberties, and interests. We have already noted the example of the march by the National Front closing down an Asian district through fear and intimidation. It is not hard to think of meritorious examples like this where the power to impose conditions is clearly justifiable; the difficulty as always which such open-ended powers is that they are likely to apply also to cases where the line between protest and protection from coercion is less clear. The advantage of having powers to set conditions is that there is greater scope for accommodating conflicting factors without simply favouring one to the exclusion of the other; the disadvantage is that the decision is likely to be made within the largely inscrutable discretion of the police.

Public protest aimed at vulnerable groups

An issue which inevitably creates difficulties in a multiracial society occurs when the object of a public demonstration is to criticize a group or individuals within a group on the basis of race, religion, ethnic factors, or other distinguishing characteristics. The Jewish community was the object of public vilification in the 1930s, while in more recent years attention has moved to the Asian and West Indian population. Where denigration of a minority group in the course of a public demonstration leads or is thought likely to lead to serious disorder, then the usual powers of prior restraint and intervention may be invoked. The law was strengthened in the Public Order Act 1936 by making it a criminal offence for a person in the course of a public demonstration to use words or other behaviour which are threatening, abusive, or insulting with intent to cause a breach of the peace, or whereby a breach of the peace is likely.[40]

The combination of these powers provides the police with ample capacity to prevent and punish violent disorder; but while that may be the outcome of some of the worst cases of public denigration of racial minorities, other demonstrations may be virulent in their criticism and yet relatively orderly. Accordingly, an attempt was made in 1965 to catch some of those cases by introducing a criminal offence of incitement to racial hatred. The main element of the offence is the stirring-up of racial hatred against a group within Britain; the offence is committed where that is a likely consequence of the use of words, or the publication of material in a public place, which are threatening, abusive, or insulting.[41] The harm sought to be prevented is the incitement to racial hatred, regardless of whether there is also a threat to public disorder. It is implicit in the creation of the offence that the prevention of that harm through the threat of punishment outweighs the consequential curtailment of free protest.

The lines of justification for such restrictions on free speech and protest are twofold.[42] One line takes as its justification the offence caused by denigration, on the grounds of race, of members of the group under attack. To be hated on the basis of alleged racial inferiority does carry a special kind of offensiveness which might be taken as harm sufficient to satisfy Mill's principle that the law should intervene only if necessary to prevent harm to others. But there are two possible objections. The first challenges the generality of the claim that it is seriously offensive to be a member of a group which is the subject of feelings of racial hatred on the part of members of another group. The claim may be true where the hated group is a small minority which is already in a weak and vulnerable position; but the claim does not seem to be true when the hatred is directed against, say, a majority group. There might still be offensiveness, but hardly harm of a serious kind. The second objection centres on the difficulty of distinguishing offensiveness based on racial hatred from offensiveness that may result from public abuse that is blasphemous, sexist, or offensive to one's basic moral or aesthetic values. And yet to allow restrictions for each of these grounds would be an unwarranted curtailment of free protest. The law attempts to meet this objection by requiring feelings not just of dislike, ridicule, or contempt, but actual racial hatred. But it must be admitted that, unless there are other factors which make race a special case, the objection is hard to overcome.

This brings us to the second line of justification for a special offence based on incitement to racial hatred. Here the case is more consequentialist: the inciting of racial hatred can trigger against the group not only feelings of offence but also a chain of harmful consequences; these may include real and tangible disadvantages in housing, employment, and education, all matters which are vital to community life and personal well-being. Provided that these harms can be made out, they satisfy both limbs of Mill's principle: they are serious enough to qualify for legal protection, and they would seem to outweigh the claims of free protest, at least in serious cases. In order to be sustained, this justification would need to satisfy the difficult task of showing empirical evidence of the causal link between incitement to racial hatred and harmful consequences. Indeed, it is only in very special cases that the link could be made out – where, for example, the racial group is a minority which is already heavily disadvantaged and discriminated against. Presumably it was the conviction of the government that just such evidence did exist in respect of certain racial minorities in Britain, and it was that conviction which led to the creation of wide-ranging regulation of racial discrimination of which the criminal offence is a minor part. But if the rationale were the prevention of consequential harm to disadvantaged and vulnerable minorities, then the criminal offence would require a definition which would be more complex, and which would restrict the range of prohibited incitements more narrowly. Since there seems little prospect of that, the present offence must be seen as based on foundations that are not entirely stable. However, in practice the offence is not often prosecuted; it requires both the initiative of the police and the consent of the Attorney-General, both of whom exercise discretion in deciding whether to proceed.

The White Paper proposed an extension of the terms of the offence to cover not just conduct which is likely to stir up racial hatred but also conduct which is intended to do so. The subsequent Act followed that proposal, and also broadened the categories of publication which will be caught by the offence.[43] The White Paper offered no detailed discussion, but it claimed that the justification for the offence is the connection with public order, meaning presumably that the stirring-up of racial hatred, while not itself constituting disorder, is a firm step towards that end. As a matter of fact this is manifestly not the case, since further disorder does not follow necessarily from racial hatred. And, furthermore, if public order is the rationale, it could be argued that there should be intervention only when disorder occurs. This would certainly demonstrate a greater concern for preserving free protest.

CONCLUSION

In the Green Paper on public order, the government asserted that

> our law does not in terms recognize a specific right to demonstrate. This is because the basic assumption in the law is that one is free to do whatever is not specifically prohibited by the law. So while there is in law no specific right to demonstrate, one is certainly free to do so, provided specific provisions of the law . . . are not contravened.[44]

If any conclusion can be drawn from the discussion in this essay, it is that that statement is highly misleading. In many areas affecting public protest the law is unsettled, incomplete, and open to interpretation; in addition, it is shot through with discretion in so many ways that the scope of protest depends increasingly on the variable judgments of officials, judgments against which there is rarely review or recourse. Moreover, if *Hubbard* v. *Pitt* is the law, then it cannot be right to say that one is free to do what is not prohibited; there is no prohibition on peaceful, non-obstructive assemblies on public roads, and yet because that is not a purpose for which the road is dedicated, it appears to be unlawful. The reality is that public protest has a more unstable and vulnerable position in the law than official appraisals recognize. The proclamation of a right to protest might go some way towards establishing a more secure legal footing, but it is surely folly to think that that in itself is the final solution. The real problem lies in the attitudes of officials – legislators, judges, police, and others; those attitudes have produced the present position, and it is only if they change that the value of public tumults will be secured.

NOTES

The author wishes to thank Genevra Richardson for comments and suggestions.

1 For discussion of the idea of public protest, see Barnum (1977: 310), Barendt (1985: 195–9), Stoykewych (1985: 43).
2 For a recent discussion of free speech, see Browne-Wilkinson L J in *Wheeler* v. *Leicester County Council* [1985] AC 1054 at 1063–5; also Lord Denning in *Hubbard* v. *Pitt* [1976] QB 142.
3 *Review of Public Order Law* (1984–5, HMSO, Cmnd 9510), p. 2. The government's position is explained further in the parliamentary debates; see especially the Home Secretary's introduction of the Public Order Bill to the second reading: *Weekly Hansard*, issue no. 1376, 13–17 January 1986, cols. 794–800.
4 See the European Convention on Human Rights (1950), Articles 10 and 11.
5 For a related discussion of the legal status of free speech, see Barendt (1985: 78–81).
6 For this approach to rights, see Dworkin (1977), and Raz (1984).
7 The following are examples of cases which raise important issues of civil liberties and yet in each the concept of rights plays at most a minor role: *Duncan* v. *Jones* [1936] 1KB 218; *Thomas* v. *Sawkins* [1935] 2 KB 249; *Hubbard* v. *Pitt* [1976] QB 142. Note also the views expressed by members of the House of Lords in *Defence Secretary* v. *Guardian Newspapers* [1985] 1 AC 339.
8 See: *R.* v. *Sang* [1980] AC 402; *Malone* v. *Metropolitan Police Commissioner* [1979] Ch. 344. The prisoners' rights cases are well discussed by Richardson (1985).
9 See *Kavanagh* v. *Hiscock* [1974] 1 QB 600.
10 *Review of Public Order Law*, op. cit. (note 3), p. 2; see also debate in the House of Commons on the Second Reading of the Public Order Bill, *Weekly Hansard*, issue no. 1367, 13–17 January 1986, especially cols. 794–815.
11 See the discussion by Scarman (1975).

12 Balancing is a familiar metaphor in judicial opinions. A notable area where balancing occurs is in deciding between the public interest in preserving certain kinds of confidentiality and the public interest in free access to evidence for the purposes of litigation; see de Smith (1980: 35–45). In civil liberties cases, rarely is the balancing process discussed overtly.

13 *Weekly Hansard*, issue no. 1367, 13–17 January 1986, cols. 794–800.

14 Dworkin (1977) offers powerful arguments for the existence of deep principles.

15 For fuller discussion of the nature of discretion, see Galligan (1986).

16 See, for example, *R*. v. *Chief Constable, ex parte CEGB* [1982] QB and *Parkin* v. *Norman* [1983] QB 92.

17 For studies of these organizational influences and the relationship with legal norms, see Manning (1977), Hawkins (1984).

18 For an account of how this might be done, see Lustgarten (1986).

19 For further development of these ideas, see Galligan (1986).

20 *R*. v. *Mansfield Justices, ex parte Sharkey* [1985] 1 AER 193.

21 *Piddington* v. *Bates* [1961] 1 WLR 162; *Lavin* v. *Albert* [1982] AC 546; *R*. v. *Howell* [1982] QB 416.

22 *Duncan* v. *Jones* [1936] 1 KB 218.

23 ibid.

24 *Piddington* v. *Bates* [1961] 1 WLR 162; *R*. v. *Mansfield Justices, ex parte Sharkey* [1985] 1 AER 193.

25 *Thomas* v. *Sawkins* [1935] 2 KB 249.

26 See Miller and Walker (1984: 19–23).

27 Seditious Meetings Act 1817, s. 23.

28 *Hubbard* v. *Pitt* [1976] QB 142. See also *Ex parte Lewis* (1988) 21 QBD 191 and the discussion in the Canadian case *Attorney General* v. *Dupond* (1978) 84 DLR (3d) 420.

29 Highways Act 1980, s. 137.

30 For critical discussion, see Wallington (1976).

31 *Review of Public Order Law*, op. cit. (note 3), p. 27.

32 ibid., p. 28.

33 For discussion of issues raised by the hostile audience, see Marshall (1971: 162–6), Barendt (1985: 206–13).

34 [1936] 1 KB 218.

35 (1882) 9 QBD 308.

36 *Humphries* v. *Connor* (1864) 17 ICLR 1.

37 Public Order Act 1986, s. 5.

38 [1974] 1 QB 600.

39 [1976] QB 142.

40 Public Order Act 1936, s. 5.

41 Race Relations Act 1976, s. 5A. These provisions have been extended in the Public Order Act 1986, part III.

42 See Barendt (1985: 161–7).

43 *Review of Public Order Law*, op. cit. (note 3), pp. 39–40; Public Order Act 1986, part III.

44 *Review of the Public Order Act 1936* (1980, HMSO, Cmnd 7891), p. 8.

REFERENCES

Barendt, E. (1985) *Freedom of Speech*, Oxford: Clarendon Press.

Barnum, D. G. (1977) 'The constitutional status of public protest activity in Britain and the United States', *Public Law* 310–44.

Benewick, R. (1967) *Political Violence and Public Order*, London: Allen Lane.

Brownlie, I. and Supperstone, M. (1981) *Brownlie's Law of Public Order and National Security*, London: Butterworths, 2nd edn.

de Smith, S. A. (1980) *Judicial Review of Administrative Action*, London: Stevens, 4th edn.

Dicey, A. V. (1961) *The Law of the Constitution*, ed. E. C. S. Wade, London: Macmillan.

Dworkin, R. M. (1977) *Taking Rights Seriously*, London: Tavistock.

Fine, B. and Millar, R. (1985) *Policing the Miners' Strike*, London: Lawrence & Wishart.

Galligan, D. J. (1986) *Discretionary Powers: A Legal Study of Official Discretion*, Oxford: Clarendon Press.

Hart, H. L. A. (1973) *Oxford Essays in Jurisprudence* ('Bentham on legal rights'), Oxford: Clarendon Press.

Hawkins, K. (1984) *Environment and Enforcement: Regulation and the Social Definition of Pollution*, Oxford: Clarendon Press.

Lustgarten, L. (1986) *The Governance of Police*, London: Sweet & Maxwell.

Machiavelli, Niccolo (1970) *The Discourses*, ed. B. Crick, Harmondsworth: Penguin Books.

Manning, P. K. (1977) *Police Work: The Social Organization of Policing*, Mass.

Marshall, G. (1971) *Constitutional Theory*, Oxford: Clarendon Press.

Mill, J. S. (1962) *On Liberty*, ed. M. Warnock, London: Fontana.

Miller, S. and Walker, M. (1984) *A State of Siege (A Report of the Yorkshire NUM)*.

Raz, J. (1984) 'Legal rights', *Oxford Journal of Legal Studies* 4: 1.

Richardson, G. (1985) 'Judicial intervention in prison life', in M. Maguire, J. Vagg, and R. Morgan (eds.) *Accountability and the Prisons: Opening Up a Closed World*, London: Tavistock.

Scarman, L. (1975) *The Red Lion Square Disorders of 15 June 1974*, London: HMSO, Cmnd 5919.

——— (1981) *The Brixton Disorders 10–12 April 1981*, London: HMSO, Cmnd 8427.

Stoykewich, R. (1985) 'Street legal: constitutional protection of public demonstration in Canada', *University of Toronto Faculty of Law Review* 43.

Wallington, P. (1976) 'Injunctions and the "right to demonstrate"', *Cambridge Law Journal* 82.

4

Trade unions and their members
Clyde Summers

Trade unions present a paradigm of the recurrent problem in our modern society of reconciling collective power and individual rights. Life is collectivized at almost every level, with economic, political, and social activities dominated by organized groups which submerge the individual, and which at times exercise a coercive power over the individual equal to that of the state. The problem is how to preserve individuality within this collectivized structure. Trade unions present the issue in complex and intractable forms because the union's functions reach the very core of the individual's existence – his or her job, economic sustenance, and life at the workplace.

It is not the union which has collectivized the employment relation and subjected the individual to controls. This is an inevitable product of modern industry and commerce. Without a union, the individual's job and life at the workplace are subject to the collective control of management, which gives it ability to restrain freedom of expression and thought, to discriminate, and to deny due process. Individual bargaining gives most employees weak protection and little choice. There is, in the absence of a union, the problem of reconciling the collective power of management and the rights of individual workers.

The union adds a counterbalancing force, limiting the employer's collective control by exercising collective power on behalf of the employees' collective interest. In seeking to further that collective interest, or its own institutional interests, the union may in turn sacrifice the interests of some individuals. To promote or protect collective interests the union may fail to protect or may deny individual rights. The fact that the union's declared purpose is to represent the interests of employees casts the problem in bold relief as a conflict between the collective and the individual.

Reconciling or accommodating the collective interests of unions and the individual rights of workers is particularly difficult because of three special characteristics of unions.

First, unions are themselves expressions and instruments of individual rights – the right of association which is fundamental if the individual is to have any voice in the collectivized structure. The right to form and join unions is protected in almost all free societies from both public and private restraints. The union, therefore, can rightfully claim that its collective activity is an expression of individual rights. This conflict is then articulated as one between competing individual rights.

Second, the union's function is to counterbalance the employer's collective economic power, and this creates a continuing potential of economic conflict. The union's relation with the employer may be, at best, one of "constructive tension," but often is an alternating cold and hot war. In this conflict, the union's effectiveness, if not its very existence, may be at stake. The individual is inescapably cast in the position of siding, or seeming to side, either with the collectivized employees or with collectivized management. The assertion of individual rights as against the union will be viewed as aiding and abetting the enemy.

Third, and most important for our purposes, is that the union serves different functions which raise different problems of collective and individual rights. The central and unique function of unions is representation of workers' interests in their jobs and life at the workplace through collective bargaining. This function is performed through negotiation with employers – a process of persuasion reinforced by the ability, actual or potential, to exert economic pressure on the employers. A secondary, but important, function of unions is to influence the political process. The political function may be in substitute for, or in aid of, collective bargaining – minimum wages, protection against dismissal, safety regulation; but it may be directed toward broader social policies not directly related to employment or limited to the interests of workers – social insurance, progressive taxation, foreign policy; and may extend to support of political parties and candidates. Finally, unions perform significant social functions of the kind which might be carried on by social clubs or voluntary associations – providing social affairs, recreation activities, adult education, insurance benefits, and aid to charitable or other non-political causes.

Analysis of individual rights in relation to a trade union requires that these different functions – the collective bargaining, political, and social functions – be examined separately. For each function, the accommodation of collective interests and individual rights requires quite different considerations. Only by examining these functions separately can we sensibly discuss how to make accommodations when the union performs all three functions.

THE COLLECTIVE BARGAINING FUNCTION AND INDIVIDUAL RIGHTS

The starting-point for analysis must be clear recognition that collective bargaining is inevitably a compulsory system, enveloping and regulating the working lives of individual employees whether they are union members or not, and whether they consent or not. In the United States this is legally explicit. The majority union is the exclusive representative of all employees in the bargaining unit, and its collective agreement legally binds members and non-members alike. The employer cannot bargain with any other union for any of the employees, and no individual can negotiate for either better or lesser terms. In addition, the union can and does negotiate for exclusive control over the individual's grievances claiming violations of the collective agreement. In West Germany an agreement binding employers of half the employees in a sector can be extended by government to all employers in that sector, and other Western European countries have similar legal devices for making collective agreements binding on non-consenting employers and employees.

Even though the legal provisions do not contain, on their face, the compulsion of exclusive representation or extension, the practical results may be much the same. In West Germany, the collective agreement legally binds only union members. However, employers commonly enter into collective agreements even though a minority of their employees are union members and then apply the collective agreement to all employees, whether members or not. Sweden starts with the same legal rule, and the employer is legally obligated to negotiate with any union which has members among the employees. The employer, however, is not obligated to sign an agreement. Swedish employers have refused to sign agreements with any but the dominant Lands organisation (LO) or Tjänstemännens Centralorganisationen (TCO) unions, even though the competing unions represented a majority of employees. The employer instead signs an agreement with the dominant union, and that agreement requires the employer to provide the same benefits to members and non-members. Workers who have expressly rejected the LO or TCO union and formed a separate union are thus governed by the agreement of the LO or the TCO union. In Japan, as in Sweden, the employer is legally required to negotiate with any union which has members among the employees, and to treat all unions equally. The employer, however, uses the requirement of equal treatment to insist that the minority union accept the same terms as agreed with the majority union.

In the United Kingdom the compulsory character of collective bargaining is less marked. The collective agreement is not legally binding on anyone; any individual can legally bargain for better or lesser terms. In addition, the importance of local bargaining through shop stewards on a day-to-day basis provides potential for variations. However, the terms and conditions in any given workplace are substantially standardized and reflect the agreements reached with the unions. Most individuals cannot practically bargain for different terms, but are in fact governed by the collective agreements.

The closeness with which the non-member or non-consenting individual is regulated by the union's bargaining varies from system to system. The individual is most rigidly bound, both legally and practically, by the exclusive representation principle in the United States. The collective agreement typically fixes individual terms which cannot be varied either up or down, and the individual can obtain an adjudication of his or her rights under the collective agreement only if the union will take the case to arbitration. In Western Europe extended agreements normally establish only minimum terms, and the individual may, at least in theory, negotiate for more. Most systems allow individuals to litigate their rights under the collective agreement or their employment contract, but without the aid of the union this may present an unbearable burden. In the British system individual claims not supported by the union may prove of little value.

The central point here is that unions, through collective bargaining, regulate in one significant measure or another the working lives of non-members. In this respect, collective bargaining effectively limits freedom of association; workers cannot, in practical terms, bargain through "representatives of their own choosing." To be sure, in almost every country, the individual remains free to join any union he or she chooses, but that choice is drained of substance. The American truck driver can join the Auto Workers, but he will still be governed by the Teamsters' collective agreement and bargaining procedure. The West German auto worker can join the Christian union, but his or her wages, hours, vacations, and pension will be negotiated by the DGB Metal Workers' Union. Swedish dockworkers can form their own union, but the controlling collective agreement will be negotiated by the LO Transport Workers. The individual's freedom to associate is freedom to join a union which either legally or practically cannot act as representative, but is also compulsion to be represented by a union with which the individual does not want to associate. In Great Britain the symbolic freedom is less sanctified; for where there is a closed shop, workers may be required to join the controlling union. Even in the absence of a closed shop, the Bridlington Principles of the Trades Union Congress seek to prevent more than one union representing a particular grade of workers, and unions may be ordered by the TUC

Disputes Committee not to admit, or even to expel, members where another union is determined to be the appropriate union.

Significantly, the compulsory character of collective bargaining has seldom been considered as violating freedom of association so long as the individual was allowed the form of freedom of choice. Challenges to exclusive representation violating fundamental freedoms have been brushed aside by the United States Supreme Court without serious discussion (*Minnesota State Board* v. *Knight*, 465 US 271, 1984). Constitutional challenges to the West German Co-determination Act of 1976 did not even mention the freedom of association of non-union members (judgment, 1 March 1979 – § 1 BUR 532 and 533/77, 419/78). When Swedish public and private employers refused to make collective agreements with any unions other than the dominant LO and TCO unions, arguments that this violated rights of association and negotiation were rejected by the Swedish Labor Court (1969 AD 114; 1972 AD5). When this decision was challenged as violating the right of association guaranteed by Article 11 of the Convention on Human Rights, it was upheld by the European Commission on Human Rights and the European Court for Human Rights (*Swedish Engine Drivers' Union*, 20 Eur. Ct H. R., 1976), with neither confronting the basic issue. Japanese courts have wrestled with this problem but in the end have allowed the employer to insist that all collective agreements follow the one with the dominant union. The Committee on Freedom of Association of the International Labour Office has recognized aspects of the problem but has declared that giving priority to "most representative" unions and certifying such unions as exclusive bargaining agents does not violate Convention No. 87 on the Freedom of Association, particularly if there is a majority vote (187th Report, Case No. 796, para. 173, 1978).

A more compulsory and less questioned limitation on the individual freedom of association of workers is presented by statutory works councils or employee representation committees. These are legally compelled collective representation systems which, within their sphere, may have exclusive representation rights. West German works councils, for example, may be created on the demand of any three employees, and when created have extensive representation functions and powers at the shop and enterprise level. By statute (Works Constitution Act of 1972) they have exclusive authority to negotiate and agree on a wide range of matters concerning the most significant day-to-day aspects of the employees' working life, including matters of safety, working hours, methods of pay, transfers, working conditions, and mass dismissals. Unions are precluded from negotiating concerning matters allocated to the works council. Individual employees are required to look to the works council for representation on these matters and cannot choose to be represented by a union. Freedom of association is limited to voting for or against a union's slate of candidates in the works council election. Individual workers are thus legally barred from bargaining through representatives of their own choosing and are compelled to be represented by a structure created and empowered by the state. Other Western European countries have varied forms of plant-level employee representation systems, but a common basic characteristic is that the statutory organizations have the authority and responsibility to act as the individual employee's collective representative regardless of his or her choice.

Recognition that collective bargaining systems, in some significant degree, deprive individual employees of the ability to bargain through representatives of their own choosing raises the question why this is accepted almost without discussion in societies in which freedom of association is a fundamental right. The answer is simply that there is no practical alternative. The employment relations is, by force of modern methods of production and business structures, collectivized. The standardization of terms and conditions of employment, the systematic assignment of work, and general rules of conduct are, in a large measure, inescapable. Individualization would invite chaos and assure arbitrariness and invidious discrimination.

The choice is not whether the employment relation shall be collectivized, but who will establish the standardized terms and general rules. In the absence of collective bargaining the employer decides the terms by which all employees will be governed. Collective bargaining, whether through a union or a works council, simply limits management's freedom to decide by giving the employee's representative a voice in those decisions.

In practical terms, one voice on the employee's side will dominate because the employer will, and in most situations must, insist that all employees doing the same work be governed by the same terms and rules. That voice may be a single union or several "most representative" unions acting together. But freedom of association in which each individual can bargain for his or her own terms through a representative of his or her own choosing is a practical impossibility. The employee's choice is between one voice and no voice. This provides the framework for examining the relation between collective power and individual rights in employment. Where the choice is for collective bargaining, the problems are not simply a two-dimensional relation of a union to its non-members, but a three-dimensional relation with the employer. The problems cannot be sensibly discussed by abstract assertions of freedom of association, apart from the union's function as a collective representative of the employees. The problems are the complex and thorny ones of the relation between a union, or other collective body, which is the effective representative in bargaining with the employer, and individual workers who willingly or unwillingly come within its sphere of control.

With this framework we can proceed to examine some of the particular problems in the union's performance of its collective bargaining function.

Selection of collective representative

Since each individual cannot bargain through a representative of his or her own choosing, the question is, how shall the representative be chosen? The immediately obvious answer is that it should be a collective choice, a process through which the right of all employees to choose is accommodated by their participation in the choosing. The most simple and direct form is the one used in the United States of a National Labor Relations Board (NLRB) election to select an exclusive representative by a majority vote of all employees in the bargaining unit. Other devices such as designation of "most representative" unions in France may be rooted in majority rule, at the same time preserving at least the form of greater freedom of choice by designating several unions as "most representative." In some countries, such as Sweden, the problem is submerged because a unified labor movement gives one union a clearly dominant majority.

Majority rule raises the question: majority of whom? Who is to be encompassed in the election or bargaining unit? The larger the unit, the more sub-groups will be submerged and denied freedom of choice; but smaller units may be ineffective in bargaining, or provide only the illusion of independence. Considerations for determining the scope of the voting unit are too complex to work out here. The most that can be said is that, from the individual rights view, the units should be as small as practicable, given the radiations of their regulatory effectiveness and the social purposes sought to be achieved.

The alternative to majority employee choice is to leave the choice either to the state (a denial of freedom of association), to the employer (a denial of employee rights), or to economic forces which gives control to that union which, because of its economic position and strength, can assert control. The latter, which is essentially the British system, avoids state intervention or employer control, but may permit a union chosen by a minority effectively to deprive a majority of their freedom of choice. Apart from its denial of individual rights, reliance on relative economic strength may invite continuing conflict in the workforce and dissipate the ability to represent effectively.

The most troublesome question arises when a majority chooses not to be represented by any union but to bargain individually. Can the majority thereby bar the minority from bargaining collectively for themselves through a representative of their own choosing? Such minority union bargaining, if effective, will in practice influence the terms of those who bargain individually. To that extent the majority will be regulated by the minority. Use of majority rule here, however, bars the minority from collective action entirely, subordinating them to employer control. This encroaches on individual rights a significant step beyond the use of the majority rule to determine which among two or more unions shall act for them collectively. In addition, society may properly make the judgment that collective bargaining as a method of regulating the labor market has social and political values sufficient to justify guaranteeing the right for all who wish to engage in it even though this may radiate effects on a majority who choose otherwise.

This principle that the majority cannot bar a minority from bargaining collectively is, so far as I know, accepted by every free society. Even in the United States, which has the most explicit majority rule, a minority union can make a "members only" contract so long as there is no majority union. Although an employer is not legally required to bargain with a minority union, a strike by a minority union to compel bargaining and to obtain a contract is a legally protected activity.

Freedom of association in the form of choosing one's own representative for collective bargaining is inescapably qualified because there cannot be multiple independent representatives. Conflicting individual rights to choose the representative can be best accommodated by designating the representative chosen by the majority. But the right to bargain collectively is an individual right not to be denied by majority vote.

The right not to strike

The question whether an individual has a right to work during a strike is particularly thorny, not so much because of core considerations, but because of special or subsidiary aspects. It is necessary, therefore, first to articulate the core considerations in the common strike. If one looks beyond abstractions to reality, it is plain that in an ordinary strike the claim by an individual or minority of the right to continue working is largely an appeal to an illusory principle. If the union is strong in the sense that the employer cannot continue operating because too few report for work, the strikers' skills are unique, or social attitudes do not accept operating during a strike – whatever the reasons – the individual or minority has no choice. The claimed right to work has no substance because there is no work. The individual or minority has a choice only when the union lacks that strength and the employer decides to operate in order to weaken or break the strike. The claimed right to work can thus be exercised by the worker only if the employer so decides, and its exercise is in aid of the employer when the union is in most need of support.

An appeal to the "right to work" is misplaced. In a fully effective strike, the right is empty; in a partially effective strike, the right is controlled by the employer. Indeed, the right involved is not the right of the individual, but a disguised right of the employer to employ striker-breakers to defeat the strike. The economic conflict is between the collective representative of the employees and the employer. An individual or minority right which can be exercised only when desired by the employer, and in aid of the employer against the employees, has little claim for recognition as a basic right.

The core considerations are quite different when the purpose of the strike is not to influence employer decisions concerning terms and conditions of employment, but to influence political decisions concerning governmental policies. The individual's right to freedom of political choice and action has a special claim of a different order from freedom of economic choice and action. In a political strike, the individual must be free to express his or her political differences by refusing to strike; the individual's voice ought not be muted or drowned by a collective voice.

Drawing a line between economic and political strikes, however, can be difficult. The fact that the employer is the government should not make a strike concerning terms and conditions of employment any less economic. This is true whether the strike is in a nationalized industry or in the postal service. On the other hand, the fact that the employers are private does not make a strike, such as refusal to load ships to protest a foreign policy, any less political. The British miners' strike, however, illustrates how difficult it can be to draw the line between economic and political strikes, and how sharp differences in how the strike should be characterized can lead to bitter disputes as to the rights of miners who wished to return to work.

An important subsidiary question is how the decision to strike should be made. If the decision is to bind all of the workers, then it should express the will of the majority. This does not, in principle, require a direct vote on the strike, although this may be a more accurate and reliable way of determining the members' desires, but the decision may be made by a representative body or the union officers, if they have been democratically elected. Either directly or indirectly, every member should have a voice. In addition, the decision should be made in accordance with the union's rules and controlling procedures, for basic to the protection of all individual rights is the observance of due process.

Finally, the most difficult question is, what action can the union take against those who work during a properly called economic strike? Although they have no right against the union to work during the strike, and the law might appropriately prohibit the operation of a business in the face of a properly called strike, the union is not entitled to use violence or mass picketing which physically prevents them from work. Such means cannot be used by private parties to enforce their rights against one another. On the other hand, the union can certainly exclude such individuals from membership, at least until they demonstrate a willingness to support the union in its conflicts with the employer. Also, it would seem appropriate for the union to fine or assess them up to their net gain from working during the strike. The fining of union members and suing to collect the fine is legally rationalized as enforcement of the contract of membership, but non-members who work during a strike damage the collective interest as much as members who work. In principle, the collective representative should be able to protect the collective interests against injurious action by all employees regardless of union membership.

Are there limits, other than force or violence, on measures which the union should be allowed to take against those who work during a strike? Should a union, by enforcing a closed shop, be allowed to bar an employee forever from obtaining employment in the enterprise or the trade, or to enforce a fine of a year's pay? Those who work during a strike can scarcely assert a moral claim to benefits won by the strike and can properly be required to share the sacrifices of the strike. This does not mean that they should bear the mark of Cain and be permanently denied the right to work. The union's sanctions should be limited to those which are remedial and corrective and prevent unjust enrichment, and should not be punitive or vindictive. Perhaps we can be no more specific than to say that the sanctions should be bounded by principles of proportionality.

The right to strike without union authorization

This problem, which is the obverse of the previous one, may take two quite different forms. First, a minority group of employees, or even a majority, may become dissatisfied with the bargaining efforts of the collective representative and strike without authorization. The employer or the union, or both, may then impose sanctions on the strikers. The question is whether the presence of a collective representative limits the employees' right to strike. In the United States, where there is a clearly designated exclusive representative, the right to call a strike becomes vested in the representative, and the striking employees can be discharged. In West Germany a strike can be legally called only by a union. In most countries, union members who strike without authorization can be fined or expelled by the union. These legal rules are built on the premise that a strike is a collective economic action; and within a working collective bargaining structure the channelling of collective action is sufficiently important to circumscribe the right to strike.

Strikes by minority or unauthorized groups are directed against the collective representative as much as, or more than, against the employer, and serve to compel attention by the collective representative to worker dissatisfaction. Although there is a basic right of workers to make their dissatisfactions known, and to have them fairly considered by the collective representative, it is difficult to argue for a basic right to use the strike for this purpose, especially if other avenues are available.

The second form of the problem arises when the collective agreement carries with it an express or implied no-strike obligation. Such provisions are universally allowed, and are statutorily imposed in many countries. They are uncommon in the United Kingdom, and the sanctions are often limited in other countries. In Sweden the maximum penalty is a 200 crown fine for each striker; in the United States the strikers are not liable in damages but may be discharged by the employer, and union members may be fined by the union. There seems to be consensus that the value of stability during the term of the collective agreement justifies this limitation on the individual's right to strike.

The right to refuse to join the union

The simple logic that freedom of association includes the freedom not to associate has little to commend it beyond its seductive verbal synonymity. It is at best a half-truth which lumps together the various elements of membership and blocks separate analysis of the different obligations of membership. The so-called "closed shop" or "compulsory unionism" issue is not a single but several issues. The question is not the indiscriminate one of whether there is a negative right of association, the question which fractured the European Court for Human Rights in *Young, James, and Webster* (44 Eur. Ct H. R., 1981). The question is, what obligations can a union properly impose on those it represents in collective bargaining?

Membership of an organization carries with it for some people a psychological quality of belonging, of being encompassed within, being a part of and taking on the qualities of that organization. For those who feel kinship with its members, share its values, and support its goals, membership is a positive value; the right to join is a significant value deserving of protection. For others, the right not to be forced into such an association and wear its identity unwillingly, to assert one's choice of association, or to declare one's independence of all such associations also has significant values equally worthy of protection. For both, the values are intensely personal, internalized values which express the individual's sense of self-worth. At this level, the right to associate and the right not to associate are substantial equivalents.

Union membership, however, involves two distinct obligations apart from the sense of belonging – the obligation to support the union financially, and the obligation to obey union rules. These obligations may exist without any sense of belonging, indeed, without any formal joining of the union. It is necessary to examine each of these obligations separately to determine whether, and to what extent, they may be compulsorily imposed on unwilling employees. In examining these it is important to remember that the union has three different functions: the collective bargaining, political, and social functions. Our focus for the moment is on the obligations to obey and to pay in the collective bargaining function.

The union's function in collective bargaining is to increase the employees' bargaining power, obtaining better terms and conditions than they could through individual bargaining. Although a few employees may sometimes not benefit, the overwhelming majority benefit from the collective bargain. Even those who gained less wages benefit from improved working conditions and the establishment of a system of industrial justice. The union has a compelling claim that all those who benefit from the bargain should help bear the cost of the bargaining. American law is built on this premise, that the union is entitled to charge all of those represented their share of the union's collective bargaining costs. No person can be required, on pain of dismissal, to join the union, take an oath of fealty, attend union meetings, or carry a union card. But no person has a right to continue working and be a "free rider." Although an individual may find contributing to an unwanted union psychologically or emotionally objectionable, or may prefer to contribute to another union, the obligation to pay a fair share of collective bargaining costs is a small encroachment on personal sensitivity, at least in the absence of religious beliefs against such contribution.

Requiring obedience to union rules directly related to collective bargaining raises a range of problems. Union rules limiting production, tools used, or kind of work performed may be economically unwise but they do not encroach on individual rights any more than equivalent provisions in collective agreements. Union prohibitions against working on non-union materials or making deliveries to non-union employees may be considered inappropriate forms of economic pressure, but they are not objectionable because they violate any basic rights of the employees. As already discussed, union fines for working during a strike do not inhibit any basic right of employees, but only curb the ability of the employer to operate during the strike.

The reasoning here, it must be emphasized, is applicable only to the union's collective bargaining function. The union does not have the same justification for compelling unwilling employees to contribute to union expenditure for purposes other than collective bargaining, or to enforce rules other than those related to its bargaining functions.

The serious encroachment on individual freedom of compulsory unionism is not in requiring an unwilling employee to pay his or her fair share of the cost of collective bargaining or requiring obedience to rules relating to collective bargaining, but in requiring an employee to become a member in the full sense. Compelling a person to swear fealty, identify themselves as a member, attend meetings, or participate in an organization with which they do not wish to associate is an assault on their personality.

The competing right of a union to function effectively as a collective representative and the right of an unwilling employee to personal integrity and individual freedom can, in this troublesome area, be largely accommodated by separating the obligations of membership. The individual can be compelled to share the cost of a union's bargaining on behalf of all employees. At the same time, the individual can refuse to join the union, to accept any token or symbol of personally belonging, to participate in any union activities, to pay any costs, or to obey any rules unrelated to collective bargaining.

The right to fair representation

The preceding discussion has built on the premise of the inescapable collectivization of the employment relation and the necessity for unions to counterbalance the employer's collective control by exercising collective power on the employees' behalf. Collective bargaining is inevitably a compulsory system with the dominant union regulating the wages and working lives of all employees within its sphere of control. Discussion of the several claimed individual rights has underlined the extent of union control. In the face of this, how can we prevent or limit the subservience of the individual to combined union and employer collective power?

One device has already been suggested – give employees the right to choose their collective representative, and the right to change their representative if it proves unsatisfactory. Majority rule, whether determined by formal elections as in the United States, or by less formal processes as in other countries, gives individuals some voice in the selection of their representative and an ability to hold that representative accountable.

Majority rule, however, may leave individuals or minority groups vulnerable to having their interests sacrificed by the majority, or by union officials. The extensive power exercised by the collective representative should, therefore, carry with it an obligation to represent all employees fairly and equally. The individual employee's lack of effective rights to be independent of the collective system should be compensated for by guaranteeing the employee a right to fair and equal treatment within the collective system. This important individual right has been explicitly recognized in the United States for forty years, and is applied in both the negotiation of collective agreements and the processing of grievances arising under the agreement.

The principle was first articulated by the Supreme Court to invalidate a provision in a collective agreement which placed black employees at the bottom of the seniority list (*Steel* v. *L. & N. Ry*, 323 US 192, 1942). The union was obligated to represent all employees for whom it bargained "without hostile discrimination, fairly, impartially and in good faith" (323 US at 204). This principle extends beyond race discrimination to other cases where a majority, or those in political control, benefit themselves at the expense of a minority or discriminate against opposition groups. The union's obligation in processing grievances is substantially greater. It cannot "arbitrarily ignore a meritorious grievance or process it in a perfunctory fashion" (*Vaca* v. *Sipes*, 386 US 171 at 191, 1967). This may include refusing to appeal grievances of particular individuals, failing to investigate the merits, or not attempting to win at arbitration. The outer boundaries of the union's duty are uncertain, but the core principle that the individual has a right to fair, equal, and honest representation is clear.

Surprisingly, there are only a few traces of equivalent principles being developed or even discussed in other countries, although the union's collective agreement may have equivalent practical control over the individual, and the individual may be highly dependent on the union in enforcing rights under the collective agreement or the employment contract.

The right to a democratic union

The most important device for reconciling the collective power of the union and the individual rights of employees is to guarantee the right to participate in democratic decision-making within the union so that the individual will have a voice in the collective decisions which affect his or her working life. The individual becomes a participant in self-government, not an object of others' control.

Democratic decision-making does not, of course, guarantee the full protection of individual rights. Intolerant or determined majorities may trample on a minority. All of the preceding discussion marking out the rights of the individual against the union has presupposed that the union's action – whether to call a strike, make a political assessment, enforce a union rule, make a collective agreement, or refuse to appeal a grievance – has been democratically decided. The fact that the individual has participated in making the decision does not ensure that his or her rights will not be invaded. Democratic processes are a necessary condition for the recognition of individual rights, but they are not a sufficient condition for their full protection.

The right to participate in democratic decision-making in the union can be guaranteed only by the recognition of its component rights. The basic threshold right is the right to be a member of the union which in fact determines the individual's terms and conditions of employment. Legal procedures, union rules or structures, or relative economic strength may determine which union is the collective representative. The threshold right of the individual is to be a member of that union.

Without being a full member an individual can have no effective voice in the continuous process of policy-making, or in the election of officers who formulate and implement bargaining policy. Limiting employee participation to referendum votes on specific issues provides at best limited voice. Voting to select or change the collective representative is an empty exercise if there is no effective competing union. Voting on whether to strike or whether to approve a proposed agreement may provide little real choice because positions taken by union spokespeople at the bargaining table may have foreclosed preferred alternatives. The effective decision is made in selecting the spokespeople and determining the bargaining policies and strategies.

The right to join and the right not to be expelled are not absolute; but because the fundamental right to participate in self-government is involved, the only reasons for exclusion should be those which would justify denying the right of franchise in a democratic society. This would include, of course, a refusal to help bear the costs of collective representation and a refusal to abide by the union's collective decisions. Participation in decisions may be direct, as in union meetings or referendums, or indirect, as in the election of officers or representatives. Democratic decision-making, whether direct or indirect, requires every member to have full and free voice and vote. This includes full freedom to speak at union meetings and otherwise, to criticize union policies and officers, and to join with other members to advocate or oppose union policies – in short, the basic democratic rights of free speech and assembly. In the election of officers, this includes the right to nominate candidates and to campaign on their behalf, the right to vote, and the right to have the votes counted honestly. All those who exercise substantial policy-making authority in the union must be selected by and answerable to an open and fair election process.

The scope and contours of these rights cannot be marked out here, but the Landrum–Griffin Act in the United States, particularly Title I (Bill of Rights of Union Members) and Title IV (Elections), is suggestive. The underlying logic is that unions acting as collective representatives in fact exercise governing influence over the working lives of those they represent. Their decision-making processes should, therefore, observe the basic rights and principles of democratic government. The analogy is, of course, not perfect, for there are significant differences, but those differences do not necessarily point toward less recognition of basic democratic rights. Indeed, the typical one-party structure of union government, with the dominating position of incumbent officers, may require greater protection of dissent and opposition groups and special safeguards in union elections. This does not mean that the internal processes of unions must be regulated by law; the union can and should recognize these basic democratic rights. But if the union fails to do so, then a democratic society has an obligation to guarantee these basic rights. This requires of unions no more than they have demanded of society and claimed for themselves.

THE POLITICAL FUNCTION OF UNIONS AND INDIVIDUAL RIGHTS

The relation between the union and the individual in political affairs is significantly different to their relation in collective bargaining. As emphasized earlier, collective bargaining is inevitably a compulsory process, with the individual bound by the union's policies and decisions. In contrast, the political process is fundamentally individual and voluntary; each individual is free to make his or her own choices of political policies, candidates, and political affiliation.

Any restriction on that freedom is a violation of fundamental democratic rights; collective decisions cannot bind the unwilling. Unions, in performing their political function, may encroach on individual autonomy in two ways. First, unions may discipline by fine or expulsion those who oppose their political program. Second, unions may use union dues to support political causes, parties, or candidates. In either case, the leverage is essentially the same – the union requires, as a condition of membership, support of its political program.

If the union were not also a collective bargaining representative, there would be little problem. Like any political organization, the union could condition membership on political conformity; those who disagreed would be free to leave. But because a union represents employees in collective bargaining, the individual cannot leave without losing his or her voice in collective bargaining decisions. Exclusion from the union of those who disagree with the union's political goals denies them the right to participate in those decisions which affect their working life. Individuals' right to political freedom ought not be conditioned on the surrender of their franchise in their industrial government. Both the right of political freedom and the right of industrial franchise are fundamental.

When the union uses the political process to protect or reinforce its collective bargaining ability (e.g. strike and picketing legislation), the union may argue that it has as much claim to compel conformity and financial support as it has when it exercises the collective bargaining function. But the political process seeks to influence the decisions of government, not private employers, and the purpose of democratic government is to give all individuals a free and independent voice. The political process, if it is to provide free voice, must be protected from private as well as public restraint.

Reconciling the right of unions to engage in political activities and the right of individual members to choose freely the political causes they support is relatively simple. The individual's participation in the union's political action should be entirely voluntary, separated from participation in the union's collective bargaining function. No individual should be excluded from membership because of political beliefs or activities different from those of the union, nor should any member be required to contribute to the union's political funds as a condition of membership. Political funds should be kept separate from funds to support collective bargaining. This device of separate funds is now required by statute in the United Kingdom and by a Supreme Court decision in the United States (*Chicago Teachers' Union Local 1* v. *Hudson*, 106 S. Ct 1066, 1986), making contributions to political funds entirely voluntary. Whether the procedure should be one of "contracting in" (that is, the member not being obligated to pay the political assessment unless he or she expressly agrees) or one of "contracting out" (by expressly objecting to the use of dues for political purposes) raises no fundamental principle, so long as the individual has an unrestrained choice.

The principle of separating collective bargaining and political functions should bar the use of regular union dues or assessments for political purposes whether those dues are exacted under the compulsion of a union security agreement or not. The basic right is not to be required to support political causes with which one disagrees as a condition of participating in collective bargaining decisions, whether or not one's job is at stake. The United States Supreme Court, however, has not gone further than to bar the political use of compulsory dues are exacted under a union security provision in a collective agreement.

The principle that a worker's right to industrial franchise ought not be conditioned on political conformity is applicable to all political activities, not just to the support of political parties and candidates, as in the United Kingdom. Indeed, basic principles of freedom of belief and expression should extend the principle to all political and ideological causes, for the individual ought not be compelled to support the advocacy of ideas with which he or she disagrees. The Supreme Court has recognized this extension of the principle for over twenty years (*Machinists* v. *Street*, 376 US 740, 1960).

THE SOCIAL FUNCTION OF UNIONS AND INDIVIDUAL RIGHTS

The social functions of unions raise problems akin to their political functions, but significantly different. Individuals are seldom, if ever, excluded or disciplined for refusing to engage in social functions. The problem is one of using union dues to support financially these non-collective bargaining activities. Individuals may understandably resist being required to finance activities they do not want or use as a condition of participating in collective bargaining decisions. However, requiring a person to contribute to a social affair, a recreation program, an adult education course, a mutual insurance plan, or other such activities does not encroach on individual conscience or personal freedom in the same way as compelled contributions to political or ideological causes. There may be some charitable or other contributions which would have this objectionable quality; those should be treated the same as political expenditures, and exceptions should be allowed for religious objectors. Otherwise, compelled contributions to the union's social functions may be an imposition on the individual's pocketbook, but they do not violate the individual's basic rights. Thus, the United States Supreme Court has found no statutory or constitutional bar to the union using compulsory dues for social activities (*Ellis* v. *Ry Clerks*, 466 US 435, 1984).

CONCLUSION

Any effort to reconcile collective and individual rights in our modern industrial society must end with unsatisfying answers. On the one side, the union, expressing the collective right of association and dedicated to promoting the rights and welfare of workers, collectively needs solidarity to fulfill its purposes, particularly in dealing with the collective control of employers. On the other side, the union's influence and control reach the individual's most crucial interests – the ability to work and conditions of daily work life. The conflict between collective and individual rights arises because some individuals do not share fully the values and interests of the collectivity, and seek to assert and exercise their individuality.

Answers cannot be found by denying collectivization and appealing to individualism. Modern industrial society is irretrievably collectivized, and even in the absence of a union the employment relation is collectively controlled by the employer, with individual rights puny and primitive. We do not even speak of the worker's rights as a member of the enterprise. It is the union which provides, through collective bargaining, rights of voice, due process, and personal freedom – rights which employers often deny through individual bargaining. Collective bargaining cannot eliminate the collective character of the system, but only gives the union an element of control, and the individual is compelled to be subject to that collective control. It is this overriding fact, too often ignored, which forecloses simple or clear answers.

Nor can answers be found in wise-sounding language of "weighing the interests of the union against the rights of the individual," as if these had measurable weights and we could objectively observe which way the heavenly scales tipped. The union has a complex of interests, and the individual's rights have several interests. The problem is not to weigh one against the other or to compromise by giving equal shares to each. The problem is to identify the various interests of the union and break down the rights into their elements and then find solutions which will give to each that which has the most value. Thus, separating the functions of unions, identifying the different obligations of membership, and articulating the elements of the right not to associate may lead us to solutions which maximize the values of both the union and the individual.

Finally, discussion of these problems may be furthered by avoiding words which have become vested with multiple meanings and freighted with emotional investment. Terms like "picketing," "right to work," "closed shop," and "political contributions" confuse discussion and obstruct reasoned analysis. They each denote complex and varied fact situations which need separate examination.

What is presented here does not purport to be a definitive analysis, but rather an effort to push part way through the problem. The answers are stated with more flatness and confidence than they deserve, for there was not the space to spell out details or doubts. Ultimately, they are built on one person's values, which many may not share, and which cannot be proved. Nor should we expect necessarily to agree, for though we may share common values we may choose different paths to fulfillment.

5

Affirmative action
Drew S. Days III

In the past ten years, the United States Supreme Court has decided nine cases involving the constitutionality or legality of programs granting preferential treatment on the basis of race, sex, or national origin.[1] All but three of the challenged programs have survived legal attack.[2] However, it would be a mistake to conclude from this record that the debate over affirmative action has been finally resolved on or off the court. For the outcomes in each of the cases presented for Supreme Court review have reflected profound disagreements among the justices over everything from the constitutional or legal authority for affirmative action programs, generally, to the propriety of specific programs, in particular. These differences on the court are significantly reflected in attitudes toward affirmative action in the society at large. In short, America has yet to arrive at a consensus on the question of whether and under what circumstances racial and sex criteria should be used to allocate limited opportunities in higher education, employment, housing, and government procurement.

I

Opposition to affirmative action can be attributed in part to white racial animus toward blacks that dates back to the landing of the first boatload of African slaves at Jamestown, Virginia, in 1619. One would have to be entirely naive to think that America's history of slavery, segregation, and discrimination has not been a powerful force in shaping white attitudes toward programs designed to benefit blacks. Other racial minorities and women have distinct but related histories of exclusion and denial that also shape the public's view of special efforts to assist those groups. Invidious motivations aside, however, the current debate over affirmative action is also an unavoidable consequence of contradictions inherent in controlling constitutional and legal provisions.

A key tenet of the American faith is that one may go as far and as fast as one's talents will allow. We are, it is often contended, a classless society in which rugged individualism and self-reliance are highly rewarded. The "self-made" man or woman is the embodiment of this creed. The opponents of affirmative action contend that it violates these cherished American values. It is at odds, they claim, with the basic concept of individual rights, namely, that each person has a right not to be discriminated against on the basis of race or certain other factors, such as color, national origin, religion, or sex, that have no bearing upon one's individual merit.

One can, upon consulting the two provisions central to the affirmative action debate, find support for the opponents' contentions. The first, the Equal Protection Clause of the Fourteenth Amendment to the US Constitution, declares that "no state shall deny to any *person* . . . within its jurisdiction the equal protection of the laws" (emphasis added).[3] By its terms, and as construed by the Supreme Court, the Equal Protection Clause applies only to governmental, not private action. The second, Title VII of the Civil Rights Act of 1964, holds, in part, that "it shall be an unlawful employment practice for an employer to fail or refuse to hire or to discharge an *individual* . . . because of such individual's race, color, religion, sex or national origin" (emphasis added).[4] Title VII's prohibitions apply to both governmental and private employers. The texts of both provisions speak quite explicitly to the right of individuals to be free from discrimination. This focus was understandable since the evil that the Equal Protection Clause sought to address in 1868 and that Title VII sought to combat in 1964 was the refusal of American society to treat blacks as individuals irrespective of their merit or capacity. Rather, they were enslaved and later subjected to the status of second-class citizens solely because of the color of their skin, because of the racial group to which they belonged.

Ironically, the proponents of affirmative action accept the opponents' characterization of the historical contexts out of which both the Equal Protection Clause and Title VII grew, namely discrimination against blacks as a group. However, there the agreements ends. For they argue that the vestiges of this history of group discrimination and disadvantage cannot be eradicated effectively without the use of group-based remedies under certain circumstances. Although they cannot cite, as can opponents, language in the Equal Protection Clause or in Title VII that provides strong support for the claim that group remedies are authorized by these provisions, the proponents do have powerful historical evidence on their side. The words of the Equal Protection Clause and of Title

VII cannot be allowed to obscure their central purpose, which was the remedying of the effects of discrimination against blacks as a group. They were designed to achieve a significant change in the condition of blacks. In the case of the Fourteenth Amendment to the Constitution (including the Equal Protection Clause), the aim was to move blacks from the status of slaves to that of citizens. And, in so far as Title VII was concerned, that legislation was directed at bringing blacks, other racial minorities, and women from a condition of economic marginality to that of full participation in the American world of work. Proponents of affirmative action argue that it does violence to both provisions to read them without these historical contexts and overall objectives in mind.

II

Irrespective of how one reacts to the foregoing legal arguments in the abstract, it is an historical fact that approaches suggested by opponents of affirmative action for eradicating discrimination have not proven successful. The end of the Civil War prompted the addition of three new amendments to the United States Constitution, the Thirteenth (1865), the Fourteenth (1868), and the Fifteenth (1870). The Fourteenth, as has already been mentioned, contains the Equal Protection Clause. Moreover, its terms establish standards for determining citizenship, afford similar "privileges and immunities" to citizens among the various states, and guarantee due process of the laws. The Thirteenth, the constitutional expression of President Lincoln's Emancipation Proclamation, freed black slaves and prohibits "slavery and involuntary servitude."[5] The Fifteenth bars the denial of the right to vote "on account of race, color, or previous condition of servitude."[6] These amendments, and legislation enacted from 1866 to 1875 pursuant to their authorization, clearly spoke in terms that did not single blacks out for any special treatment. Rather, they appeared to reflect the view that protecting *everyone* from racial discrimination would serve to guard against systematic discrimination against blacks or any other racial group.

These hopes proved unfounded. With relatively few exceptions[7] the Supreme Court construed the Civil War Amendments and legislation enacted by the Reconstruction Congress restrictively, leaving blacks largely unprotected against mob violence and official efforts to reduce them once again to positions of subservience to whites.[8] In the 1896 decision, *Plessy* v. *Ferguson*,[9] the Supreme Court upheld the constitutionality of racial segregation in public transportation. The "separate-but-equal" doctrine approved in *Plessy* was thereafter applied to almost every phase of life in southern and border states for over the next half-century. Despite the language of the Civil War Amendments and federal civil rights legislation guaranteeing individual rights against discrimination, blacks were subjected to segregation and discrimination because of their race, as a group. All blacks went to black schools, irrespective of ability or motivation or residence. Blacks were excluded from job and professional opportunities no matter what their individual qualifications.

The Supreme Court's decisions in *Brown* v. *Board of Education*[10] in 1954 striking down the "separate-but-equal" doctrine in public education was viewed by many as the beginning of the return to a focus upon individual merit and away from discrimination based upon one's race. It was felt that if children were assigned on a nonracial basis, say to the school closest to their homes, significant desegregation would occur. Barriers to employment opportunity for blacks could be achieved by ensuring that "opportunities were open to talent," that segregated plants and lines of progression were forbidden, and that no discrimination in pay or other terms and conditions was allowed. Removing overt barriers to black participation in the electoral process was seen as the answer to discrimination in voting. From *Brown* through the early 1970s, a period during which the major modern civil rights legislation, including Title VII, was enacted, the focus, therefore, was upon individual access. Discrimination was not perceived as a systemic problem.

By the early 1970s, those involved in the fight against discrimination were forced to acknowledge several realities. First, constitutional and statutory provisions prohibiting discrimination against "persons" or "individuals" were being widely violated. Children were not being assigned to schools on a nonracial basis. Employers were continuing to deny opportunities to blacks, other minorities, and women irrespective of their individual merit. And election officials persisted in their efforts to exclude blacks from the political process.

Second, even where nondiscriminatory standards were arguably in effect, it was found that longstanding conditions produced by a regime of segregation and racial exclusion could not be so easily overcome. In school districts that offered all students the option of deciding which school they would attend, the vast majority decided to remain in their traditionally one-race facilities. Black applicants familiar with a company's long history of discrimination remained reluctant to test the employer's newly expressed commitment to nondiscriminatory hiring and promotion. Black access to the polling booth did not translate immediately into political power because of certain electoral schemes, most notably the at-large election, and of restrictive requirements for getting on the ballot, even where black voters represented a significant minority.

Third, the long history of segregation and discrimination had left many blacks unprepared to satisfy requirements imposed by employers, election laws, and institutions of higher education. Employment, literacy, and admissions tests all disproportionately excluded blacks from job, voting, and educational opportunities enjoyed by whites. Unless effective responses to these barriers could be devised, it would be difficult to conclude that blacks had derived any practical benefits from the formal end to official racial segregation.

These circumstances made unavoidable the conclusion that discrimination was a systemic problem requiring systemic remedies. The responses were severalfold. In the school desegregation area, courts and administrative agencies began to impose upon affected school districts an *affirmative* responsibility for ensuring that their previously dual systems were effectively dismantled and that children went to "just schools" rather than "white schools" or "black schools."[11] Where necessary to achieve this result, school boards were required to make racial assignments of students measured against pre-established ratios of whites and blacks in each school. To the extent that meaningful desegregation could not be accomplished by the assignment of students to neighborhood schools, school boards were expected to transport them to schools further away from their homes.[12]

In employment, court decisions interpreting the terms of Title VII concluded that screening devices such as tests or educational requirements could not be utilized where they disproportionately excluded blacks, other racial minorities, and women unless they could be shown to be "job-related" or justified by "business necessity."[13] In other words, employers would have to show that applicants who performed well against these standards would predictably perform well on the job. Moreover, persons claiming employment discrimination found courts becoming increasingly receptive to the use of statistics to prove their allegations. Gross underrepresentation of minorities or women in an employer's workforce where adequate pools of qualified candidates from such groups existed created a presumption that the law had been violated.[14] Additionally, in cases where there was evidence of long-standing, deep-seated, and resistant racial discrimination in violation of Title VII or other provisions, lower federal courts and administrative agencies began to impose remedies upon employers that required that they meet certain "goals and timetables" for hiring blacks, other racial minorities, and women.[15] Most courts found these remedies consistent with their duty to see to it not only that present discrimination was ended and that victims were compensated for their injuries but also that every effort was made to prevent the recurrence of discriminatory practices.

From its passage in 1965 until the late 1960s, the Federal Voting Rights Act[16] barring racial discrimination in the electoral process was used primarily to prevent or remedy blatant forms of interference with blacks' exercise of the franchise. Thereafter, however, its provisions were directed against other, apparently race-neutral practices that effectively minimized or cancelled out blacks' ability to elect candidates of their choice.[17] Under one section of the Act, for example, certain states and localities are required to obtain prior approval from the federal government or federal courts before making any changes relating to voting. Changes that have the "purpose or effect" of restricting minority political participation must be disapproved. During the 1970s, this process was used to prevent thousands of changes that would have adversely affected blacks in particular, as well as Hispanics, Asian-Americans, and American Indians. Covered jurisdictions and courts or agencies routinely and explicitly considered the racial consequences of proposed voting changes in determining their legality.

More generally, the early 1970s was a period during which many American institutions initiated voluntary efforts to make up for the striking absence of blacks, other racial minorities, and women in important areas of our national life. Riots in several major cities both before and after the assassination of the civil rights leader and Nobel Peace Prize Laureate Dr Martin Luther King Jr undoubtedly contributed significantly to the feeling among concerned whites that black poverty and isolation had to be addressed immediately. These "affirmative action" programs covered a wide spectrum. At one end, employers, housing officials, and colleges and universities instituted special recruitment measures to ensure that minority group members were aware of their services and were encouraged to take advantage of them. Others provided special assistance to minorities to aid them in acquiring the skills or experience necessary for them to compete along with non-minority candidates for employment or educational opportunities. Some educational institutions provided special financial assistance in the forms of loans, grants, or scholarships to minority students to ensure their attending college despite economic hardship. Employers and housing officials established goals for minority hiring or apartment occupancy. And at the other end, colleges and universities set up "special admissions programs" to increase minority representation in higher education utilizing admission criteria and selection procedures that differed from those used to choose nonminority applicants.

There was reason to believe that these affirmative action programs were making headway in altering, in at least relative if not absolute terms, the caste-like character of race relations in the United States. Blacks, and other racial minorities, were finding employment in sectors of the economy and at levels previously closed to them. The number of black elected officials had increased markedly. And black and other racial minority representation in undergraduate, graduate, and professional education institutions had also grown appreciably. However, some of these measures became the subject of legal challenge before they had any real opportunity to become fully effective.

III

In 1974, the Supreme Court agreed to consider an attack upon the constitutionality of a state law school's special admissions program brought by an unsuccessful white applicant. Although the merits of that case were not reached by the court for technical reasons,[18] the court's, and the nation's attention has been focused ever since upon major challenges to the constitutionality or legality of affirmative action plans in education, employment, and government contracting.

It is difficult to put one's finger on exactly why the controversy over affirmative action arose when it did. Clearly, by the mid-1970s, whatever impact the riots of the late 1960s had made upon the conscience or enlightened self-interest of white America had dissipated. Whites' fear of what James Baldwin called "the fire next time,"[19] the concern that black frustration would result in civil unrest of cataclysmic proportions, was no longer present. Economic conditions at that time also provide some explanation. The country was experiencing a recession, employment was low, interest rates were high, and government support for social programs was being drastically reduced. Under these circumstances, white commitment to affirmative action became seriously strained.

It also bears noting that, by the mid-1970s, affirmative action programs had begun to affect a different group of whites than had been the case previously. First, civil rights enforcement, which for almost two decades after *Brown* v. *Board of Education* had focused upon southern and border states where official racial segregation had existed, came north. Northern school districts were facing desegregation suits, and northern employers were being charged with Title VII violations. Whites who had been supportive of vigorous enforcement in the South of civil rights laws were suddenly forced to reconsider their attitudes when their lives and livelihoods were directly affected. Second, affirmative action programs, whether imposed by courts or administrative agencies or established voluntarily, were having an impact upon a generation of whites with little or no understanding of the civil rights struggles of the 1950s and

1960s to eradicate official racism in America. These whites took the position that, since they had not violated the civil rights of black or other racial minorities, they should have no responsibility for remedying the consequences of those violations, particularly at their own expense.

Whatever the explanation for the growth of affirmative action challenges and whatever the motivation for such attacks, the use of race-conscious criteria raises serious legal and political problems that cannot be ignored. The question of whether the Equal Protection Clause and Title VII can properly be read to authorize such practices has already been addressed. Legalism aside, however, it is not surprising that critics of affirmative action question whether the "cure" is not worse than the disease. Is there not reason to believe, they contend, that the use of race-conscious criteria stigmatizes those it is designed to benefit, that it reintroduces racial and ethnic distinctions that *Brown* sought to banish from our public discourse, and that it creates new victims of discrimination, innocent whites, in the name of remedying civil rights violations against racial minorities? Are we not being asked, they argue, to unlearn the lesson that considerations of race, ethnic origin, color, sex, and religion, as opposed to individual merit, have no place in our national life? Proponents of affirmative action either deny the relevance of these considerations or assert that, whatever their force, the risks of doing nothing in the face of increasing racial polarization far outweigh those presented by taking race into consideration.

Although it is hard to separate the merits of this debate over affirmative action from the politics and personalities of the antagonists, once done, one can see that it is a subject about which honorable people can honestly disagree. Opponents of race-conscious remedies are prepared to forgo whatever short-term gains might be achieved by affirmative action programs in order to create, in the long run, a society where considerations other than individual merit are irrelevant and where opportunities are open to all in a real, not merely theoretical, sense. Proponents of race-conscious remedies are unwilling to pass up the *certainty* of minority advancement in education, employment, housing, and other areas in the short run for the *possibility* of achieving a color-blind society in the long run. To complicate the matter further, the lines between the proponents and opponents of affirmative action, on and off the Supreme Court, are not nearly so bright as the foregoing discussion suggests. Proponents of race-conscious remedies in one setting may oppose them in others.

IV

Not much would be achieved by providing a case-by-case description here of how shifting coalitions of Supreme Court justices have determined the course of affirmative action since 1974. However, a discussion of general areas of dispute and, where possible, of how the court has dealt with them, may prove helpful to the reader. First, the court has clearly held that, under certain circumstances, race-conscious and sex-conscious criteria may be employed consistent with both the Equal Protection Clause and Title VII. The consensus falls apart, however, when it comes to the question of what those circumstances are. Remedying racial discrimination has been found to justify the use of race-conscious criteria. But what type of evidence will suffice to establish racial discrimination has not been agreed upon.

In civil rights jurisprudence, one can identify at least three ways of defining discrimination. The most straightforward form of discrimination is where one person intentionally and purposefully denies another equal treatment because of the latter's race, color, national origin, sex, religion, or other personal characteristic. Such discrimination may be overt, as in the case of the laws in parts of the United States that required racial segregation until they were struck down by the Supreme Court's *Brown* decision. It may also be covert where laws appear neutral "on their face" (or by their explicit terms) but are administered or implemented in a fashion that disadvantages some and not others depending upon their respective racial or other characteristics. A law that required that everyone be able to read and write in order to vote but was administered to allow only literate whites, not blacks, to cast ballots would be an example of covert intentional discrimination.[20] In order to establish a violation of the Equal Protection Clause of the Fourteenth Amendment, one must, according to the Supreme Court, prove the existence of either overt or covert intentional discrimination.[21] Where that form of discrimination has been proved, the court has held that race-conscious remedies may be utilized to rectify the situation.

The second form of discrimination is defined not by the intent or purpose behind it but rather by its impact. The Supreme Court has held that, at least in so far as Title VII of the Civil Rights Act of 1964 is concerned, a law or practice that has a disparate or disproportionate impact upon one racial or ethnic group as opposed to its effect upon another, or upon women more heavily than upon men, may constitute illegal discrimination. Thus, for example, if an employer utilizes a written test to screen applicants that disproportionately excludes blacks as opposed to whites, that test may be found illegal under Title VII.[22]

According to the court, Congress envisioned this definition of discrimination in the context of Title VII enforcement because of its desire to eradicate effectively the consequences of many generations of denial to blacks of jobs solely on the basis of race. Given the extent to which segregation and other forms of exclusion deprived blacks of opportunities to prepare themselves for employment, Congress intended that racially neutral tests that disproportionately excluded blacks would not be permitted under Title VII unless the employer could prove that they were "job-related," that is, that performance on the test correlated closely with subsequent performance on the job. Where this form of discrimination exists or where strong evidence suggests its presence, the Supreme Court has upheld at least voluntary programs to correct for the disproportionate exclusion of racial minorities and women.[23]

The third form of discrimination is generally referred to as "societal discrimination." Unlike the other two forms of discrimination, societal discrimination does not depend upon showing that a particular individual or institution acted in a fashion that had the purpose or effect of disadvantaging others because of their personal characteristic. Rather, it is a recognition that certain racial groups, especially blacks, and women have been the victims of long-standing, deep-seated, and pervasive discrimination in almost every area of American life. Consequently, proponents of the societal discrimination concept argue that race-conscious or sex-conscious measures to alleviate the present effects of the discrimination are thoroughly justifiable, without the need to show that the institution establishing such programs was itself guilty of practices which by intent or in effect resulted in exclusion or disadvantage. The Supreme Court has, however, explicitly rejected the notion of societal discrimination as a sufficient basis for establishing programs that utilize race or sex criteria. According to the Court, if "societal discrimination" were accepted, almost any affirmative action program would be legitimate and immune to meaningful judicial review.[24]

Although proponents of affirmative action have presented the Supreme Court with justifications for the use of race-conscious or sex-conscious criteria other than discrimination, these alternative rationales have failed to gain any significant support among the justices. In the first affirmative action case to be considered fully by the court, a medical school's special admissions program was defended on the grounds, among others, that it promoted the compelling educational objective of "ethnic diversity." Ensuring the presence of blacks, Hispanics, and several other racial ethnic group members in medical school classes would allow for valuable exchanges of ideas and experiences that would not be possible in an all-white or virtually all-white academic setting. The challenged program was struck down by the Supreme Court, however, and only one justice found the goal of "ethnic diversity" a sufficient justification for race-conscious admissions programs in higher education.[25]

More recently, a school board sought to justify its race-conscious program affecting teacher lay-offs on the grounds that it was necessary to achieve the goal of providing "role models" of different races for its students. The board argued that ensuring the presence of minority group teachers in the classroom would provide minority students with palpable evidence that, with proper educational preparation, they, too, could expect to achieve professional success. As a result, it was argued, those students would be more highly motivated to apply themselves to their studies. The Supreme Court rejected that argument and declared the board's plan unconstitutional.[26]

The court has acknowledged the surface appeal of both the "ethnic diversity" and "role-model" justifications for affirmative action programs. However, it has not been persuaded that there is sufficient empirical or other probative evidence that such goals would be achieved by using race-conscious criteria or that they could not be achieved to an acceptable degree without the need to rely upon such criteria. Moreover, even were proponents able to satisfy these burdens, it is questionable whether the court would be willing to conclude that the benefits of ethnic diversity or role-models outweighed the burdens imposed upon affected persons because of their race, ethnic origin, or sex.

The Supreme Court has devoted substantial attention in its affirmative action cases to the question of who may appropriately benefit and who may permissibly suffer the burden of race-conscious or sex-conscious remedies. There is total consensus among the justices that persons who have been the direct victims of racial or sex discrimination are entitled to receive remedies that make them "whole" for the disadvantage they have suffered, that fully compensate them for their loss.[27] However, the court has not arrived at anything approaching agreement on when and on what terms so-called non-victims of discrimination should benefit from affirmative action programs.

The problem arises in the following way. Let us assume that an employer has been found to have discriminated against black applicants for a number of years in violation of Title VII. A court may without question provide black applicants who were illegally denied jobs with a range of remedies including payment of lost wages and employment at the level they would have enjoyed but for the employer's discrimination. But may the court order the employer to meet, where there are qualified applicants, a percentage goal for hiring blacks over a certain period of time – for example, having a 20 percent black workforce by the end of five years? Opponents of such remedies have argued that they violate both the Constitution and Title VII because they reward blacks who were not victims themselves of the employer's discriminatory practices. For these blacks, critics claim, the hiring goal is a windfall justified only on the basis of their race rather than because of any need to make them whole for their own injuries.

Employing various linguistic formulations and rationales, a majority of justices on the Supreme Court have concluded that remedies that benefit non-victims of discrimination are permitted by both the Constitution and Title VII. Thus far, at least, where the affirmative action is imposed by a court as part of a remedy for proven constitutional or statutory violations rather than voluntarily established, the Supreme Court has approved the inclusion of non-victims only where there is evidence of "persistent or egregious discrimination."[28] However, even justices who have granted the legitimacy of goal and timetable remedies which benefit non-victims have parted company when confronted by particular affirmative action plans. In a debate more semantic than logical, justices generally supportive of such plans have argued that the percentages and timetables were flexible "goals" (not required to be met if qualified candidates are unavailable) whereas the dissenters have characterized them as "rigid quotas" designed to achieve "racial balance."

At the heart of this debate is a basic disagreement over what percentages are required to remedy the effects of proven discrimination, that is, to create a condition with respect to the presence of minority group or female workers that would have obtained in the absence of the illegal employer practices. Put more directly, would the percentage of blacks in an employer's workforce have been 30 or 25 or 10 percent in the absence of racial discrimination? If 10 percent, goals set at 30 or 25 percent, say the dissenting justices, are not remedial at all but designed instead to achieve racial balance or parity between the availability of black workers in the labor pool and their presence in an employer's workforce.

The intense debate on the court over whether and under what circumstances non-victims should benefit from affirmative action is fueled, in part, by a concern for the impact of such programs upon "innocent third parties," whites or males who are not themselves guilty of any discrimination toward racial minorities or women. Generally, there has been greatest consensus in favor of plans that involve race-conscious recruitment and training programs,[29] less support for those relating to hiring and promotion,[30] and greatest opposition to arrangements that require lay-offs according to racial or sex criteria.[31] The rationale for this calibrated response on the part of some justices is that acceptable affirmative action plans should, in their view, distribute the burdens upon the widest group of whites or males as possible and have the smallest impact upon settled expectations. Recruitment and training fall at the acceptable end of this spectrum, lay-offs at the extreme opposite end. Promotions fall somewhere in the middle.

V

The foregoing discussion addresses only a few of the major areas of contention on the Supreme Court with respect to affirmative action. But it should suffice to reinforce the observation made at the outset of this essay about the lack of consensus in the United States over the use of racial or other similar criteria to allocate scarce opportunities and resources. And one is hard put to predict with confidence what the ultimate outcome of this debate will be.

Part of the answer lies with the United States Congress. For there are certain provisions of Title VII, now the subject of bitter controversy among the justices, that might be amended to make clear once and for all whether race-conscious criteria may legally be used to remedy the consequences of discrimination in employment. Congress took exactly this approach in 1982 when it amended the Voting Rights Act of 1965 to overcome an interpretation of the statute that it found unduly narrow. However, it has appeared quite willing to leave resolution of the disagreement over Title VII's interpretation to the courts. There are several possible explanations for this state of affairs.

First, proponents of affirmative action have been successful in defeating all efforts by opponents to add to Title VII language that would further restrict the use of race-conscious or sex-conscious criteria. They have reason to fear that any opening up of Title VII to the amending process at their initiative would be seized by opponents as an invitation to revise the statute drastically. Second, they may see no pressing need to amend Title VII since, as a practical matter, Supreme Court decisions have been basically supportive of affirmative action. Third, and somewhat ironically, opponents of affirmative action have not, in recent years, actively sought to amend Title VII, anticipating that the court itself would impose severe restraints upon race-conscious or sex-conscious programs. Given the closeness of the votes by the justices upholding affirmative action plans, opponents undoubtedly continue to hope that additions to the court through death or resignation will produce a new majority prepared to overrule existing precedents.

A solution to the dispute over the degree to which the Equal Protection Clause authorizes or at least tolerates the use of race-conscious or sex-conscious criteria is more problematic. Only a constitutional amendment either expressly approving of or rejecting affirmative action would do the job. The new Canadian Constitution, for example, contains a provision that explicitly authorizes affirmative action programs for both individuals and groups.[32] Amending the US Constitution has never been a simple proposition, however, as is attested to by the fact that there have only been twenty-six amendments during the Constitution's 200-year existence. And the recent unsuccessful effort to add an amendment guaranteeing equal rights for both men and women, the so-called Equal Rights Amendment,[33] suggests that the amending process has not become any easier than it has ever been. Consequently, the future of affirmative action as a constitutional matter is likely to remain solely in the hands of the Supreme Court.

How the affirmative action controversy turns out is clearly of great importance to everyone in the United States and of justifiable interest to people elsewhere around the world. But this controversy should not be allowed to obscure from the view of the American public or observers abroad larger and much more important questions, in this writer's estimation. Given the intense scholarly and public attention accorded the Supreme Court's affirmative action decisions, it is not surprising that many Americans have come to think that the outcome of the debate over the legality of race-conscious or sex-conscious criteria will, standing alone, determine the future status of blacks, other minorities, and women in this society. Certainly, if the court were to prohibit all affirmative action, even that modest effort to improve the conditions of disadvantaged groups and women would no longer be available. But favorable rulings on affirmative action are not likely to result in the near future in significant improvements in the inferior status of racial minorities, measured against any of the important socio-economic indices, or of women in employment.

America has many millions of blacks and other racial minorities who rank far below whites with respect to education, health, housing, and employment. Women continue to earn only about two-thirds the wages of men and can be found increasingly among the poorest members of the society. Affirmative action programs that provide a few minority seats in colleges or graduate schools, goals and timetables for employment of minorities and women, set-asides in government contracts for minority entrepreneurs, or minority quotas for rental housing cannot be expected realistically to lift large numbers of minorities and women from social marginality into the mainstream of American life. There are many reasons why the United States is so starkly split along race and sex lines. But one undeniable explanation is that historic discrimination has dropped roots deep in our culture that will be difficult to extirpate.

The important questions, therefore, relate to what America is prepared to do faced with the knowledge that affirmative action is, at best, a palliative and stopgap response to profound societal problems. Is it willing to provide heretofore unavailable resources to ensure that the majority of racial minorities receive levels of education, health care, housing and employment assistance that will make it possible for them to become productive citizens? Is it prepared to provide women who are living in poverty and heading single-parent families with training and child care that will allow them to enter the workforce and earn money to support themselves in dignity? One would think that opponents of affirmative action would find these more global approaches attractive, for there is no reason why these assistance programs could not be provided in a way that focused upon the socio-economic conditions of those being served, rather than upon their race, national origin, or sex. Programs designed to help the poorest and least educated would unavoidably reach large numbers of blacks, Hispanics, other minorities, and women, groups that have been the target of affirmative action efforts. Unlike affirmative action, however, these programs could be race- and sex-neutral, thereby avoiding some of the current Equal Protection Clause and Title VII problems. Proponents of affirmative actions might also be expected to embrace comprehensive responses to disadvantages disproportionately experienced by minorities and women, if only to reinforce their claims that race-conscious and sex-conscious programs are merely "interim," as opposed to permanent, remedial measures.

In the current United States political environment, however, the chances of mobilizing adequate public support for the establishment of comprehensive social welfare programs are almost nil. In the past, one could expect liberals to be the champions of increased spending for social programs, particularly those designed to assist racial minorities and women. However, times have changed. Civil rights issues are not on the agenda of either of the two major national political parties. And there seems to be general agreement, with only a few notable dissents, that government should operate on a balanced budget and that taxes should be kept down. Moreover, it is now the conventional political wisdom, despite significant evidence to the contrary, that attempts in the mid-1960s to address problems of poverty through massive federal government spending programs were a dismal failure and should not be repeated. Consequently, the political will and leadership are simply not present to mount any major initiatives to improve the conditions of America's poor and disadvantaged.

CONCLUSION

The noted constitutional scholar, Alexander Bickel, became, during the last few years of his life, one of the most outspoken critics of the use of race-conscious criteria in allocating scarce opportunities and resources.[34] In his earlier writings, however, Bickel suggested that, although it might violate the constitutional principle of "color-blindness," the country might find it necessary to be color-conscious for a time in an attempt to rid America of its shameful legacy of slavery and segregation. He thought that some period of "muddling through," of trial and error, might be unavoidable in order for America to arrive at "an effective and peaceable outcome" on the problem of race relations.[35]

Given the current state of the affirmative action debate in the United States, Bickel's phrase, "muddling through," captures as well as any what we are about. How that debate is resolved is certain to have profound symbolic consequences, for in a sense it will tell blacks, other racial minorities, and women whether the society is prepared to make even modest efforts to improve their inferior status. But even if affirmative action survives attack, the "effective and peaceable outcome" Bickel hoped for is likely to elude us unless far more ambitious social welfare programs are undertaken.

NOTES

1 *Johnson* v. *Transportation Agency*, 107 S.Ct. 1442 (1987); *United States* v. *Paradise*, 107 S.Ct. 1053 (1987); *Local 93, International Association of Firefighters* v. *Cleveland*, 106 S.Ct. 3063 (1986); *Local 28 of the Sheet Metal Workers' International Association* v. *EEOC*, 106 S.Ct. 3019 (1986); *Wygant* v. *Jackson Board of Education*, 106 S.Ct. 1842 (1986); *Firefighters Local Union No. 1784* v. *Stotts*, 467 US 561 (1984); *Fullilove* v. *Klutznick*, 448 US 448 (1980); *United Steelworkers of America* v. *Weber*, 443 US 193 (1979); and *Regents of the University of California* v. *Bakke*, 438 US 265 (1978).
2 *Wygant*, *Stotts*, and *Bakke*, *supra* note 1.
3 US Const. amend. XIV.
4 42 USC § 2000-e 2(a).
5 US Const. amend. XIII.
6 US Const. amend. XV.
7 *Ex Parte Virginia*, 109 US 339 (1880) and *Strauder* v. *West Virginia*, 100 US 303 (1880).
8 *Civil Rights Cases*, 109 US 3 (1883); *United States* v. *Cruikshank*, 92 US 542 (1876); and *United States* v. *Reese*, 92 US 214 (1876).
9 163 US 537 (1896).
10 347 US 483 (1954).
11 *Green* v. *County School Board of New Kent County*, 391 US 430 (1968).
12 *Swann* v. *Charlotte-Mecklenburg Board of Education*, 402 US 1 (1971).
13 *Griggs* v. *Duke Power Co.*, 401 US 424 (1971).
14 *Teamsters* v. *United States*, 431 US 324 (1977).

15 *Morrow* v. *Crisler*, 491 F.2d 1053 (5th Cir.) (en banc), *cert. denied*, 419 US 895 (1974).
16 Pub. L. No. 89–110, 79 Stat. 437.
17 *Perkins* v. *Matthews*, 400 US 379 (1971); *Allen* v. *State Bd. of Elections*, 393 US 544 (1969).
18 *DeFunis* v. *Odegaard*, 416 US 312 (1974).
19 J. Baldwin, *The Fire Next Time* (1963).
20 *Louisiana* v. *United States*, 380 US 145 (1965).
21 *Washington* v. *Davis*, 426 US 229 (1976).
22 *Griggs* v. *Duke Power*, *supra* note 13.
23 *Weber* and *Johnson*, *supra* note 1.
24 *Wygant*, *supra* note 1.
25 *Bakke*, *supra* note 1.
26 *Wygant*, *supra* note 1.
27 *Stotts*, *supra* note 1 and *Franks* v. *Bowman Transportation Co., Inc.*, 424 US 747 (1976).
28 *Paradise* and *Local 28*, *supra* note 1.
29 *Weber*, *supra* note 1.
30 *Paradise*, *supra* note 1.
31 *Wygant*, *supra* note 1.
32 Section 15 (2), Canadian Charter of Rights and Freedoms, Canada Act 1982 (UK), 1982, c. 11.
33 US Const. amend. XXVII (proposed).
34 A.M. Bickel, *The Morality of Consent* (1975), New Haven: Yale University Press, 133.
35 A.M. Bickel, *The Least Dangerous Branch* (1962), New York: Bobbs, 64–5.

6
Politics, socialism, and civil liberties
Bernard Crick

We socialists, I am sorry to remind you in mixed company, can have a bad name with some libertarians. And, to the surprise of anarchists, 'libertarian' has become a bad name to many of us. Libertarian philosophy is often associated with those of the radical Right who believe in an uncontrolled market economy but who also, with greater logical consistency than traditional conservatives, dislike censorship and almost any controls on personal life and private morals. But it is equally sensible to talk of 'libertarian socialists' and of 'libertarian conservatives'. I simply want to restate the case why liberty is never a sufficient condition for social justice (unless you are an anarchist, whether of the left- or right-wing variety) yet is always and everywhere a necessary condition for social justice.

I am equally angry with neo-liberals who say that democratic socialists are either hypocritical or muddled to think that equality and liberty can go together and with Marxists who say that individual liberty is possible only in a classless society (or that 'bourgeois liberty' is not really liberty). There are still fellow socialists who, despite all the awful object lessons of oppression using or misusing the name of socialism, take terrible liberties with liberty: no liberty, they say, for fascists, racists, perhaps even 'scabs' (the comprehensive term used to be 'no liberty for the enemies of the people').

Far from seeing equality as a pre-condition for a future liberty, the early socialists, the pre-Marxian socialists, saw the aggressive assertion of actual, existing popular liberties as being thwarted by gross inequalities. Greater equality of condition had to be achieved in order to maximize liberty. There was no glimmer of an opinion that popular liberties had to be restrained for the sake of equality. Poverty and oppression prevented people acting freely, or certainly limited drastically the effective limits of free action. But liberty, none the less, was seen as the greatest goal. A poor man, it was said, could scarcely call his soul his own. So an egalitarian society would allow much greater freedom of action for more people, not just freedom for the fortunate few. Early socialists, like Proudhon in France and Robert Owen in Britain, believed not merely that the main object of the struggle against oppression and the class system was to maximize human freedom, but that the struggle must take the form of asserting popular liberties. And they believed that socialist communities would, in a decentralized society in which the role of the state was minimal, order their affairs very differently.

There were, unhappily, two other traditions of early socialism: that of the followers of Saint-Simon and that of Blanqui. Saint-Simon was the great rationalist: a just society would be created by the knowledge and administrative skills of a specially educated élite controlling the state in the true interests of society (not what selfish people clamoured for or the ignorant thought they wanted). Blanqui was the eternal revolutionist and militant (he spent over half his life in prison): a small band of dedicated working-class revolutionaries could choose the right tactical moment to seize the state power and use it to smash the old social order for ever. For once the artificial order was violently demolished, a natural order of spontaneous harmony would follow. (Some modern terrorists exhibit just this potent mixture of delinquency and innocence.)

Yet even Saint-Simon and Blanqui professed that part of their aim was liberty (though there were good grounds for not trusting either). They offered no unusual definition of it. Liberty for all was not to be attained in either a traditional or a capitalist system, but qualitatively the liberty there was and the liberty to come were much the same thing. It was only Marxists who began to argue (not even Marx himself consistently) that bourgeois liberty was not really liberty at all and that true liberty could be found only in a classless society after the revolution. Bourgeois liberty was used only against the working class and was only ever of tactical, temporary, opportunistic use to them. Parliaments were only devices by which the bourgeoisie made use of their leisure, gained from exploitation and surplus value, to deceive and control the working class. I am not concerned here with how this argument entered into socialist tradition. I want only to identify it and to point to some consequences. The international socialist movement became split between libertarian and democratic socialists and authoritarian socialists who believed that the party embodies the will of the working class and that there must be no liberty to oppose or delay their emancipation.

FORCING TO BE FREE

The Marxist view of liberty was, however, only a specific formulation in class terms of an older and more general argument. Saint-Just in the days of the Jacobin ascendancy had cried that there was no liberty to stand aside. 'Those who are not for us are against us,' he declaimed to the Assembly. 'What are they but enemies of the people?' The fearsome concept was born that allows no appeal and leaves an individual no space in which to move. The idea of privacy as anti-social was invented almost at the same time that privacy itself became a concept to be valued. And you also had to be clerical or anti-clerical; middle positions of indifference or suspended judgment were dogmatically and violently denounced. Robespierre explained that

> The terror is nothing but justice, prompt, severe and inflexible, it is thus an emanation of virtue; it is less a special principle than a consequence of the general principle of democracy applied to the most pressing needs of our country.   (Talmon 1952: 114–15)

But it was Rousseau who had given this idea its more acceptable classic formulation, actually intending to strengthen democracy. For his idea of the 'General Will' was that social justice was not to be found in reason by educated philosophers. Rather it was to be found in the hearts and sentiments of ordinary people, the common people, when they stripped their minds of all pre-conceived knowledge, of book learning, and of all vested interests. Thus what was good for all, not for one's selfish self or corporate interest, would prevail. The common man would be more able to achieve this empathy or uncorrupted innocence than the educated or the aristocrat. But what if some poor wretch was to be so insensitive as not to experience, or so perverse as consciously to disobey, this beneficent General Will?

> Whosoever shall refuse to obey the general will must be constrained by the whole body of his fellow citizens to do so: which is no more than to say that it may be necessary to force a man to be free – freedom being that condition which, by giving each citizen to his country, guarantees him from all personal dependence and is the foundation upon which the whole political machine rests and supplies the power which works it.
>
> (Rousseau 1947: 261–2)

Now, there are many occasions on which it is right and just to use force against a fellow citizen: to resist a violent attack or to arrest or detain a thief, and so on. But something is wrong when we say that the person who is forced is therefore made free. We may be more free when a killer is locked up, but it is dangerous to believe that constraints on others make them free. Many things limit freedom, but the idea of it as lack of constraint is essential. Rousseau does not solve the problems of 'dependence' and 'oppression'; he substitutes one kind of oppression for another.

Consider the consequences. Oppressive commands must be not merely suffered and obeyed but applauded and internalized. Everything is class ideology, and 'the ideologically correct' is determined not by Rousseau's imagined beneficent Legislator but by an actual political party. On this logic not merely is there no liberty to criticize the party of the people, but liberty itself becomes everything the party decides to do, and nothing else. Consider a poignant and astonishing example.

In 1936 a Russian music critic called Olesha was commanded to recant publicly his admiration for the music of Shostakovich:

> The article in *Pravda* deals with a question of principle. It is the opinion of the Communist Party; either I am wrong or the Party is wrong. The line of least resistance would have been to say to oneself, 'I am not wrong', and mentally reject *Pravda*'s opinion. In other words by keeping to the conviction that in the case in question the Party had not spoken correctly, I would have granted the possibility that the Party was wrong.
>
> What would have been the result? There would have been serious psychological consequences. The whole framework of our social life is very closely knit together, comrades. In the life and activity of our state nothing moves or develops independently. . . .
>
> If I do not agree with the Party in a single point, the whole picture of life must be dimmed for me, because all parts, all details of the picture are bound together and arise out of each other, therefore there must not be a single false line anywhere.
>
> That is why I agree and say in this matter, in the matter of art, the Party is always right. And it is from this point of view that I begin to think of Shostakovich's music. I continue to enjoy it. But I begin to recollect that in certain places it always seemed to me somewhat, it is difficult to get the right word, contemptuous.
>
> (Olesha 1936: 88)

He must have been very frightened but he must also have been a very clever time-server. He was clever not to claim an implausibly sudden conversion to Stalin's dislike of modern music; and equally clever to grasp so well and state so slavishly the full logic of the Communist theory of ideology. He exhibits the bottom of the slippery slope on which any one of us can find ourself once we get into the habit of telling lies for the good of the cause, or more generally accepting that free actions and judgments must always be an 'ideologically' correct calculation of class (more often party) interest.

Modern Marxists might dismiss this as the personal philistinism of Stalin. But the more profound problem arises if one believes that freedom is a mere product of material circumstances, not a means of shaping them. For then free actions can be only those that further the true cause, not those of critics or opponents. Their actions become not free but somehow unnatural, perverse, anti-social. Those who adhere to this ideological theory of truth can offer no guarantees against the abuse of power by whatever person or group is trusted to speak for the cause authoritatively, precisely what John Stuart Mill called 'the fallacy of infallibility' (Mill 1859). It is dangerous as well as morally wrong to demand freedom for oneself but not for opponents. Single parties so often turn inwards to fight against themselves for power: 'the revolution devours its own children'.

I am, of course, discussing freedom of speech, assembly, and movement: the rights of citizenship, rights which if not exercised will wither away. I am not discussing rights of rebellion. Some states are so oppressive that it is the positive duty of their subjects to try to overthrow them, to act like citizens, if all other remedies have failed. But socialists have no special privilege, nor has anyone else, to break down laws or even to overwork non-violent civil disobedience (which if over-used as more than a symbolic gesture can hardly fail to involve or to provoke violence). Those who wish to transform society have a special duty to be tolerant and thick-skinned against criticism. It is not merely a question of tolerantly suffering 'reasonable criticism' or graciously welcoming 'helpful criticism'; one needs the civic toughness to accept slander. Our mothers well taught us that

> Sticks and stones may hurt my bones,
> But names they never will do.

Orwell said that 'Liberty is telling people what they do not want to hear' – ridiculously insufficient but certainly a necessary part of any definition of liberty.

So liberty is liberty. There is no exclusive socialist, liberal, nor yet conservative liberty. One modern Marxist has seized this point well – in contrast to so many prudes among us who feel tainted by any talk of 'things in common' and will not, unlike Marx himself, praise the bourgeoisie for their great achievements in their time:

> Regimes which depend on the suppression of all opposition and the stifling of all civic freedoms must be taken to represent a disastrous regression in political terms from bourgeois democracy. . . . But the civic freedoms which, however inadequately and precariously, form part of bourgeois democracy are the product of

centuries of unremitting popular struggles. The task of Marxist politics is to defend these freedoms: and to make possible their extension by the removal of class barriers. (Miliband 1977: 212)

If this is true, then it has implications for those of us who wish to defend and extend liberty as well as to promote particular causes.

Common ground can and should be found between socialists and non-socialists in taking up all cases where the civil liberties of anyone are threatened, whatever their politics. Even tactically it is usually best to make working alliances if the object is, indeed, to win a point of law of general application, to see that justice is done and not (as has sometimes happened in some famous campaigns) to make a martyr to publicize the cause. Socialists discredit themselves and devalue liberty when they make socialism a condition for supporting bodies like the National Council for Civil Liberties. The insistence that the NCCL, for instance, moves beyond 'negative objectives' and 'campaigns positively' (for socialist objectives and trade union discipline) is damaging both to civil liberties and to democratic socialism. Bodies like Amnesty International sometimes face the same problems – that is, some members who are more keen to attack oppression in general with their mouths than to do what is more quietly and thoughtfully needed to help actual individuals in prison. Take-overs of voluntary bodies by socialists can be very damaging, obviously to the bodies in question, which need to be able to convince non-socialists, but also to socialists themselves. The public can come to view them as irresponsible wreckers and trouble-makers, as people who fail to demonstrate that 'socialist institutions' work but can demonstrate that socialists can stop coalitions for specific causes working. (I am sometimes tempted to think of much of this as play-acting at revolution in a safe playground in leisure time, in which no one will get hurt.)

Of course the defence and assertion of civil liberties are not enough. Everyone has other values and needs. Socialists have a quite specific combination of values. We think that society needs reform-ing towards both egalitarian and libertarian objectives, building through and towards a great sociability and sense of community. Society needs reforming. But everything can't be done at once, still less in the same forum. We need to differentiate and discriminate tasks and roles, if we are serious and not just play-acting. We need to keep the basic constitutional and procedural concerns of civil liberties apart from agitation for substantive socialist reforms. Otherwise the tragedy of Soviet communism, not just of Stalinism, will be repeated for ever.

Special theories are invented to explain why the Russian Communist Party proved, contrary to socialist expectations, grimly repressive. Most of them seem far-fetched, and many have always been special pleading. One reason at least why one-party states become one-party states is that the leaders of a determined party want it to be that way: a matter of human will. More subtly, they developed an ideology that at a particular point of time crudely conceptualized all civil liberties and constitutional restraints as part of the exploitative mechanisms of the superstructure of capitalist states. But we now live in a world in which there are many capitalist autocracies and many socialist autocracies, most of them not even pretending to be parliamentary, democratic, or liberal. Neither the mode of production nor the class structure determines everything (nor are they ever as simple as once thought).

Truth to tell, even the British Labour movement, while intensely libertarian, has always had a rather simple theory of the constitution: that if a party gets a working majority in the House of Commons it can legislate as it pleases. Popular sovereignty legitimizes parliamentary sovereignty. There has been little concern with limiting parliamentary sovereignty itself – despite its use to privatize vast amounts of public property and to destroy local democracy in the capital city itself. I fancy that this may be changing. A reaction against centralized planning and excessive state control in favour of more local autonomy is taking place. It begins to dawn on even the most traditionalist socialists that to protect local and community rights some structure of public law, entrenched in the courts, might be preferable to the alternating risk of everything being undone again next time. It is doubtful if there could be a thoroughgoing decentralization of the polity and the economy without something like a Bill of Rights. But that is, of course, some Marxists would object, a liberal concept; so it is. So what? We should not deny historical fact. But we should try to make something better of it for all.

A REAL DIFFERENCE IN EMPHASIS

None the less, there is a real difference in emphasis between liberal and democratic socialist accounts of liberty. Sir Isaiah Berlin in his famous essay, *Two Concepts of Liberty* (1958), argued powerfully against what he called 'the positive theory of liberty' – theories that, in various ways, identify liberty with the positive achievement of some chosen state of affairs or, at least, with a comprehensive avoidance of error. 'In thy service, Lord, is the only perfect freedom' and 'The truth shall set you free' are both, whether in religious or secular mode, paradigmatic of positive liberty. A sociological version of the argument was Harold Laski's 'liberty is the existence of those

conditions in society which enable me to become myself at my best'
(Laski 1948: 142). The fallacy of this is quite simply that not being
unhealthy, not being unemployed, or not being in poverty cannot,
however lengthy the benign list, constitute or guarantee freedom.
(But in other writings Laski offered, as if he saw no difference, a
negative formulation: that liberty is the absence of those conditions
which can prevent me becoming myself at my best – Laski: 1937.)
Liberty, indeed, means being left alone and not interfered with,
even if sometimes other values lead us to curtail but never to deny
liberty.

> The 'negative' liberty they strive to realise seems to me a truer and
> more humane ideal than the goals of those who seek in the great,
> disciplined authoritarian structures the idea of 'positive' self-
> mastery, by classes, by peoples or the whole of mankind.
>
> (Berlin 1958: 56)

Yet something is missing from Berlin's account, not about the
nature of liberty but about the conditions for liberty. Either we must
say that Berlin puts too much stress on the protection of individual
liberty, the liberal ideal of being protected by law from the state, and
not enough on *the exercise of liberty* – the price of liberty is more than
eternal vigilance, it is eternal activity. Otherwise, we must argue for
an unobjectionable sense of 'positive liberty' which is not
authoritarian at all but is republican. Authoritarianism identifies
liberty with some chosen and obligatory version of truth or
righteousness; but the republican tradition identifies liberty with the
positive exercise of citizenship, popular participation, the perpetual
challenging of authority, the election of leaders but always criticizing
them and holding them to account. The republican tradition
aggressively seeks to politicize issues and to democratize institutions;
the liberal tradition gently seeks to take issues out of politics and to
put a wall of law between a legislature and, say, education, religious
observance, or property rights. To the republican while a good life
cannot be wholly political, yet nothing can be taken out of politics
a priori; but everything must be settled politically – that is, by public
debate, argument, persuasion, bargaining, and compromise.

Free actions are the actions of individuals not of organic groups
or homogeneous classes. Socialists must never forget that. They are
themselves individuals, usually rather innovative and unusual
individuals. But individuals interact with other individuals. This the
liberal sometimes forgets. My identity consists not in asserting the
uniqueness of my wretched personality to the height, nor in repress-
ing it sternly into some single and conventional social role, but in
how I am recognized by others. When we act we interact. You are
what you are because I, and many others, see you in that way. I am

what I am because of the reactions and recognitions of others. Free political actions are not merely free actions, they are interactions between people acting in a political manner: citizenship. Acting in a political manner is not simply acting effectively towards realizing some policy or ideal, but it is acting through public debate, using persuasion, recognizing other people's differing values, reaching sensible compromises, being resolute about ends but open-minded about means, and seeking to avoid all violence except the counter-violence of self-defence.

In the republican tradition the sword of liberty, it was always said, will rust in its sheath if not used – the true socialist might add – not just for other people but *by* those other people. 'We are all here on earth to help each other,' the poet Auden once gibed, 'but what the others are here for I can't imagine.' The liberal is stronger on 'the shield of the laws', but the republican (and democratic socialist who inherits this Roman, Dutch, French, and early American tradition) is stronger on William Blake's 'sword of burning fire': assertion, challenge, positive action. All are needed. In the republican tradition politics is not a minor disagreeable necessity, as it is to liberals; it is one of the marks of the good life and an educative activity in itself (Crick 1982). A person becomes more fully human by public debate and interaction with his or her fellows. Citizenship, free citizenship, acting for the common good, is the most noble image of humanity. Socialists in free societies commonly exhibit in their own behaviour this rugged and active republican individualism; but then they sometimes fatuously claim not to be acting freely but as the impersonal agent of some great abstraction like *the* people or *the* working class.

Politics, like freedom, in some thin sense can exist anywhere – in the Kremlin or in the court of the Great Dictator. But in a fuller, richer sense its existence as a public method of government, as a *system*, is limited. Most governments in the modern world seek to repress political activity, some endure it, and a very few encourage it. Politics comprises the public actions of free people, and freedom can be maximised only in political democracies (Crick 1973). That is minimal political justice.

Social justice consists in the procedures of reconciling in a political manner the plurality of different values and interests found in any complex society. Socialism is one such substantive view or, rather, to be fully honest and let a cat go running from the theoretical bag, is many such views. Democratic socialists believe not merely that socialist societies can be achieved by democratic means, but that they can only be achieved thus. It may seem foolish not to call the Soviet Union a socialist society. This is not a very serious theoretical issue. For if we do call it socialist, then it is a bad socialist society in the primary sense that it is not a free society. Conservatives often argue, like old Stalinists, that any socialism must impose changes so drastic that freedom suffers. But in the history of socialist thought, and in the possibilities raised by democratic socialist governments, this view is easily refutable – whether one is a socialist or not. It is as silly as to claim that all Conservative or capitalist governments are really, in some deep sense, authoritarian ('almost' fascist) or tend that way (according to a polemical pamphlet that Lenin wrote in a hurry in a peculiar circumstance).

Thus liberty deserves almost fanatic support from democratic socialists, not just if it appears to help a favoured cause of the moment. A truly socialist movement is so committed to liberty and open government that at times it can seem almost incoherent amid the multitude of voices which speak for it and the variety of different policies advocated. It can at times seem almost paranoid in its belief that anything less than totally open government conceals weapons of oppression and conspiracies against the people behind closed doors. And liberty is an unpredictable and exuberant thing. Give people liberty and you never know what they will do with it. The actions of free men and women are always unpredictable – which is why some teachers prefer teaching 'the rule of law' rather than the disruptive skills necessary for effective participation. Now, I am all for the rule of law. We should always give the benefit of doubt to laws that have been properly passed. But it is also in our tradition, in the republican tradition long before socialism even, to ask whether the laws are just and to challenge unjust laws. That is the difference between the good citizen and the good subject.

Berlin's (1958) concept of negative liberty does well to stress that many doors must always be left open. The socialist should know that many roads lead to Rome, not just one. Some may take longer, for instance, but prove less bloody. But it is not enough to purr with pleasure that there are so many doors; doors are to be passed through, though we should never slam them behind us. People who use their liberty in order to avoid political life are more often done down than left in peace. The price of liberty is active citizenship both in the formal polity and in all other associations (Crick 1984: 13–16). The sword can never rest at our side until everyone can and will act as equal citizens: women in general, the black population in particular, the Catholic minority in Northern Ireland, the Arab minority in Israel (or majorities in a different context).

CONCLUSION

The poor, the disadvantaged, and the dispossessed do not merely need injustices removed, they need positive discrimination to help them off the ground to act freely and politically for themselves. Freedom needs its antique, republican, pre-liberal cutting edge resharpened for modern conditions. Welfare is not secure if it is a gift and not a collective achievement. Freedom is positive action in a specific manner: that of a citizen acting as if among equals, and not merely to preserve the rights of existing citizens (say we socialists) but to extend them to the wretched of the earth. Far from there being an inherent contradiction between the ideals of liberty and equality, without social equality active liberty (which I call freedom) can never be achieved. But we need to watch it. It is so easy to take liberties with other people's liberties, especially if one means well by them. Without active liberty for all, the activists will always constitute a 'new class' or an élite of the elect – benign, arrogant, and reckless.

Lastly, without liberty truth can suffer. Socialists should not repeat the mistake of pre-industrial autocrats in seeking, grandly, to freeze knowledge and to hold it constant and, pettily, to excuse themselves from simple moral rules like telling the truth. What is 'ideologically correct', comrade, not merely has to be enforced but can then destroy the sense of reality of the leadership itself. That was Orwell's profound argument in his satires *Animal Farm* and *Nineteen Eighty-Four*. A somewhat similar egalitarian and libertarian to Orwell, Ignazio Silone attended the Comintern in the 1920s as a delegate of the Italian Communist Party. He provided a concrete example of all I have been warning against quite as extraordinary as poor Comrade Olesha adjusting his views on Shostakovich to those of Stalin (Olesha 1936).

They were discussing one day, in a special commission of the Executive, the ultimatum issued by the [British TUC] ordering its local branches not to support the Communist-led minority movement on pain of expulsion. After the representative of the British Communist Party had explained the serious disadvantage of both solutions, because one meant the liquidation of the minority movement and the other the exit of the minority from the trade union, the Russian delegate Piatnisky put forward a suggestion which seemed to him as obvious as Columbus' egg: 'The branches', he said, 'should declare that they submit to the discipline demanded, and then, in practice, should do exactly the contrary.' The English Communist interrupted: 'But that would be a lie.' Loud laughter greeted this ingenuous objection, frank, cordial, interminable laughter, the like of which the gloomy offices of the Communist International had perhaps never heard before. The joke quickly spread all over Moscow, for the Englishman's entertaining and incredible reply was telephoned at once to Stalin and to the most important offices of State, provoking new waves of mirth everywhere. The general hilarity gave the English Communist's timid, ingenuous objection its true meaning. And that is why, in my memory, the storm of laughter aroused by that short, almost childishly simple little expression – 'But that would be a lie' – outweighs all the long, heavy, oppressive speeches I heard during the sittings of the Communist International, and became a kind of symbol for me.   (Crossman 1950: 109)

I have never forgotten hearing that fine, scholarly socialist Harold Laski reading that passage from the newly published book in one of the last lectures he ever gave. It worries me because laughter is usually on the side of liberty, it is a form of liberty, so often satirizing autocrats. But this was not the satirical laughter of free men, which makes a moral point, but the laughter of cynics, which sees nothing in the world but naked power. 'They that live by the sword shall die by the sword.' Any socialism that neglects the liberties of others destroys itself.

REFERENCES

Berlin, I. (1958) *Two Concepts of Liberty*, Oxford: Clarendon Press.
Crick, B. R. (1973) *Political Theory and Practice*, London: Allen Lane.
—— (1982) *In Defence of Politics*, London: Penguin Books, 2nd edn.
—— (1984) *Socialist Values and Time*, London: Fabian Society.
Crossman, R. H. S. (ed.) (1950) *The God That Failed*, London: Hamish Hamilton.
Laski, H. (1937) *Liberty in the Modern State*, London: Penguin Books.
—— (1948) *A Grammar of Politics*, London: Allen & Unwin, 5th edn.
Miliband, R. (1977) *Marxism and Politics*, Oxford: Oxford University Press.
Mill, J. S. (1947; first published 1859) *On Liberty and Considerations on Representative Government*, Oxford: Blackwell.
Olesha, P. (1936) 'On Shostakovich', *International Literature* 6 (June): 85–7.
Rousseau, J. J. (1947; first published) in E. Barker (ed.) *The Social Contract*, Oxford World Classics.
Talmon, J. L. (1952) *The Rise of Totalitarian Democracy*, London: Secker & Warburg.

PART II

Free expression and
freedom of information

Editor's notes
The conflicting views of two national civil liberties organizations

A characteristic feature of modern civil liberties movements is the surge of identity among groups of people seeking recognition and respect for their rights and dignity. Jews, blacks, women, and gays have each asserted their rights not to be the subject of hatred, ridicule, and worse, harm and discrimination. Individuals and groups on the extreme political Right still openly purport to exercise their freedom of expression to offend and degrade these groups. Neo-Nazi organizations such as the National Front in Great Britain and the Klu Klux Klan in the United States still band together to demonstrate their racial and ethnic superiority. The result of the exercise of such freedoms can give offence, intimidate, incite, or even cause actual injury.

Civil libertarians espouse two, often conflicting sets of rights – freedom of expression and anti-discrimination. At what point does free expression yield to protect minorities from the hurtful lash of the tongue or waving of the swastika? Moreover, which group has the right to claim the assistance of respected and well-known organizations devoted to protecting civil liberties?

This conflict was presented to two of the largest civil liberties organizations in the west – the American Civil Liberties Union (ACLU) and the National Council for Civil Liberties in England and Wales (NCCL). The two organizations resolved the conflict in diametrically, and dramatically, opposite ways.

NCCL ADVICE POLICY

In 1984 NCCL gave advice to a member of a neo-Nazi organization, the National Front. In one instance, Joseph Pearce, a prominent member of the Front and editor of its magazine *Bulldog*, had his apartment searched by the police. It did not appear that the police had probable cause to believe that Mr Pearce had committed any offence which justified the search. The search was conducted violently with considerable personal and property damage; photographs and address books were seized.

In the second instance, a bus carrying members of the National Front was detained by the police for half a day in a lay-by, heading north to an anti-IRA march. The police, without giving reason, then forced the bus to travel in the other direction (south), blocking all exits on the motorway.

In the first case, legitimate civil liberties issues concerning unlawful search, privacy, and freedom from harm to person and property were involved. The second case involved apparent restrictions on the freedoms to associate and travel for a lawful purpose. (In the same year, NCCL had campaigned vigorously against police actions to stop Kent coal-miners from travelling to the north of England in order to picket – see Chapter 1.) Both cases, then, would have warranted NCCL's advice if the violation of civil liberties had occurred in relation to individuals or groups other than the National Front or its members.

On 22 March 1984 *The Guardian* published a prominent story about NCCL's decision to give advice to the National Front which stirred considerable controversy. The NCCL Executive Committee supported the General Secretary's decision to give advice, but was overruled by the organization's Annual General Meeting in April 1984.

The AGM passed several motions:

- In view of recent publicity given to reports of NCCL advising the National Front and one of its leaders, NCCL reaffirms its total commitment to opposing racism, which infringes the rights and liberties of racial minorities. This annual meeting accordingly resolves that NCCL should not knowingly aid organisations or individuals representing organisations whose primary objectives are opposed to civil liberties within a multi-racial society.

- This Annual General Meeting expresses concern at the aid given by officers of the Council to members of the National Front. Whilst acknowledging the civil liberties of all, it would seem inappropriate for this Council to provide aid of any kind to an organisation or individual whose publicly stated objectives include the removal of civil liberties from a large section of society and a substantial portion of the membership of this Council. The AGM believes that the provision of such aid could ultimately help bring about the denial of rights to others.

NCCL's Executive Committee subsequently interpreted these resolutions as proscribing the staff from giving any advice to individuals with 'well-known racist views', whether or not such individuals belonged to a racist organization. The resolutions were also held to extend to racist individuals or groups even if the advice sought was unrelated to their racist objectives – for example, access to school records under NCCL's freedom of information policy.

Two cases illustrated the painful decisions which NCCL had to take following the 1984 AGM. The first was a transsexual who had been prominent in the League of St George, a racist organization. She was being discriminated against in the benefits to which she was entitled by the Department of Health and Social Security. NCCL refused to give advice until she renounced her racist beliefs. The second case involved an ordinary member of the National Front who had her home searched by the police without a warrant; she was treated roughly and had property destroyed. In this instance advice was refused pursuant to the policy.

In the General Secretary's speech to the AGM in April 1985, I argued that

> if we are to hold ourselves out as being a civil liberties organisa-
> tion, then the only issue for us to consider is the civil liberties
> principle posed. It should not be our place to reserve our aid for
> those we approve of. The resolutions passed last year meant that
> we had to refrain from giving assistance in those areas where a civil
> liberties organisation has a duty to be fair and even-handed. By
> doing so we lost a bit of our self-dignity and a great deal of our
> political credibility.

The AGM of the NCCL in April 1985 modified the policy for giving advice. It tried to make a clearer distinction between giving advice to racist individuals and to groups. The AGM prohibited giving advice to 'an organisation, or an individual representing an organisa-tion, whose known objectives involve the denial of basic rights to others'. However, the AGM supported giving advice and, where appropriate, assistance to individuals irrespective of their beliefs.

The new policy failed to answer a number of questions. Clearly the intent of the resolution was to proscribe giving advice to groups on the extreme political Right. But the language of the resolution arguably covered any organization whose objectives involve the denial of basic rights to others, including those that NCCL has historically (and properly) supported. Organizations (and their representatives) such as the Irish Republican Army, the Palestinian Liberation Organization, and militant groups on the extreme political Left advocate means which restrict the freedoms of, and harm, other people. These and other organizations such as Protestant loyalists in Northern Ireland or Libyan or Iranian freedom fighters have racial, ethnic, or religious hatred as an undercurrent of their ideological beliefs. Many organizations and their representatives stand for, and express, beliefs which, if implemented, would rob others of their civil rights and liberties.

Once a civil liberties organization stands in judgment over the political platforms and content of speech of other groups, it will be seen to advocate an ideological set of beliefs, and undermine its own legitimacy in defending the principle of free expression.

NCCL's new policy also failed to guide its officers as to whether to advise an individual who represents a fascist group, but whose enquiry is not strictly related to the activities of that group. Leaders of the National Front, for example, may organize a demonstration against the IRA or nuclear installations. This does not necessarily advocate a denial of civil liberties to others. Or National Front officers may have their property and persons harmed during a police search for pornography and racist literature. Does the policy prohibiting advice extend to these cases?

In 1985 it was not publicly known that members of the National Front sought membership in NCCL, presumably for the purposes of speaking, and voting, against the advice policy resolutions. This raised the different question as to whether a civil liberties organization is bound to accept as members those who are not committed to its own constitutional principles. The Executive Committee, after a thorough hearing in relation to each application for membership, decided to reject the applications.

ACLU ADVICE POLICY

NCCL's initial decision, before it was overruled at the normal meeting, was only to give advice to members of the National Front. ACLU in 1977–8 went further by representing Frank Collin, the head of the National Socialist Party of America, which espouses a platform calling for the forcible deportation of Jews, blacks, Latinos, and other non-whites from the United States.

Mr Collin sought to demonstrate with his group in Marquette Park in Chicago. The Park District required a posting of $250,000 worth of insurance prior to the issuance of a demonstration permit. Mr Collin obtained ACLU's agreement to challenge in court the district's insurance requirement.

Mr Collin then sought to obtain permission to demonstrate in park districts in the suburbs of Chicago. He was rejected in the village of Skokie, north of Chicago. Skokie's population is 50 per cent Jewish and had thousands of survivors of Hitler's concentration camps. The

Skokie Park District told Frank Collin that $350,000 in insurance was required for a rally in the park. One further prerequisite for a permit was a finding by appropriate officials that the assembly 'will not portray criminality, depravity, or lack of virtue in, or incite violence, hatred, abuse or hostility toward, a person or a group by reason of religious, racial, ethnic, or national affiliation'.

Mr Collin's permit stated that the march would involve 30 to 50 demonstrators wearing uniforms including swastikas and carrying a party banner with a swastika and placards with statements such as 'White Free Speech'.

The Federal Court of Appeals in *Collin* v. *Smith*, 578 F. 2d 1197 (7th Cir. 1978), upheld ACLU's claim: (1) wearing of armbands and display of party flag are entitled to comprehensive protection under the constitution; (2) a village ordinance regulating demonstrations could not be justified as 'time, place or manner' regulations, where the ordinance turned on the content of demonstration; and (3) the asserted falseness of Nazi dogma and its general repudiation did not justify prohibiting the dissemination of materials which would promote hatred towards persons on the basis of their heritage.

Below, two of the most prominent proponents of their organization's policies present their arguments: Professor Norman Dorsen, President of the ACLU, and Stephen Sedley, who proposed the successful NCCL resolutions.

7

Is there a right to stop offensive speech? The case of the Nazis at Skokie

Norman Dorsen

I

A small group of right-wing extremists call themselves "Nazis." They profess to follow the tenets of Adolph Hitler. They adopt the swastika as a symbol and wear uniforms reminiscent of World War II stormtroopers. In 1977 they seek to hold a rally, in full regalia, in a Chicago suburb in which reside many thousands of Jews, including about six hundred who survived Hitler's death camps. Should they be permitted to do so? That is, should their interest in presenting themselves and their point of view in an avowedly peaceful manner prevail over the resistance of the residents of the town who regard such a performance as inherently assaultive, a psychological threat, a reminder of what they survived but so many of their co-religionists did not?

In brief compass, these are the facts that gave rise to the most controversial and publicized case that the American Civil Liberties Union (ACLU) undertook in many years, perhaps ever. The residents of Skokie fought fiercely in the courts and media to stop the planned demonstration. They found allies, including many ACLU members who resigned in protest from the organization, as well as newspapers, individual journalists, and others customarily devoted to the strong protection of free speech. But they eventually lost in court, and the American Nazis were free to demonstrate. In the end, however, the Nazis chose not to demonstrate in Skokie and instead mounted a small, brief, and uneventful ceremony in front of the federal building in downtown Chicago.

Those who opposed the demonstration sought repeatedly to place it "in context." The context to which they referred was the barbarism of the Hitler regime and particularly the unprecedented and almost unimaginable cruelties inflicted on entire portions of the population – Jews most numerously, but also communists, homosexuals, gypsies, the mentally retarded, and others. Throughout the episode there was extensive testimony from Skokie residents as to their deep resentment and rage; no one could fail to be moved by these feelings.

Why then did the interest in free speech, pressed by the ACLU, prevail in American courts presided over by judges who surely could not be accused of insensitivity to the horrors of Hitler's Germany or the despair of its survivors? The explanation requires attention to another "context" in which the case arose – the long tradition in the United States of a principled protection of free expression even when formidable interests are arrayed against it.

Four examples will suffice to illustrate the tradition:

National security is an important value. But in the Pentagon Papers case[1] the Supreme Court refused to enjoin the *New York Times* and other newspapers from publishing a history of the Vietnam war whose publicity the government claimed would have drastic consequences for the United States military position and diplomatic relations. (As to the tension between civil liberties and national security, see Chapter 11.)

Privacy is an important value. But the court has refused to prevent or punish the disclosure of confidential health information, the broadcasting of the name of a rape victim in violation of a state statute, or the details of an incident embarrassing to a family that had been held hostage by kidnappers.[2]

Personal reputation is an important value. But the court has erected significant constitutional barriers to public figures seeking to recover damages for defamation by the media.[3]

The maintenance of order in schools is an important value. But the court has rejected a school's attempt on this ground to bar a pupil from wearing to class a black armband protesting the Vietnam war.[4]

In all these cases the free speech interest was held to outweigh admittedly substantial opposing interests. This is not to say that assertions of the primacy of free speech are, or should be, automatically accepted. In other cases the Supreme Court has rejected free expression claims in which national security, reputation, and school discipline were implicated.[5] The court, no doubt, would in future reject free expression if it concluded that other interests were compelling. In other words, free speech is not absolutely protected, and should not be. But it should be inviolate unless the values on the other side are powerful and can be vindicated only by restricting speech. As Justice Cardozo once put it, the right to freedom of expression guaranteed by the First Amendment of the US Constitution is "the matrix, the indispensable condition" of a free society.[6] The reasons for that high status are worth recalling.

The first is that free speech permits the fulfillment of individuals by presenting their views (and therefore themselves) without legal restraint. This is a goal of the highest order. As one Supreme Court justice put it, "the final end of the State [is] to make men free to develop their faculties."[7]

A second major justification of free expression stresses the concept of democratic self-government, the "profound national commitment to the principle that debate on public issues should be uninhibited, robust, and wide open."[8] Indeed, a democracy cannot claim to be legitimate without freedom of speech; it cannot enjoy the consent of the governed if the governed cannot discuss and ponder matters that the government wants to exclude from public debate. Further, such debate helps to maintain "the precarious balance between healthy cleavage and necessary consensus" by facilitating social reform. The movements on behalf of labor unions, racial minorities, and women are the most important examples of desirable social reforms advanced by the ability of people to persuade, agitate, and implore.

A third purpose of free speech is its "checking value" against possible government corruption and excess by exposing and questioning official actions.

A fourth major purpose is to advance knowledge and reveal truth. Justice Oliver Wendell Holmes said that the "best test of truth is the power of the thought to get itself accepted in the competition of the market."[9] While this may seem unduly optimistic at times, the purifying quality of speech has been evident for centuries in many spheres of human endeavor, especially the arts and sciences.

It is for these reasons that great thinkers throughout recorded history have celebrated the freedom of speech: Socrates, Milton, Locke, Jefferson, Montesquieu, and Mill. It is the keystone of our liberty. Indeed, in the course of academic discourse and courtroom combat I have rarely found a person who openly belittles the constitutional guarantee. To the contrary, everyone professes to support it. Why, then, does the First Amendment need an advocate? I suggest that the key is not whether the disputants accept the purposes of free speech but rather the *degree* to which they embrace them. Intensity of this sort cannot be measured mathematically, but it is palpable in judicial opinions, the briefs of lawyers, and articles by lawyers and journalists. I am not extolling mere emotionalism but rather laud a simple yet compelling confidence in speech values and a full sensitivity to their significance.[10]

A key question in balancing rights concerns the burden of proof. The framers of the US Constitution made this decision, and made it wisely, in favor of free speech values. The powerful words of Justice Louis Brandeis illustrates the intensity of which I speak:

Those who won our independence believed that freedom to think as you will and to speak as you think are means indispensable to the discovery and spread of political truth . . . that without free speech and assembly discussion would be futile; that the greatest menace to freedom is an inert people; that public discussion is a political duty; and that this should be a fundamental principle of the American government.[11]

Without this intense commitment, the judge or scholar, after paying the obligatory homage to free expression, will nevertheless regretfully conclude that "in *this* case" it must yield for reasons of national security, or domestic order, or government efficiency, or the other reasons that are regularly advanced to overwhelm our fragile constitutional guarantee. Indeed, the Skokie incident is a good example of a situation in which some people were willing to say "in this case" free expression must yield. This is why it is useful to examine the case now, a decade later; its difficult facts test allegiance to free speech.

And of course there are reasons that make a full commitment to free speech seem difficult. People do say foolish and vicious things, and we may suspect that their words cause foolish and vicious acts. But to conclude that speculative harm traced to language justifies restrictions on free speech is to reverse the value judgment made by those who wrote the First Amendment to the US Constitution and lived through the turbulent times that begot it; they said by all means punish the lawless act but protect the freedom of speech.

These considerations provide the background to the Skokie controversy. But they do not resolve it because, to paraphrase Justice Holmes, they are too general to decide the concrete case. To explain why free expression triumphed, and deserved to triumph, requires a closer look at the Skokie incident.

The well-established starting-point, recognized even by those who opposed the demonstration, is that the streets and parks "have immemorially been held in trust for the use of the public and, time out of mind, have been used for purposes of assembly, communicating thought between citizens, and discussing public questions."[12] It was not always thus. An earlier philosophy of exclusion held that people had no more right to march, speak, and demonstrate in publicly owned streets and parks than they would on the grounds of a private landowner. This is past history, and the right of individuals and groups to gather in "public forums" to speak out on public issues is now unquestioned. (As to the legal right to use public thoroughfares for protest in the United Kingdom, see Chapter 3.)

But the right is not absolute and may be subject to reasonable conditions even-handedly applied to all groups. Thus, if the Nazis sought to march in a residential area at night time or during rush-hour traffic, they could have been stopped. No such claim was made in Skokie, because the city in fact objected to the demonstration on content grounds and not because of the time, place, or manner of the demonstration.

The arguments offered for prohibiting the march fell in two groups. The first was that Nazis should be prohibited from presenting their message regardless of where it is said and who hears it. The second argument conceded that the Nazis' speech should be protected in general but would permit its restraint in a town like Skokie, where many Jews reside who were persecuted by the German Nazis. Parts II and III of this essay examine these contentions.

II

The most extreme position is that American Nazis have wholly forfeited their right to speak because they associate themselves with Hitler's murders and their message is too dangerous and odious to permit. Rabbi Meir Kahane summed up the idea in a Skokie synagogue when he said, "Rights? They have rights? What person has the right to demand that others be put into ovens?"[13] An essentially similar argument was made by Skokie officials who argued for a ban on the swastika because it is a symbol of genocide. A closely related position is that those who attack freedom of speech (like the Nazis) seek to destroy our democracy and thus should not be allowed to speak if we wish to preserve civil liberties. Professor Ernest van den Haag made the point, "if freedom is to be inalienable . . . invitations to alienate it [cannot] be recognized as a legitimate part of the democratic process."[14]

These arguments ultimately fail for several reasons. Initially, as a factual matter, it is questionable whether we properly can attribute the crimes of Hitler's Germany to those who were not even born when they occurred and have not been proved to have committed a crime or even the intention to do so despite the similarity of their message. To do otherwise is guilt by association, a form of critical judgment that fair-minded people have come to reject, most notably after the ravages of the McCarthy period in the 1950s. Because Americans were horrified by Stalin's crimes, and because they feared communism, they silenced thousands of voices, sent people to prison, and deprived many others of jobs for their words. As Aryeh Neier has pointed out, Senator McCarthy and his allies did a "clumsy job,"[15] persecuting not only Stalinist communists, but anti-Stalinist communists, socialists, fellow travelers, and liberals, all to the detriment of free speech and lawful political behavior.

In short, government will often confuse the enemies of its policies with the enemies of freedom. This occurred early in the United States' history when Congress enacted the Sedition Laws. It could happen tomorrow if public animosity toward a particular minority made it politically popular to victimize it. Who can deny the possibility that Black Panthers, homosexuals, unconvicted "terrorists," and the like would feel the lash of censorship if conditions were ripe?

Another theory to justify suppression rests on the ground that speech that attacks or casts contempt on a racial group does not merit legal protection. This argument was sustained by the US Supreme Court in 1952 in the *Beauharnais* case when it upheld a conviction of an outspoken bigot under the Illinois Criminal Group Libel Law.[16] Noting that libel of individuals was unprotected by the First Amendment, the court held that libels of a racial or religious group should be accorded similar treatment. Today there is a substantial question in the USA whether *Beauharnais* remains good constitutional law in light of subsequent Supreme Court decisions providing First Amendment protection to defamation of individuals. Further, such group defamation laws are dangerous because they accord public officials wide discretion to invoke them. For example, in over fifty years Illinois prosecuted no one under its law but Beauharnais, although there must have been others whose speech fell within the language of the law. In fact, Illinois has now repealed the law.

My late colleague, Edmond Cahn, spoke of the Illinois law in an address at the Hebrew University of Jerusalem in 1962. He pointed out that, if the group libel law were vigorously enforced,

The officials could begin by prosecuting anyone who distributed the Christian Gospels, because they contain many defamatory statements not only about Jews but also about Christians; they show Christians failing Jesus in his hour of deepest tragedy. Then officials could ban Greek literature for calling the rest of the world "barbarians." Roman authors would be suppressed because when they were not defaming the Gallic and Teutonic tribes they were disparaging the Italians. For obvious reasons, all Christian writers of the Middle Ages and quite a few modern ones could meet a similar fate. Even if an exceptional Catholic should fail to mention the Jews, the officials would have to proceed against his works for what he said about the Protestants and, of course, the same would apply to Protestant views on the subject of Catholics. Then there is Shakespeare who openly affronted the French, the Welsh, the Danes. . . . Dozens of British writers from Sheridan and Dickens to Shaw and Joyce insulted the Irish. Finally, almost every worthwhile item of prose and poetry published by an American

Negro would fall under the ban because it either whispered, spoke, or shouted unkind statements about the group called "white." Literally applied, a group-libel law would leave our bookshelves empty and us without desire to fill them.[17]

The pervasive censorship throughout recorded history, including contemporary history, suggests that Professor Cahn's fears were not idle.

A variant of the group defamation argument is that hateful speech is not expression worthy of protection. The philosopher Joel Feinberg, while nevertheless concluding that the Nazis were correctly permitted to march in Skokie, has made this argument forcefully. After observing that the purpose of Nazi speech (in Skokie and presumably elsewhere) is merely "to affront the sensibilities of the Jews," he said that "Only some speech acts are acts of advocacy, or assertions of belief; others are pure menacing insult, no less and no more." With particular reference to the Illinois Supreme Court's opinion that the display of the swastika is symbolic political speech, Feinberg says:

> That is almost as absurd as saying that a nose thumbing, or a giving of "the finger," or a raspberry jeer is a form of "political speech," or that "Death to the Niggers!" is the expression of a political opinion.[18]

This argument, if accepted, would curb the Nazis by sweeping the chess-piece of free speech entirely off the table. But it cannot fairly be accepted, as Professor Amdur has convincingly argued:

> "Jews are scum" is a political opinion – a nasty opinion to be sure, but just as political as "corn dealers are starvers of the poor," "private property is theft," and "abortion is murder." "Death to the Niggers" is political expression, at least if "death to the Klan," "smash capitalism," and "fuck the draft" are political expression. The swastika *is* symbolic political speech; it sends an unmistakeable message, indicating support for certain values and a certain political program. Like Feinberg, I find the message, values, and program odious, but that is not the issue here. If the red flag, the hammer-and-sickle, the black armband, and the Black Power salute are examples of symbolic political speech, then why not the swastika?[19]

The dispute over whether what the Nazis are saying is "speech" points up a more general reason to reject attempts to enjoin their right to demonstrate. Such injunctions are "prior restraints" because they are imposed before the speech actually occurs. David Goldberger, the ACLU attorney who represented the American

Nazis in the Skokie case, observed that such restraints "touch a raw nerve in the American legal system,"[20] as epitomized by former Chief Justice Burger's opinion for the US Supreme Court in a 1971 picketing case: "Any system of prior restraints of expression comes to this Court with a heavy presumption against its constitutional validity."[21]

The reasons for this "heavy presumption," which the Illinois courts stressed in the Skokie case, are that they entirely prevent the expression of would-be speakers and deprive the public of its interest in knowing what the speakers would have said. Prior restraints also decisively alter the legal rules in favor of censorship by permitting the state to enforce its injunction through a civil proceeding for contempt against the speaker rather than through the criminal process (for breach of the peace or the like). In criminal cases, the defendant is protected by procedural safeguards such as the right to trial by jury and the obligation of the state to prove its case beyond a reasonable doubt rather than by a preponderance of the evidence. The evils of prior restraint were illustrated in the *Pentagon Papers* case,[22] where the Nixon administration sought to enjoin materials relating to the Vietnam War on the ground that national security would be compromised. The US Supreme Court rejected the plea, and when the papers were eventually published they revealed misdeeds by government, but there was no damage to national security.

A final general argument against speech by Nazis was not, as far as I know, put forward in the Skokie case itself. It proceeds from the premise that free speech (indeed civil liberties generally) is an adjunct to remedying the unequal distribution of power in society. It is argued that civil liberties should be concerned with redressing this maldistribution (see Chapter 7). What does this mean? What body is to be charged with deciding who lacks power? The answer surely is that the very groups who today possess power would make the determination. Can one believe that they would protect only those who sought to displace them?

It is not clear that extreme right-wing groups in the United States or Great Britain have less power than minority groups such as Jews or blacks. On a practical level, experience in Great Britain shows that the decision of the National Council for Civil Liberties not to defend free speech for racist organizations and the laws which prohibit incitement to racial hatred (see Chapter 3) has had no discernible effect on the National Front and other neo-Nazi groups. Moreover, statutes and police actions designed to curb free expression of these groups because they are offensive to the black community have back-fired and are now used against blacks in their communities, trade unions on the picket lines, and the Campaign for Nuclear Disarmament.

It is argued that civil liberties generally should be concerned with rectifying the unequal distribution of power, and not merely with free speech. Do "powerful" groups thereby forfeit other liberties such as the right to a jury trial, to practice their religion, or to privacy in their own homes? To limit civil liberties according to the nebulousness of social power would invite confusion, inequality, and ultimately the destruction of liberty.

III

The arguments that would concede the general right of Nazis to exercise free speech, but deny them the right to speak in Skokie, where thousands of Jewish survivors of Hitler or their children make their home, also are unpersuasive.

The first argument is based on the societal policy against incitement to riot. The governing rule under the First Amendment to the US Constitution is that speech advocating illegal action (including riot) cannot be punished except where such advocacy "is directed to inciting or producing imminent lawless action and is likely to produce such action."[23] There was no evidence that the Nazis met this test, and indeed there could not be since they had not yet spoken or held their demonstration. The true issue here is whether they could be barred from speaking because of the possibility, perhaps the likelihood, that the *listeners* – Jewish residents of Skokie and their allies – would create a disturbance by reacting violently to the hateful words. In American constitutional parlance, this is called the "heckler's veto," whereby those who disapprove of certain speech can, by threatening violence against the speakers, silence them. It should be self-evident that to accept such limitations would fatally wound free speech because speakers could always be prevented from speaking by those who object. (For a comparable view in the British context, see Chapter 3.) In recent years the Supreme Court has consistently rejected the idea, and it merits little discussion as a matter of principle.

A second contention rests on a famous dictum by US Supreme Court Justice Oliver Wendell Holmes. Employing a version of the "clear and present danger test" that he later discarded, Holmes said that "free speech would not protect a man in falsely shouting fire in a crowded theater and causing a panic."[24] But the analogy to Skokie is inapt. In the crowded theater there is an audience that has no opportunity to avoid the cry of fire, to determine its truth or to respond to it. Speech on the public street of Skokie, given with ample notice, does not engage a captive audience. People are free to attend or stay away. If it appears that unlawful action will occur as a result of the Nazis' speech, the police should promptly intervene, and if unlawful action takes place it should be punished. This approach is consistent with the views of Justices Brandeis and Holmes:

> To courageous, self-reliant men, with confidence in the power of free and fearless reasoning applied through the processes of popular government, no danger flowing from speech can be deemed clear and present, unless the incidence of the evil apprehended is so imminent that it may befall before there is opportunity for free discussion. If there be time to expose through discussion the falsehood and fallacies, to avert the evil by the processes of education, the remedy to be applied is more speech, not enforced silence.[25]

A third argument under this rubric would rely on the 1942 US Supreme Court *Chaplinsky* case that permitted punishment for "fighting" words.[26] In that case the court upheld the conviction of a man who got into an argument with a police officer and said to him, "You are a God-damned racketeer [and] a damned Fascist and the whole government of Rochester are Fascists or agents of Fascists." The court's theory was that such utterances are unrelated to self-government (a somewhat doubtful proposition on the facts) and that such insulting words trigger violence in the same automatic way that a cry of fire in a crowded theater triggers panic. But the Supreme Court has subsequently limited this doctrine, vacating convictions that would have expanded it beyond individual, face-to-face encounters.[27] Nor has the court applied the concept to non-verbal symbols like a red flag or peace symbol (or swastika). To do so would broadly undermine protection of speech that is obnoxious or distasteful to a particular group. In a society composed of myriad such groups – racial, religious, and others – the consequences for free speech would be dire.

A final argument for censorship, which surfaced during the Skokie case, would expand existing law under which it is an actionable private wrong for a person intentionally to inflict emotional harm on another. Liability has been imposed, for example, for falsely telling a person that a loved one has been killed or directing racial slurs at an individual.

One thoughtful commentator, Donald Downs, has developed a similar theory. Recognizing the potential for major inroads on free speech, his theory would allow liability only in cases in which speech in a public forum involves the unprovoked advocacy of death or violence to, or the vilification of, a racial or ethnic group and is "directed at an individual, home, neighborhood, or community in such a way as to single out an individual or specified group as the definite target of the expression."[28] This "targeting" approach is tailored to finding a principled way to restrict the Nazis' speech. But it invites more questions than it answers: Why should only racial and ethnic slurs be included, and not religious slurs or slurs directed at women or homosexuals? Why should liability exist only if the speech occurs in a "public forum"? How does one determine whether a group is the "definite target" of the expression?* The opportunity for arbitrary responses to these questions is evident. This means, once again, reposing in the hands of government officials wide discretion as to who would be permitted to speak and who would not. No truly free system could survive this process.

IV

A tragic feature of human history is the relentless persecution of people for racial, religious, and ethnic reasons. Should all speech on the part of groups who have engaged in crimes against other groups be banned? When this question is put to those who would have censored the Nazis at Skokie, a few say yes, but most say no. They would ban only the Nazis because, it is said, they epitomize evil in a unique way.

This position is not sustainable. As mentioned earlier, there is a vast leap in assimilating the Nazis at Skokie with those who served Hitler. However abhorrent the former's views, they have committed no genocide or other crime; if they do commit unlawful acts, they should be convicted and punished. Beyond this, a special rule for "Nazis" is wholly ahistorical. In our own century, Turks decimated Armenians, the Soviets wiped out Ukrainians, and African tribes have slaughtered rival groups. The United States has

---

* In the Skokie case, although it was widely believed that the Nazis selected Skokie as a particular target, this is doubtful. Frank Collin, the Nazi leader, wrote letters requesting permission to demonstrate in local parks for "white power" to several Chicago suburbs, including many with few Jews in residence. The Skokie Park District was the only government entity to reply to the letter, denying permission for the demonstration. Only then did Collin announce that there would be a demonstration in front of Skokie Village Hall. His letter said that they would

> obey all laws and they would not obstruct traffic. In protest against the denial of the permit to demonstrate in Skokie's parks, the Nazis planned to carry signs with such slogans as "White Free Speech," "Free Speech for White Americans," and "Free Speech for the White Man." . . . The demonstrators would make no derogatory statements, either orally or in writing, directed at any ethnic or religious group. They would, however, march in uniforms. The Nazi uniforms include a swastika emblem on the armband.
>
> (A. Neier, *Defending My Enemy*, New York: E.P. Dutton, 1979: 39)

This history negates the widely held perception that the Nazis pre-selected Skokie for their demonstration because of its high proportion of Jewish residents.

seen unspeakable cruelties to black slaves and American Indians. How can a rule on free expression ignore these crimes and acknowledge only what the Nazis did?

At the core of the genuine feelings of rage and despair inspired by the Nazi demonstration at Skokie was a wish: that the Nazis would disappear, that the kind of evil they exemplify would cease to exist. Most of us share that hope, but preventing Nazis from speaking will not exorcise them. They will continue to speak racial hatred wherever they are. Is it not better to expose this venom and to respond to it, rather than drive it underground to fester? The best defense against hateful speech is counter-speech upholding democratic values which appeals to the good sense and decency of the people. As Professor Franklyn Haiman has observed, if we begin to ban expression that

> disrespects the rationality, autonomy and dignity of its audiences . . . what about all the commercial advertising, political campaigning, and religious cult evangelizing which exploits and manipulates the fears, hates and other irrationalities of its audiences and uses people as means rather than ends?[29]

There was another deep-seated objection to the Nazis at Skokie: their success in securing vast publicity by dramatically confronting Jews on their home turf. Apart from the question whether that was the original plan, such direct confrontation is common when speakers seek public attention for an unpopular point of view. Radical labor unionists entered company towns; Benjamin Spock protested Vietnam on army bases; Martin Luther King expounded civil rights at the white bastions of Selma and Cicero. In all these cases, outraged citizens sought to prevent the unpopular demonstrations, just as today different groups seek to prevent peaceful marches by homosexuals against the Roman Catholic Church or pro- or anti-abortion groups against their opponents. It must be constantly borne in mind, as Justice William O. Douglas said some years ago, that

> a function of free speech under our system of government is to invite dispute. It may indeed best serve its high purpose when it induces a condition of unrest, creates dissatisfaction with conditions as they are, or even stirs people to anger. Speech is often provocative and challenging. It may strike at prejudice and preconceptions and have profound unsettling effects.[30]

There are limits that can be imposed on hate groups that are consistent with a system of free expression. During the Skokie episode, the ACLU refused to defend a Nazi who was prosecuted for offering a cash bounty for killing a Jew. The reward linked the speech to unlawful action in an impermissible way. Nor would we defend a Nazi (or anyone else) whose speech interfered with a Jewish religious service or who said, "There is a Jew; let's get him." And it is questionable whether we would defend a Nazi group that sought to march every week in a Jewish neighborhood or to do so without notice (so that it could not be avoided). Contrary to one assertion, the Nazis did not "successfully put the ACLU on retainer."[31]

It is common knowledge that thousands of members and contributors to the ACLU withdrew their support because of Skokie. It is less widely known that the organization very quickly recouped both members and dollars and that the Skokie case became a long-term asset for the ACLU.* Americans who did not understand or care about the fine points of civil liberties could still respect a decision based on principle. They recognized that the ACLU was undergoing financial hardship because it would not sacrifice the First Amendment even for the most despised and unpopular. That is precisely the function envisaged by the Constitution in a free and open society.

NOTES

I am pleased to acknowledge the valuable research assistance of Kerwin E. Tesdell, my former fellow in the Arthur Garfield Hays Civil Liberties Program at New York University School of Law.

1 *New York Times Co.* v. *United States*, 403 US 713 (1971).
2 The cases are *Whalen* v. *Roe*, 429 US 589 (1977); *Cox Broadcasting Corp.* v. *Cohn*, 420 US 469 (1975); *Time, Inc.* v. *Hill*, 385 US 374 (1967).
3 The seminal case was *New York Times Co.* v. *Sullivan*, 376 US 254 (1964).
4 *Tinker* v. *Des Moines School District*, 393 US 503 (1969).
5 E.g. *Haig* v. *Agee*, 453 US 280 (1981); *Gertz* v. *Robert Welch, Inc.*, 418 US 323 (1974); *Bethel School District* v. *Fraser*, 106 S. Ct 3159 (1986).
6 *Palko* v. *Connecticut*, 302 US 319, 327 (1937).
7 Justice Brandeis, concurring in *Whitney* v. *California*, 274 US 357, 375 (1927).
8 *New York Times Co.* v. *Sullivan*, (*supra* note 3) at 270.
9 *Abrams* v. *United States*, 250 US 616, 630 (1919).
10 Professor Joel Gora and I have discussed this point more fully in our article 'The Burger court and the freedom of speech,' in V. Blasi (ed.) *The Burger Court* (1983) New Haven: Yale University Press, 42–4.
11 *Whitney* v. *California* (*supra* note 7) at 377.
12 *Hague* v. *CIO*, 307 US 496, 515 (1939) (opinion of Justice Roberts).

* It is my judgment, based on numerous exchanges with the public, that, if the ACLU had decided to represent the Nazis in Skokie, the credibility of the organization would have been severely harmed and its economic loss would have been greater and less easily retrievable. On a related point, some critics faulted the ACLU on the ground that even if the Nazis should be permitted to speak, it was wrong for the ACLU to expend scarce institutional resources for this purpose. But in fact the resources required to litigate demonstration cases of this type are trivial. Most important, if the First Amendment interest in the Skokie case were allowed to perish by default, the case would have been a precedent employable thereafter by the opponents of free speech in all sorts of cases.

13 Quoted in A. Neier, *Defending My Enemy* (1979) New York: E. P. Dutton, 125. Neier was executive director of the American Civil Liberties Union during the Skokie episode. The executive director of the Illinois Civil Liberties Union also wrote an account – D. Hamlin, *The Nazi/Skokie Conflict: A Civil Liberties Struggle* (1980) Boston: Beacon Press.

14 A. Neier (*supra* note 13): 145.

15 A. Neier (*supra* note 13): 146.

16 *Beauharnais* v. *Illinois*, 343 US 250 (1952).

17 Quoted in A. Neier (*supra* note 13): 139–40.

18 J. Feinberg, *Offense to Others* (1985) New York: Oxford University Press, 86–93.

19 Amdur, book review, 'Harm offense, and the limits of liberty,' *Harvard Law Review* 98 (1985): 1946, 1956–7.

20 Goldberger, 'Skokie: the First Amendment under attack by its friends,' *Mercer Law Review* 29 (1978): 761, 765.

21 *Bantam Books* v. *Sullivan*, 372 US 58, 70 (1963).

22 *New York Times Co.* v. *United States*, 403 US 713 (1971).

23 *Brandenburg* v. *Ohio*, 395 US 444 (1969).

24 *Schenck* v. *United States*, 249 US 47, 52 (1919).

25 *Whitney* v. *California* (*supra* note 11) at 377.

26 *Chaplinsky* v. *New Hampshire*, 315 US 568, 572 (1942).

27 *Rosenfeld* v. *New Jersey*, 408 US 901 (1972); *Lewis* v. *New Orleans*, 408 US 913 (1972); *Brown* v. *Oklahoma*, 408 US 914 (1972). See also *Papish* v. *Board of Curators of Univ. of Missouri*, 410 US 667 (1973).

28 D. Downs, *Nazis in Skokie* (1985) London: University of Notre Dame Press, 163.

29 Haiman, book review of D. Downs, *Nazis in Skokie* (1985), manuscript, p. 4.

30 *Terminiello* v. *Chicago*, 337 US 1, 4 (1949).

31 Nessen 'Slouching toward Skokie,' *Village Voice*, 31 July 1978, p. 26.

8

The spider and the fly: a question of principle

Stephen Sedley

Nothing in the Convention may be interpreted as implying for any State, group or person any right to engage in any activity or perform any act aimed at the destruction of any of the rights and freedoms set forth herein or at their limitation to a greater extent than is provided for in the Convention.

(European Convention on Human Rights, Article 17)

A tone of high principle comes readily to those of us who campaign for justice and decency in the murky business of politics and social control. I am not being sarcastic. It is both easier and more compelling to say, 'This should never happen: it is wrong in principle', than to say, 'It is wrong to let X do this; it is right to let everybody else do it.' In the second approach lurks every vice from inconsistency to hypocrisy. If principles are constant and universal truths, it is an approach which must be unprincipled. And pragmatically, when the endeavour to influence public opinion necessarily depends on press coverage, to offer such a ready target to an often hostile press seems almost suicidal.

Yet it seems to me, as to many others, that the American Civil Liberties Union suffered a self-inflicted wound when it decided to back the constitutional right of the American Nazi Party to march through Skokie, a predominantly Jewish suburb of Chicago. More important perhaps, it damaged the philosophy and constricted the growth of civil liberties in our era. Of course it won itself a good press, but it acted on what I want to suggest was a mistaken understanding of principle. Britain's National Council for Civil Liberties after bitter debate in 1984 and 1985 decided not to go down a similar road. It did not assert that racists should be denied rights enjoyed by others, but it decided that NCCL's advice should not be made available to them. The decision was predictably attacked by a press not exactly distinguished by daily espousal of the rights of racial minorities.

There is little to be learnt about either the philosophy or the policy of civil liberties from the run of the mass media, and danger in letting political commentators and leader writers dictate or even shape the work of a body which has to pioneer. Most of the principles now accepted and voiced by the media were fought for and won by people whom their predecessors either ignored or attacked. The obvious exception, press freedom, was not echoed by much press stridency in favour of the freedom of others to voice their views; those elements of society had and still have to fight and win their own battles. Conventional wisdom, the stock-in-trade of most political journalism, has in its time in the name of liberty – the same type of liberty as the press enjoys – opposed almost every measure to protect the powerless, from the outlawing of slavery to the extension of the franchise, from the banning of mantraps and of the use of child sweeps to the ten-hour working day, from the abolition of flogging in prisons to the abolition of beating in state schools. In this vocabulary freedom stands for the perpetuation of power in the hands of those who already possess it. It is not the seed-bed in which civil liberties grow. The changes which have altered our fundamental thinking about freedom, in particular freedom for whom, have originated neither in Fleet Street nor at Westminster but in the reaches of society barely frequented by historians and journalists, where currents flow, tides shift, and occasionally great waves are generated on the surface. The way we have been taught our own history has a direct and distorting effect on our comprehension of how liberties and principles evolve, because it substitutes effect (the great man, the ardent reformer) for cause.

It behoves a civil liberty organization to remember that the good opinion and trust of the victims of racism may be more important to the achievement of its aims than a good press. In Britain today a number of militant racist organizations exist and (importantly) thrive in the political and social atmosphere. If now one of them wants to march through Spitalfields or some other poor quarter with a large ethnic-minority population, it will not have the aid of NCCL in asserting its right to do so. The issue is not, of course, and never has been whether the march would infringe the law of public order, for legality is not the yardstick of civil liberty. It is whether the occurrence of the march – national flags used as nationalist emblems, military drums, phalanges of aggressive young white males – would itself be an assault on the right of the people of the locality to live free from fear. The answer itself is too plain for argument: fascist and racist organizations choose to march through such areas in preference to main thoroughfares precisely because they are out not to persuade or convert but to intimidate.

NCCL in its present stance does not contest their right to march.

I am not the only person, however, to whom it appears that the entitlement of racist organizations to NCCL's aid is logically continuous with their entitlement to carry on their activities. The line at present drawn between the two is a reasonable but pragmatic one, reflecting as much as anything else the delicacy of NCCL's own position. In opposition to both stances, and in support of the right of racists to march as they wish within the law, principle is invoked and its opponents are consigned to the ranks of the unprincipled and the opportunist – manipulators who are all in favour of civil liberty so long as it works for them and against their enemies. That this cap undeniably fits some of those on the left who support the policy I am advocating does not, however, condemn the policy. It has more acceptable underpinnings.

I want to suggest that principle *is* fundamental, but that far from being a unitary body of timeless criteria, principle is a complex and shifting concept.

Racial discrimination is currently condemned publicly by effectively everybody from far Left to centre Right. The degree to which it is rejected privately and politically varies substantially. The common denominator of the public consensus is probably a positivist notion about equality before the law. Beyond that point I doubt whether the consensus goes. For example, there is a view, not confined to the political Right, that although black people have a right to equality of opportunity, their intellectual and personal potential is less than that of whites. There is an equal and opposite form of racism in parts of the Left where black workers are seen as fresh troops in an ongoing struggle, with no historical experience or cultural identity entitled to separate respect. Correspondingly an account of why racism is wrong will vary from a moral denunciation of the denial of human rights to a political denunciation of practices which split the working class.

Of the many aspects of what we unhesitatingly recognize as the principle of anti-racism, perhaps the most readily forgotten is its novelty. The post-war generation in which I grew up knew black people mainly as savages in school textbooks and in boys' adventure books which contained words like 'nigger' and 'coon'. We have watched the racial and cultural composition of British society change drastically since the 1950s, and have slowly and imperfectly understood some of the racism programmed into us – for example, the habit of speaking as I have just done of white society as 'we'. There is a long way to go, but if you look back, white-dominated societies have come a certain distance. It is not easy therefore to invest the commandment 'Thou shalt not discriminate' with the durability (you could hardly say the inviolability) of 'Thou shalt not kill'. The truth, it seems to me, is that today in Britain as in the USA anti-racism is a principle because consensus has made it one, and its genesis, content, and rationale are a great and complex web of divergent ideas and movements.

In making this suggestion I am not trying to belittle the importance of anti-racism, but am pointing out that it is neither absolute nor timeless. It is a function of history, of social movement, of culture, of politics, and above all of struggle – of the refusal of black people to be pushed to and beyond the margins of white-dominated societies. It is one of those great waves which currents, tides, and winds will generate. I am happy to go on calling it a principle because I do not think that it differs in character or origin from any of the other principles which developed societies like to think of as ageless ground-rules of collective existence. Most of all is this true of those truths which the founding fathers of modern American society held to be self-evident. Not only were they not evident at all to most of the rest of the world; looking back we can see that the new ground they were breaking in terms of political and social codes was not ground intended for occupation by women, who were excluded by the very language in which the self-evident truths of equality were expressed, or by the slaves owned by some of those who proclaimed them.

Examples can be multiplied. Among them, freedom of speech and of association, as much as freedom from racial discrimination, are the products of historic struggles, in this instance against authoritarians and censors. They are fundamental because in our society we have made them so. (They are also heavily qualified because our society has prized other rights – property, passage, an unblemished reputation – more highly.) In the abstract language of high principle you might say that radical dissenters from William Penn to John Wilkes, from William Hone to George Loveless, stood in the dock in their time so that Oswald Mosley and Colin Jordan could preach and practise race hatred in ours. Politically, historically, and ethically you could say no such thing. These are freedoms which became subjects of contest and matters of principle because the growing and moving components of society demanded them and the static and resistant elements eventually accommodated them. Few states bother to penalize the merely eccentric. What those in power could not tolerate was not the bare freedom of speech and association, which are always available to those in power, but the threat of what the dissenters spoke and organized for. It was what Penn preached, what Wilkes and Hone published, and what Loveless practised that brought them into the dock. It is history – as lived, not as written – which has transformed their heresy into our orthodoxy. But it is a lack of principle that now tries to translate the eventual success of those who resisted tyranny into the instrument of new tyrannies.

I am well aware how subjective this approach seems in theory and how double-edged in practice. Every political divide has one side accusing the other of representing a new tyranny. Is the civil liberty movement therefore going to allow whichever side has the political muscle to do so to silence its opponents? Or is it to arbitrate; and if so, by what criteria? The questions are logical, but they are not abstract, and neither are the answers. Injustice and oppression flow from the unequal distribution of power, whether within one household or across the face of the planet. Civil liberties ought above all to be concerned with means of redressing or mitigating this maldistribution. In practice they generally are so concerned: all human rights and civil liberty organizations that I know of have been concerned both in their origins and in their orientation with the victims and casualties of developed societies. This is morally and historically as it should be. The undoubted gap that exists in some places and some minds between practice and theory is, I would argue, the product of an ahistorical understanding of civil liberties and of a resort to language which has the virtue of unassailability and the vice of unreality. One repeated example is the reduction of racist activity to an issue of "speech" or "expression", shorn of the physical intimidation and concrete foreclosure of opportunity which it constitutes for the individuals and communities it is aimed at. (The debate about its wider causative effects is a comforting fallback but misses this central point.) This in turn reduces the entire argument to a debate about censorship, which is actually one of its most marginal features but has the advantage of being the easy terrain for a concept of principle which does not cope very readily with rough country.

One reflection of this, or possibly one symptom of it, is the traditional article of faith that civil liberties are concerned only with the distribution of power between the individual and the state, and that the regulation of relations between citizens is a matter for substantive law and conventional politics. I question this division. In a state which in a variety of ways generates and tolerates racism, the activities of militant racists are not simple exercises of civil rights: they are a virulent form of an endemic oppression of racial minorities – a prime concern of civil liberties – and their weapons include the entrenched and institutional power of racial privilege, prejudice and fear. In Britain they feed off social decline and the mentality of a lost empire; they appeal to the xenophobia and élitism of poor whites. But the ideology which they both draw on and contribute to is the ideology which has also given us racially discriminatory employment structures, nationality and immigration laws, and administrative controls; which has worked for two decades mainly by inertia and sometimes by political, official, or judicial obstruction to frustrate the implementation of constructive race relations initiatives; and which has closed the eyes and ears of those in positions of power to the continuance of widespread racial disadvantage and victimization in a society which claims to be free and equal. To treat such organizations as simply another political minority, and so as another client for civil liberties, is to accept the very myth of formal equality which it is the fundamental premiss and role of civil liberties to challenge.

Further, limiting the arena of civil liberties to relations between the individual and the state accepts as essentially valid the state's own pose as a neutral governor and arbiter. The civil liberty challenge then becomes a challenge to the state to stick to its assumed role and to assure the equal distribution of individual rights. The first part of this challenge may well be correct, but the second part of it fails to address the fact that the state is not the only repository of power in our society and not the only author of oppression. A state which leaves the bully and the victim, the fit and the disabled, the rich and the poor, to sort out their differences within the law is ensuring the continuance of injustice. A civil liberty organization which simply acts as umpire in such a contest is betraying its trust. It is precisely because the law is not the yardstick of civil rights that civil liberty organizations have to take sides. Their very reason for existence is that there is a certain one-sidedness in the majestic impartiality, on which Anatole France remarked, with which the law forbids rich and poor alike to sleep under bridges, to beg in the streets and to steal bread. The distribution and the intensity of wealth and poverty, of strength and weakness, are themselves a responsibility of the state.

The equation of all minorities with one another is only one aspect of the democratic fallacy. Its implicit exclusion of majorities from the ambit of civil rights is another. Civil liberties have successfully made the underprivilege and oppression of women a major concern, because their formal voting status in political democracies has not been matched by social and personal emancipation. But the movement's practice, here as elsewhere, has run ahead of its theory. Civil liberty organizations are now locked into what seem to many of their stalwarts intractable dilemmas as feminism's opposition to pornography collides with the lobby for freedom of expression. Both are civil liberty issues, but the movement lacks a tenable and accepted theoretical basis for espousing one such cause and contemplating the exclusion or rejection of the other. It lacks it because it is trapped in the idealistic notion that there is a natural harmony or balance of the freedoms we recognize as basic, when the fact is that there is not. What there is, and will always be in any but a monolithic society, is competition for the status of civil rights or liberties, and more competition for the ability to enjoy them. I want to learn from protagonists of the 'purist' position why freedom of individual enterprise, for example, should not be recognized as a civil liberty. Perhaps they would say it should, although the more usual response is the unargued one that economic rights do not rank. From the position I argue for, however, there is a principled answer: in western society this is a dominant and well-protected freedom, for the exercise of which other freedoms – to have a job and a home – require protection. In our time and place it is the latter which therefore call for recognition and which may make legislative protection of jobs and homes a civil liberty issue. Whether in another time or place, for instance in a society which does not allow private enterprise at all, freedom of individual enterprise, in our western sense of the right to accumulate wealth and the power that goes with it, will become a civil liberty issue, is a function of the great social and political movements of our epoch. We do not know how they will end or when. But we do know that civil liberties are not a simplistic process of upturning power relations: the abolition of slavery has not made the right to own slaves a civil liberty. The tide of history carries with it our standards of collective existence; they suffer sea-changes.

To understand this process is to recognize a truth which I believe *is* evident: that in real life principles come and go; that in the process they can clash with one another; and that tests of priority have to be found which are themselves principled. I have quoted at the head of this chapter the seventeenth article of the European Convention on Human Rights and Fundamental Freedoms because it recognizes one such test, the need for compatibility in the exercise of assured rights, and expresses it as a denial of rights to those who try to use their freedoms to injure the freedom of others. The Universal Declaration makes similar provision. But while the principle is, I would think, both acceptable and necessary, it is vague: how will it resolve the clash between feminism and pornography, or between militant racism and racial minorities? The idea that it should operate by allowing each some territory and erecting a fence between them, like rival football supporters, although absurd, is actually the unspoken minor premiss of the 'pure' civil liberty philosophy. By purporting to be neutral it assumes the role of arbiter; as arbiter it accords equal legitimacy to aggressor and victim; and in so doing it lends itself to oppression. The NCCL has perhaps seen this contradiction at its sharpest in recent moves to gain its support for the freedom to propagate paedophilia. I do not know on what basis of principle (other than the desire for a good press) the advocates of a 'pure' civil liberty policy joined in resisting these moves; but I do know that the protection of the powerless against people who want to use their experience, age, and status for self-gratification is the principled basis on which it was right to resist. (The fact that the right of the young to grow and discover themselves without unwarranted imposition is threatened by far more than paedophilia may also be a reminder that civil liberty issues often go unrecognized until – like blacks, women, gypsies – the sufferers start making waves and rocking boats.)

Although it has seemed to me better to start from the question of underlying principle rather than accepted practice, I have pointed out that the latter is in many ways more consistent and correct than the former. This is not a debating point. It reflects the same proper pragmatism as colours all normative civil rights documents. The Article 17 'rights with rights' regulation comes, as in the Universal Declaration, after a string of substantive rights practically all of which are loopholed with exceptions of which the state is the primary arbiter. It is a matter for debate how many of these loopholes themselves represent protections for other civil liberties. Leaving aside the claims of strong-state theory that all state necessity exceptions are means of indirectly protecting individual freedoms, there is little doubt that exceptions in favour of public order can be operated either to enhance or to inhibit other freedoms; it all depends on who, when, where, and how, and it is in the perennial debates about these factors that civil liberty organizations have their natural role. They are not going credibly to discharge it by taking the attitude either that the state, usually through its police force, will neutrally arbitrate, or that as between hostile groups of citizens there is nothing to choose on civil rights grounds – because in many cases there is everything to choose and abdication in failure to do so. How would the ACLU have chosen if the Jewish residents of Skokie had come to it for help at the same time as the Nazi Party did?

Equally, it tends to be forgotten in Britain that the crime of incitement to racial hatred which was introduced by the Race Relations Act 1965 carries within it both the present problem and a resolution of it. It evoked opposition initially from 'pure' civil libertarians precisely because it was a fetter on freedom of speech. Today it has long since ceased to be a live issue because experience and consensus have affirmed the critical need to protect racial minorities from overt abuse. Nobody credibly argues that the balance between freedom from fear and freedom of speech somehow demands or permits room for both in this area. In other words, where legislation has for once taken an appropriate initiative, we have recognized the rightness of its constriction of free speech; but the civil liberty movement has been unduly slow to theorize why this is so. It is stuck between recognition of the accurate but awkward power principle and adherence to the less assailable but less tenable purist principle of civil liberties. It tends still to preach the second and practise the first.

The inequality of power, carrying a denial of many basic rights, is the concern of civil liberties. The concern has no logical connection with whether the source lies in individuals or in the state; and if there were a logical connection, the answer would be both. The power of white males to assert themselves and intimidate others is socially generated and socially sanctioned. Black pride is not: it is the self-help of people whom western white society in general does not either help or welcome. A concept of civil liberty which equates the two has fallen victim to the fiction of formal equality which ends by conceding every race to the swift and every battle to the strong. Of course there is no single arbiter in what I have argued is the alternative contest for protection and priority in the exercise of civil liberties. That role is necessarily denied to the state. I have sought to show that it is performed, often imperceptibly, by all the processes that go to form opinion and guide action in society and which add up to our history. It does not follow that those of us who try to do something in aid of civil liberties are corks on the waves, carried about by a shifting and sometimes undetectable consensus. It does mean that we have to understand and agree on the concept of civil liberties as an antidote to the maldistribution of social power.

Until we do so, the spider will continue to preach the indivisibility of all freedoms, the fly's as much as her own. To the fly it will continue to be evident that the spider's freedom spells the fly's unfreedom. What concerns me, and should concern everyone who cares about civil liberties, is that the fly's point of view is a lot more objective than the spider's. The division of freedom according to the division of power is the constant reality which the unprivileged face daily and which any formulation of principle must address if it is to avoid mere piety. The first right in NCCL's Charter is to live in freedom and safe from personal harm. It will be the first casualty for the black and ethnic-minority communities of Britain unless the defence of it is recognized as a matter of principle in a society where racism still calls a lot of the shots.

Editor's notes
Unravelling the conflict

SHOULD FREE EXPRESSION YIELD TO A COMPELLING STATE OR PRIVATE INTEREST?

Freedom of expression is a central civil liberties tenet, but it is not absolute. There are several interests which, if sufficiently compelling, could override free expression: national security (Chapter 11), privacy, personal reputation, harm to individuals or groups such as racial groups (Chapters 7 and 8), or women (Chapters 9 and 10), and the maintenance of public order (Chapter 3). In cases where a court finds that free expression seriously undermines a compelling interest, the freedom may have to yield. In such cases, free expression should not yield at the mere claim that it would affect an important countervailing interest. A speculative or tangential assertion of that interest is insufficient to subordinate free speech under a traditional civil liberties analysis. Clear evidence of a significant and unavoidable harm of some magnitude is necessary if free speech is to be given the weight it deserves in a vigorous democracy.

IS THE HARM TO MINORITIES OR WOMEN FROM OFFENSIVE SPEECH SUFFICIENT TO OVERRIDE FREE EXPRESSION?

At the heart of this traditional civil liberties analysis is the belief that racially or sexually offensive speech, while thoroughly repugnant, does not produce a real and serious harm sufficient to override free expression. Pornography and other degrading images of women offend our sensibilities, and some have argued that pornography is causally related to sexual violence (Chapter 9); permitting offenders to write about their heinous crimes and to reap financial rewards for so doing is repugnant to most of us; warmongering and calls for hatred against other people equally so – yet, despite the unpopularity of such speech, it has generally been defended in liberal democracies.

Racially offensive speech may generate hatred, discrimination, and even violence against minorities. The law rightly proscribes actual discrimination or harm. But the association between offensive speech and these unlawful acts is difficult to demonstrate. If free expression is an important value to be protected against government interference, it should not be swept aside where the evil it causes is speculative.

At the heart of the conflict between free expression and the rights of women and minorities is a factual dispute as to whether speech itself causes discrimination and injury. That factual issue cannot be resolved here. Could it be argued, however, that the societal value favouring racial and sexual equality is, in itself, sufficiently compelling to override free expression? NCCL's balancing of interests places great weight on the right not to be devalued and dehumanized on such morally irrelevant grounds as race or gender. It is argued that a fascist march in a black area is an assault on the right of the people in the community to human respect and dignity; and it makes them the object of hostility and the subjects of fear. Pornography which treats women as an object of sexual violence also is inhuman and degrading. Is an inherent respect for the essential humanity and dignity of all human beings now so powerful a social value that it should prevail over free expression? To many the answer is yes, but there are three problems with the argument.

First, censoring all expression, including speech, marches, and demonstrations, which carries the message of racial hatred or sexual exploitation, will not begin to achieve the objective of respect for all races and genders. The abhorrent racial or sexual beliefs that many people in the United States and Great Britain hold cannot be changed by preventing their expression or by banning associations among and expressions by people who hold those beliefs. Isn't it better for offensive beliefs to be exposed as evil in open communication, rather than repressed by government?

Second, if racially or sexually offensive speech is to be curtailed because it demeans blacks or women, how much other offensive speech among antagonistic individuals and groups would be suppressed under the same test? Professor Dorsen critically examines the utter lack of consistency in applying the criterion of racially offensive speech (Chapter 7).

Third, if government were given the power to suppress speech which it considered morally offensive, the liberty of many political and religious groups would be dangerously at risk. In the current political climate, arguments by the Left for a curtailment of speech to be imposed on the far Right will certainly rebound to its disadvantage.

HECKLER'S VETO

Demonstrations which attack the very humanity of people in a local community may spark a violent reaction. Counter-demonstrations could form with the potential for heated conflict, or individuals or groups of residents may spontaneously retaliate. Is it so speculative to suggest that intentionally choosing to preach racial bigotry in a black area will result in violence? Norman Dorsen suggests that if the freedom of expression of the demonstration depended upon the behaviour of the listener, it would 'fatally wound' free speech; the heckler who disapproved of certain speech could, by threatening violence against them silence the speakers. Does this attribute an intentionality to the behaviour of a crowd which isn't there? Could free expression which did not encourage violence be legitimately curbed if it caused genuine and overwhelming feelings of spontaneous anger which could spill over into violence within the crowd? Is there justification for infringement of speech if the words and behaviour of the demonstrators cause alarm and fear in the community through the sheer venom of the message?

DRAWING A LINE: IS CONSISTENCY A VIRTUE OR A WEAKNESS?

Stephen Sedley (Chapter 8) believes that ACLU takes the easy course when it regards the right to free expression as virtually inviolable. ACLU's position shows immaculate consistency but in actuality is unprincipled. ACLU regards this consistency as a virtue; NCCL regards it as a weakness. There is a voluminous historical and contemporary literature, as Norman Dorsen points out, which expresses hatred and contempt for certain racial, ethnic, or religious groups – Christians against Jews, Jews against Arabs, Irish Catholic against Protestant, Turks against Greeks. Should all such expressions, and much more, be curtailed because of their prejudicial and offensive content? If not, how are contemporary white fascist demonstrations against blacks, or the pornographer's pictorial assault of women, to be distinguished from the offensive messages of other groups?

For Stephen Sedley, civil liberties principles are not fixed and timeless but are born of struggle. When rights to free expression and anti-racism clash, it *is* necessary to seek a principled resolution. He maintains that it is a lack of principle to translate the eventual success of those who resisted tyranny into an instrument of those who are promoting new tyrannies. Civil liberties principles, under this argument, would not guard against tyrannical speech. But no group perceives its own message as tyrannical. Is it not entirely possible that conservative governments would view, say, speech by Trotskyites, or even Marxists, as promoting tyranny? Once speech is to be judged by its content, it is well to remember that those who stand in judgment may take very different views of its merit.

THE 'INCITEMENT' PRINCIPLE

Traditional civil libertarians would allow restrictions where speech incites an unlawful act. If the future harm caused by free expression is not speculative, but imminent and real, the incitement principle may justify restrictions. The incitement principle is most often used to prevent an imminent violent act or other unlawful behaviour.

Race relations legislation in England and Wales proscribes incitement to racial hatred. Racial hatred itself is not unlawful. Further, it is not reasonably likely that an utterance which stirs up racial hatred will, in turn, lead to actual harm. Is incitement to racial hatred an overly broad application of the incitement principle? The answer is no if one accepts that racial hatred *per se* is the harm to be avoided. But it must be exceedingly difficult to demonstrate that any speech is so persuasive that it would incite the listener to a belief which he or she previously did not have.

DO GROUPS OPPOSED TO CIVIL LIBERTIES HAVE ENFORCEABLE LIBERTIES THEMSELVES?

NCCL's policy withholds advice from groups 'whose publicly stated objectives include the removal of civil liberties from a large section of society'. Should political organizations enjoy the benefit of civil liberties principles to which they do not themselves subscribe? And are such organizations entitled to complain when those principles are violated? John Rawls would not tolerate the intolerant: 'A person's right to complain is limited to violations of principles he acknowledges himself. A complaint is a protest addressed to another in good faith. It claims a violation of a principle which both parties accept.'

The platform of the National Front and other extremist political groups – both Right and Left – often do not admit to a belief in censorship. As indicated earlier, it would create a dangerous precedent to give any government, or any other entity, the power to decide whether the major objectives of a political organization were opposed to liberty, thus justifying the infringement of its liberty.

Norman Dorsen expresses the fear that the government may confuse the enemy of its policies with the enemies of freedom.

Clearly, NCCL's understandable concern is with the racism engendered by neo-fascist groups and not with judging the political platforms of various groups. But under its advice policy, how can it single out fascist groups from the many others who believe in violent revolution or authoritarian rule? NCCL's dilemma is that its own policy invites the organization to judge the content of a group's core set of beliefs to determine whether they respect civil liberties. This is neither something which a civil liberties organization should want, nor something which it can afford to be perceived as wanting.

DO CIVIL LIBERTIES PRINCIPLES FAVOUR THE POWERLESS?

Cass Sunstein (Chapter 9) argues that censorship of 'low-value' speech is justified by the position of strength of whites and the pornography industry, and the powerlessness of blacks and women. Civil liberties, according to Stephen Sedley, ought above all to be concerned with redressing a maldistribution of power.

This is a conflict resolution which favours the party which is less strong. The argument runs as follows. To be treated as a person of lesser worth because of the colour of one's skin or one's gender is a negation of civil rights. When a conflict arises between this civil right and the free speech of a relatively advantaged group, the balance should be weighted in favour of blacks and women because they already enjoy less than equal power.

This argument has a respectable pedigree. But it should be based upon a socio-political, not a civil liberties, framework. Norman Dorsen asks, who is to determine whether a group lacks power? He suggests that those in power will decide, and they will not provide additional advantage to those who seek to replace them. It is not clear in any case that extreme right-wing groups or publishers of hard pornography do have more significant political power and support than the blacks and the women's movement in the United States and Great Britain.

Increasingly, civil liberties organizations are adopting arguments relating to inequality in wealth and power as part of their civil liberties analysis. ACLU's national biennial conference and its affiliates have passed resolutions claiming that there is a civil liberty to certain economic entitlements such as housing or employment. (ACLU's national board of directors has thus far rejected the view that poverty *per se* is a civil liberties issue.) It is argued that powerless individuals cannot effectively exercise their liberties until they have a fair share of political, social, and economic power.

It is generally true that the more economic and social power one has, the greater the ability to influence others through the exercise of civil liberties. If a person has an overriding concern with poverty and obtaining basic life necessities, he or she will not have the same time, will, or resources to communicate and engage effectively in the political process. The disparity in the power to use communication media can be seen at almost all economic levels. A middle-income person, for example, will not be able to support political candidates financially, run for election, or control the mass media as effectively as a rich individual. Cass Sunstein uses a variation of this argument in his essay: 'it is fanciful to suggest that disparities in private power do not undermine the operation of a system of free expression' (p. 165).

While relative powerlessness or poverty may lessen a person's influence in the exercise of civil liberties, it does not prevent or restrict their exercise.

COMMANDING THE RESOURCES OF A CIVIL LIBERTIES ORGANIZATION

NCCL does not explicitly contest the right of fascist groups to march, but it does not think they are entitled to the organization's advice or representation. Implicit in this argument is that NCCL and ACLU are voluntary organizations with limited resources; they are entitled to choose the groups and issues to which they provide assistance. There are many competing individuals and groups seeking the support of national civil liberties groups. Is it unreasonable to deny aid and comfort to fascists? NCCL's initial decision to provide advice to fascists alienated many black groups, which wrote widely of the betrayal they felt. It was unthinkable to these groups that NCCL would devote its energies to assisting fascists, particularly since Jews, blacks, women and other discriminated-against groups have remained loyal supporters of NCCL. The damage that advising the National Front had done to NCCL's anti-discrimination work was for many at the heart of the issue. NCCL was seen as paying more attention to the abstract principle of free expression than to the realities of contemporary racism.

NCCL sought a principled position in alliance with minorities – the core of a civil liberties coalition. But in the long term this served neither the interests of the organization nor those of minorities. Once it is acknowledged that all individuals and groups have rights to free expression, then there should be a commitment to defend those rights. That is the *raison d'être* of a civil liberties organization; namely, its advice policy will be based solely upon an objective assessment of the threat to liberty posed by the case in question. This is not, as Stephen Sedley insists a betrayal of the powerless, but a principled fulfilment of the purpose of the organization.

Ironically, insistence that NCCL should not support the enemies of the political Left makes it a weaker organization to defend the increasing attacks on the Left. It should be the task of civil liberties organizations to make the case for a balanced, non-ideological framework for civil liberties. Even if those in the organization have a wider political sympathy for the Left, they must stand firm when their friends are occasionally intolerant. This is necessary not only for credibility and public respect for the organization, but also because it is in defence of the long-term interests of a free society.

9

Pornography, sex discrimination, and free speech*
Cass R. Sunstein

Until quite recently, it would have seemed quite peculiar to suggest that efforts to regulate pornography create a conflict between civil rights. The argument for censorship of sexually explicit materials appeared to depend on a kind of prudishness or moralism. The conflict was thus between freedom of speech on the one hand and attempts to prevent offensiveness to the community on the other. In these circumstances it should not be surprising that most of those concerned with civil rights and civil liberties argued in favor of the elimination of restrictions on the dissemination of sexually explicit materials.

In a short time all this has changed. The argument for the regulation of sexually explicit materials is made not in terms of offensiveness, but in terms of gender-related harms.[1] Thus pornography is said both to reflect and to perpetuate inequality on the basis of gender, inequality that is manifested in discrimination of various sorts and in sexual violence. Cast in these terms, the dispute over pornography regulation turns out to pose a conflict between freedom of speech and basic antidiscrimination principles.

The purpose of this essay is to discuss this conflict. In the process, it will be necessary to touch on general themes connected with freedom of speech and equality. Although these themes will be explored largely through the lens of American constitutional law, the conclusions should hold for any system generally dedicated to freedom of expression. In the first part of the essay I argue that pornography is a serious social problem that justifies legal concern. In the second part I contend that pornography should be understood as "low-value" speech, entitled to less protection from government control than other kinds of speech. This analysis, combined with that in the first part of the essay, supports the general conclusion that regulation of pornography, narrowly defined, would not seriously threaten a well-functioning

* Parts of this essay were previously published in *Duke Law Journal* 1986 and are reprinted by permission of the Journal.

system of free expression. I go on to examine and reject the view that antipornography regulation is especially dangerous because it regulates on the basis of "content" or "viewpoint," supporting the view that regulation of pornography actually enhances free speech. Finally, I explore some possible limitations on the reach of antipornography legislation.

PORNOGRAPHY, OBSCENITY, AND HARMS

Defining pornography is notoriously difficult; indeed, the difficulty of definition is a familiar problem in any attempt to design acceptable regulation. I will argue, however, that a definition can be framed so as to include only properly regulable materials. In short, regulable pornography must at a minimum (a) be sexually explicit, (b) depict women as enjoying or deserving some form of physical abuse, and (c) have the purpose and effect of producing sexual arousal.

This definition draws on feminist approaches to the problem of pornography and represents a departure from current American law, which is directed at "obscenity." Though built-in ambiguities are inevitable in light of the limitations of language, the basic concept should not be obscure. The central concern is that pornography both sexualizes violence and defines women as sexually subordinate to men. Pornographic materials feature rape, explicitly or implicitly, as a fundamental theme. The approach proposed here excludes sexually explicit materials that do not sexualize violence against women, and it ties the definition closely to the principal harms caused by pornography. The definition also excludes the vast range of materials that are not sexually explicit but that do contain implicit rape themes. The requirement of sexual explicitness is thus a means of confining the definition. Part of the definition, moreover, requires that the appeal of the materials be noncognitive – hence the requirement that the purpose and effect be to produce sexual arousal.

Examples of pornography as defined here can be found in such magazines as *Hustler* and numerous "adult" movies. It is difficult to capture the nature of genuine pornography without presenting examples which easily fulfill the stated conditions. One such example is the "Beaver Hunters" advertisement in *Hustler*, which shows a nude woman strapped to the top of the car; the copy below the photograph states that the woman would be "stuffed and mounted" as soon as the "hunters" got her home. But pornographic materials cannot always be easily characterized as such. There is a continuum from the most violent forms of pornography to materials that to some degree sexualize violence but cause less harm and are not low-value speech. Many popular movies and novels that combine eroticism and domination should be protected. A common plot in both books and films involves a romantic encounter in which a woman initially resists a forcible sexual assault and then submits. Although harmful, many such materials do not fall within the definition of pornography used here. Of course, there will be difficult intermediate cases.

The initial question is whether pornography, as defined here, is a cause for social concern. Until recently it was common to dismiss the case against pornography as a product of prudishness or inhibition, a kind of aesthetic distaste not grounded in concrete showings of harm. Regulation of sexually explicit material has thus been based on its offensiveness. Under almost any view, regulation of speech merely because it is offensive is problematic.

Only recently has pornography come to be regarded as posing any problem at all in terms of concrete harm – and that approach remains controversial in some circles. Constitutional consideration of the pornography problem has almost always been obscured by the gender-neutral term "obscenity." Mirroring the aesthetic concerns referred to above, the American Supreme Court treats "obscenity" as unprotected because it has nothing to do with the underlying purposes of free speech and hence is not truly "speech." Under the approach set forth in *Miller* v. *California*,[2] materials can be regulated as "obscene" when: (1) taken as a whole, they appeal to the prurient interest; (2) they portray sexual conduct in a patently offensive way, measured by "contemporary community standards"; and (3) taken as a whole, they lack serious social value, whether literary, artistic, political, or scientific. Under the court's approach to obscenity, sexually explicit materials can be regulated merely because of environmental or aesthetic objections, and considerations of gender are irrelevant.

An approach directed at pornography differs in important respects from one directed at obscenity. The term "obscenity" refers to indecency and filth; the term "pornography" – derived from the Greek word for "writing about whores" – refers to materials that focus on the role of women in providing sexual pleasure to men. The underlying rationale for regulation therefore differs depending on the definition involved, and the coverage of regulation will differ somewhat as well. In contrast to the vague basis of the obscenity doctrine, the reasoning behind antipornography legislation is found in three categories of concrete, gender-related harms: harms to those who participate in the production of pornography; harms to the victims of sex crimes that would not have been committed in the absence of pornography; and harms to society through social conditioning that fosters discrimination and other unlawful activities.[3] Although it is not possible to describe all the available data here, some of the relevant evidence can be outlined.

First, pornography harms those women who are coerced into and brutalized in the process of producing pornography. Evidence of these harms is only beginning to come to light. But in many cases, women, mostly very young and often the victims of sexual abuse as children, are forced into pornography and brutally mistreated thereafter. The participants have been beaten, forced to commit sex acts, imprisoned, bound and gagged, and tortured. Abuses appear widespread.[4]

Under a system dedicated to free speech, the usual remedy in such situations is to regulate the conduct directly – as current law in fact does – rather than to regulate the expression. Thus, for example, the state might enforce civil and criminal remedies against assault, kidnapping, and sexual abuse rather than direct the force of law against the pornographic materials themselves. Banning the unlawful conduct, however, is unlikely to eliminate it in light of the enormous profits to be made from pornography and the difficulty and cost of ferreting out and punishing particular abuses. The case for a ban on these materials depends on a conclusion that abusive practices are widespread and that the elimination of financial incentives is the only way to control those practices. The American Supreme Court endorsed this view in the context of child pornography in *New York* v. *Ferber*.[5]

Because the people to be protected are women rather than children, however, the claim of universal legal involuntariness is untenable. Many women participate in the production of pornography "voluntarily" as that term is ordinarily understood in the law. But some of them do not, and others are subject to grotesque abuse thereafter. These considerations support regulation of the materials themselves.

This justification for regulation may point to one of two conclusions. First, one might conclude that the government should be permitted to ban the distribution of those materials that have been produced through unlawful means. Thus, for example, scenes that involve actual rape, or that are the product of coercion, might be actionable. Alternatively, one might conclude that the distribution of pornography generally should be regulated through civil or criminal sanctions as a less expensive way of eliminating the problem of coercion and mistreatment.

The second harmful effect that pornography produces is a general increase in sexual violence against women, violence that would not have occurred but for the massive circulation of pornography. To say that there is such a connection is hardly to say that pornography lies at the root of most sexual violence. Nor is it to say that most or even a significant percentage of men will perpetrate acts of sexual violence as a result of exposure to pornography. But it is to say that the existence of pornography increases the aggregate level of sexual violence. Pornography is at least as much a symptom as a cause; but it is a cause as well.

The methodological problems in proving causation are considerable. Even if direct causation in fact existed, it would be difficult to demonstrate; undoubtedly there are multiple causes of sexual violence. In these circumstances the burden of proof becomes critical. If legislators may not regulate pornography in the absence of an unimpeachable showing of proof, they simply cannot regulate it; current data are insufficient to support such a showing. But if highly suggestive evidence of harm suffices – as it does in most areas of the law – the case for regulation is powerful. The evidence linking pornography and sexual violence falls in three categories: laboratory studies, victim accounts, and reports based on the experience of states and countries that have changed their practices with respect to pornography.

Some laboratory studies show a reduced sensitivity to sexual violence on the part of men who have been exposed to pornography.[6] Men questioned after such exposure seem more prepared to accept rape and other forms of violence against women, to believe that women derive pleasure from violence, and to associate sex with violence; they also report a greater likelihood of committing rape themselves. And after being exposed to violent pornography, some men report having aggressive sexual fantasies. For these reasons, some social psychologists have concluded that men exposed to pornography have a greater predisposition toward rape than men who have not been exposed.[7] In light of the relevant findings, it is highly plausible to believe that the general climate reinforced by pornography contributes to an increased level of sexual violence against women.

Laboratory results, however, do not reflect the real world with certainty. The decreased sensitivity of men may be only temporary; the subjects' reports of the effects of pornography could be inaccurate or overstated; and other causal factors may dwarf exposure to pornography in importance. Though informative, the laboratory evidence alone does not reveal the extent of the connection between pornography and sexual violence.[8]

But other evidence shows an association between the growth of pornography in particular areas with increases in rape and other forms of sexual violence. In the United States, for example, the incidence of reported rape within states is closely correlated with the mass circulation of pornography.[9] The liberalization of pornography laws in the United States, Britain, Australia, and the Scandinavian countries has been accompanied by a rise in reported rape rates. This finding becomes more striking when compared to the experience in other countries. In countries where pornography laws have not been liberalized, there has been a less steep rise in reported rapes. And in countries where restrictions have been adopted, reported rapes have decreased. The increase in reported rapes, where it has occurred, has not been matched by an increase in serious nonsexual offenses. Furthermore, there appears to be a temporal relationship between changes in pornography regulation and changes in the level of reported rapes.[10] Finally, recent studies have found a correlation between pornography and sexual violence even when controls are instituted for possible confounding variables, such as police practices, propensity to report rape, and so forth.[11]

But again, these comparisons alone do not clearly establish the causal link. The simultaneous rise of pornography and sexual violence may stem from some external factor; it does not demonstrate beyond doubt the existence of a causal connection. Other social factors, including demographic and ethical trends, may account for the simultaneous increases in both pornography and violence – though some of the studies try to control for these possible distortions. Objections of these sorts of course do not disprove a connection; they do suggest, however, that the empirical data are imperfect.

A final source of evidence concerning the harm caused by pornography is victim testimony showing that many perpetrators of sexual violence use pornography. Police reports attest to the connection, and there is evidence showing the relationship between pornography and abuse of women.[12] One cannot fully appreciate the grotesque nature of these harms without hearing or reading the testimony itself. Frequently the temporal and spatial connection is extremely close; pornography is sometimes used as a kind of "how-to" manual for sexual assault. Recent hearings on the subject before the US Attorney General's Commission on Pornography provided striking evidence to this effect.

There are, of course, dangers in relying on evidence of this sort. Reports from victims tell little about the extent of the problem and the precise nature of the causal links. Much of the reported violence may have occurred without pornography. Most consumers of pornography do not commit acts of sexual violence. In short, we do not know how widespread the phenomenon is.

We are therefore confronted with three kinds of evidence indicating a link between pornography and violence, all of them suggestive, but none of them alone dispositive. For critics of antipornography regulation, the problems of proof suffice to refute the existence of a causal connection between pornography and sexual violence. Uncertainty about the nature and extent of the link, however, hardly counsels inaction. In the context of carcinogens, for example, regulatory action is undertaken in cases in which one cannot be sure of the precise causal connection between a particular substance and cancer – even when the regulation is extraordinarily costly. Pornography may be at least as harmful as many carcinogens currently subject to regulation. If for the moment we put issues of free expression to one side, the analogy is close: the nature and extent of the link between act and harm are difficult to establish; but suggestive evidence might well, in the face of potentially severe harm, justify immediate governmental action. Inaction pending the accumulation of definitive proof has costs of its own. The question, a familiar one in the regulatory context, is: who should bear the burden of uncertainty – the pornography industry or the potential victims of sexual violence?

A third harmful effect of pornography stems from the role it plays as a conditioning factor in the lives of both men and women. Pornography acts as a filter through which men and women perceive gender roles and relationships between the sexes. Of course, pornography is only one of a number of conditioning factors, and others are of greater importance. If pornography were abolished, sexual inequality would hardly disappear. The connection between inequality, unlawful discrimination, and pornography cannot be firmly established. But pornography undeniably reflects inequality and, through its reinforcing power, helps to perpetuate it.

All of these factors support the conclusion that pornography is a significant social problem – producing serious harm, mostly to women – and that substantial benefits would result if the pornography industry were regulated. It is important to recognize that the various different harms point to different avenues for legal regulation. If the harm to women who participate in pornography is emphasized, regulation will depend on whether such harm has occurred. If the causal connection is emphasized, the question will be whether the material at issue is likely to cause sexual violence and subordination. I will return to these issues below.

LOW-VALUE AND HIGH-VALUE SPEECH

Although the harms generated by pornography are serious, they are insufficient, standing alone, to justify regulation under the usual standards applied to political speech in American law. Speech – not including obscenity – cannot be regulated because of the harm it produces unless it is shown that the speech is directed to produce harm that is both imminent and extremely likely to occur.[13] Moreover, the American Supreme Court has rejected the notion that this showing can be made by linking a class of harm with a class of speech; it is necessary to connect particular harms to particular speech. These conclusions are appropriate in any system dedicated to free expression, although they do have powerful adverse implications for antipornography legislation. If these standards are applied, a particular pornographic film or magazine might be beyond regulation unless the harms that result from the particular material are imminent, intended, and likely to occur. Demonstrating this, of course, will be hard to do.

But acceptance of these doctrinal conclusions does not resolve the question whether antipornography regulation should be permitted. The American Supreme Court has drawn a distinction between speech that may be banned only on the basis of an extremely powerful showing of government interest, and speech that may be regulated on the basis of a far less powerful demonstration of harm. Commercial speech, labor speech, and possibly group libel, for example, fall within the category of "low-value" speech. Whether particular speech falls within the low-value category cannot be determined by a precise test, and under any standards there will be difficult intermediate cases. Indeed the theory of free expression appears to lack a carefully developed approach for distinguishing between categories of speech. In the absence of such an approach, we might begin with four factors.

First, the speech must be far afield from the central concern of the basic commitment to freedom of expression, which, broadly speaking, is effective popular control of public affairs. Speech that concerns governmental process is entitled to the highest level of protection;[14] speech that has little or nothing to do with public affairs may be accorded less protection. Second, a distinction is drawn between cognitive and noncognitive aspects of speech. Speech that has purely noncognitive appeal will be entitled to less constitutional protection. Third, the purpose of the speaker is relevant: if the speaker is seeking to communicate a message, he or she will be treated more favorably than if he or she is not. Fourth, the various classes of low-value speech reflect judgments that in certain areas government is unlikely to be acting for constitutionally impermissible reasons or to be producing constitutionally troublesome harms. In the cases of commercial speech, private libel, and fighting words, for example, government regulation is particularly likely to be based on legitimate reasons. Judicial scrutiny is therefore more deferential in these areas.

In American law, the exclusion of obscene materials from protection stems largely from an act of definition. Obscene materials, to the court, do not count as "speech" within the meaning of the First Amendment.[15] But this definitional distinction can be viewed as reflecting the same considerations that define the low-value speech category. If the materials are defined narrowly, only nonpolitical and noncognitive material will be prohibited. The limitation of obscenity law to speech not having "serious literary, artistic, political, or scientific value" fits comfortably with our understanding.

This four-factor analysis is, of course, controversial. The distinction between political and nonpolitical speech, for example, is often unclear and may ultimately depend on the political view of the decision-maker. The difficulty inherent in such line drawing, moreover, may support abandoning any attempt to do so. Perhaps more importantly, distinctions between cognitive and emotive aspects of speech are thin and in some respects pernicious. Furthermore, approaches based on the purpose of the speaker are troublesome for familiar reasons. Finally, freedom of speech might be thought to promote self-realization; and, on that ground, attempts to make distinctions among categories of speech might be questioned.

But it would be difficult to imagine a sensible system of free expression that did not distinguish among categories of speech in accordance with their importance to the underlying purposes of the free speech guarantee. A system that granted absolute protection to speech would be unduly mechanical, treading unjustifiably on important values and goals. Consider laws forbidding threats, bribes, misleading commercial speech, and conspiracies. Any system that recognizes the need for some regulation but does not draw lines could be driven to deny full protection to speech that merits it – because the burden of justification imposed on the government would have to be lightened in order to allow the regulation of, for example, commercial speech, conspiracies, and private libel. By hypothesis, that lighter burden would have to be extended across the board. The alternative would be to apply the standards for political speech to all speech, and thus to require the government to meet a test so stringent as to preclude most forms of regulation that are currently accepted. In these circumstances the most likely outcome would be that judgments about low value would be made tacitly, and the articulated rationales for decisions would fail to reflect all the factors actually considered relevant by the court.

There is thus a two-stage argument for the regulation of pornography. First, pornography is entitled to only a lower level of solicitude. Under any standard, pornography is far afield from the kind of speech conventionally protected by freedom of expression. The effect and intent of pornography are to produce sexual arousal, not to affect self-government. Though comprised of words and pictures, pornography has few of the qualities that single out speech for special protection; it is more akin to a sexual aid than a communicative expression. The fact that pornography has an implicit "ideology" does not qualify it as high-value speech; such a conclusion would immunize all speech; the purposes and means of communication make pornography distinctively regulable. Second, the harms produced by pornographic materials are sufficient to justify regulation. Admittedly, there will be difficult intermediate cases and analogies that test the persuasiveness and reach of the argument. The crucial point, however, is that traditional principles furnish the basis for an argument in favor of restricting pornography.

THE PROBLEM OF VIEWPOINT DISCRIMINATION

The only American court that has faced a challenge to antipornography legislation found it unnecessary to examine either the issue of low-value categorization or the issue of harm. In *American Booksellers Association* v. *Hudnut*,[16] the United States Court of Appeals for the Seventh Circuit invalidated antipornography legislation on the ground that it discriminated on the basis of viewpoint. In the court's view, the Indianapolis ordinance amounted to "thought control," since it "establish[es] an approved view of women, of how they may react to sexual encounters, [and] . . . of how the sexes may relate to each other."

This basic approach is familiar in American law. Modern doctrine distinguishes among three categories of restriction: those that are based on viewpoint, or that single out and suppress particular opinions concerning a particular subject; those that are based on content, or that regulate any speech concerning a subject, regardless of viewpoint; and those that are both content- and viewpoint-neutral. The most intense constitutional hostility is reserved for measures that discriminate on the basis of viewpoint, even though such measures may suppress less speech than do other sorts of restriction. Thus, for example, a statute that prohibits all speech on billboards stands a far greater chance of constitutional success than a statute that prohibits speech on billboards that is critical of Republicans.

Under a standard view, restrictions based on viewpoint are necessarily content-based, but the converse need not always be true. A statute that prohibits speech critical of the President is directed at both viewpoint and content; the speaker's point of view is critical to the sanction, for speech supportive of the President is lawful. A statute that forbids false commercial advertising is said to be directed at content but not at viewpoint; although the meaning of the words decides the legal question, the statute does not appear to exclude a particular point of view. Finally, a statute that forbids all speech is directed at neither content nor viewpoint. Under current law, viewpoint-based restrictions are the most difficult to justify; indeed, they sometimes encounter a *per se* rule of unconstitutionality. Content-neutral rules, in contrast, receive the most lenient review. Content-based regulations that are neutral with respect to viewpoint occupy an intermediate category.

The special constitutional hostility toward viewpoint restrictions is not easy to explain, but it is generally sound. One reason for the hostility toward viewpoint discrimination is that the government may have a motive for excising a particular point of view that is unrelated to the public welfare; the government may excise a point of view simply because it disagrees with it, and that is illegitimate.

Viewpoint restrictions are also inconsistent with a central premise of any system of free expression – that the usual remedy for harmful speech is more speech rather than enforced silence. Thus, for example, when government prohibits people from criticizing a war effort in the presence of soldiers, the concern is that the government has bypassed the ordinary processes for decision, which include persuasion by other citizens, and has attempted to impose a solution of its own. The proper solution in such a case is to allow response through "counterspeech" rather than through regulation.

The initial response to a claim that antipornography legislation is viewpoint-based should be straightforward. The legislation aimed at pornography as defined here would be directed at harm rather than at viewpoint. Its purpose would be to prevent sexual violence and discrimination, not to suppress expression of a point of view. Only pornography – not sexist material in general or material that reinforces notions of female subordination – is regulated. Because of its focus on harm, antipornography legislation would not pose the dangers associated with viewpoint-based restrictions. The government, in effect, would have concrete data to back its legitimate purposes.[17]

Statutes that might appear viewpoint based should be upheld when they respond, not to point of view, but to harms that the government has power to prevent. In upholding regulation of labor speech, for example, the court indicated that the government was aiming not at viewpoint but at coercion of employees. The existence of genuine and substantial harm allayed concern about impermissible motivation. In the areas of bribes, threats, and fighting words, the government is also attempting to combat obvious harms. Analysis of suppression of speech advocating the immediate and violent overthrow of the government would be similar: the government is attempting to eradicate a harm, not attempting to impose a particular point of view. Bans on false or misleading commercial speech, cigarette advertising, or casino gambling are analyzed in substantially the same way. In the obscenity context, the reasoning is more obscure, but the central point remains: in some contexts, statutes that appear to be viewpoint-based are justified and accepted because of the harms involved. The harms are so obvious and immediate that claims that the government is attempting to silence one position in a "debate" do not have time even to register.

One might go further and suggest that the distinction between content-based and viewpoint-based restrictions is at best elusive and more likely nonexistent – and that the distinction itself will depend on viewpoint. Obscenity, commercial speech, fighting words, and perhaps even labor speech are said to involve viewpoint-neutral restrictions because the "viewpoint" of the speaker is deemed irrelevant to regulation. But the line drawn by the regulation does, in all these contexts, depend on point of view. One does not "see" a viewpoint-based restriction when the harms invoked in defense of a regulation are obvious and so widely supported by social consensus that they allay any concern about impermissible government motivation. Whether a classification is viewpoint-based thus ultimately turns on the viewpoint of the decision-maker.

It is for this reason that obscenity law is regarded as viewpoint-neutral and antipornography law as viewpoint-based. Obscenity law, particularly in so far as it is tied to community standards, is deemed "objective" because the class of prohibited speech is defined by reference to an existing social consensus. Antipornography legislation is deemed "subjective" because the prohibited class of speech is defined by less widely accepted values favoring the protection of the relatively powerless. But this distinction between objectivity and subjectivity is hard to sustain. Indeed, one could imagine a world in which the harms produced by pornography were so widely acknowledged and so generally condemned that an antipornography ordinance would not be regarded as viewpoint-based at all.

All this suggests that the problem of identifying impermissible viewpoint regulation is far more complex than it at first appears. Regulation based on point of view is common in the law. The terms "viewpoint-based" and "viewpoint-neutral" often represent conclusions rather than analytical tools. In the hard cases, further analysis is needed. Specifically, three factors help identify impermissible viewpoint-based legislation.

The first factor is the connection between means and ends. If the harm invoked is minimal, or if it is implausible to think that the regulation will remedy the harm, it will be more likely that the regulation is in fact based on viewpoint. The second factor is the nature of the process by which the message is communicated. Regulation of harms that derive from types of persuasion appealing to cognitive faculties is presumptively disfavored; more speech is the preferred remedy here. Regulation of antiwar speeches in the presence of soldiers is impermissible because any harm that results is derived from persuasion. More speech should be the solution. Finally, whether the speech is low- or high-value is also relevant. The low-value issue, therefore, is not made irrelevant on the ground that antipornography legislation discriminates on the basis of viewpoint. The viewpoint issue depends, in part, on whether the speech is low-value. Viewpoint-based regulation of high-value speech raises especially intense concerns about governmental motivation.

Under these criteria, antipornography legislation is defensible. First, the means–ends connection is quite close. Such legislation could be tightly targeted to the cause of the harm: the production and dissemination of portrayals of sexual violence. Second, the "message" of pornography is communicated indirectly and not through rational persuasion. The harm it produces cannot easily be countered by more speech because it bypasses the process of public consideration and debate that underlies the concept of the marketplace of ideas. Finally, pornography falls in the general category of low-value speech. Under these circumstances, anti-pornography legislation should be regarded not as an effort to exclude a point of view, but instead as an effort to prevent harm. In this respect, the best analogy is to labor speech – with the important caveat that labor speech, which touches public affairs, is far closer to the heart of the First Amendment concern than is pornography.

SUBSTANTIVITY, FORMALITY, AND THE FREE SPEECH GUARANTEE

The argument thus far has been somewhat technical, and it operates within the framework of traditional principles. But proponents of antipornography legislation argue not only that such legislation will combat related harms, but also that restrictions on pornography will promote freedom of speech. At first glance, the argument is mysterious. Conventional doctrine is based on the assumption that restrictions on speech cannot promote freedom of expression. As we shall see, that assumption ultimately stems from a belief that serious threats to free expression come mostly or exclusively from the public sphere, and that one should always distinguish the public and private spheres for purposes of analyzing free speech.

The argument that antipornography legislation can promote free speech touches on more fundamental issues than have been discussed here thus far. Essentially, the claim is that an attack on antipornography legislation represents legal formalism. An abstract notion of equality is decisive, though a substantive examination of issues of power and powerlessness would lead to a conclusion that the abstract notion is untenable. Legal doctrine that refuses to examine issues of substantive power and substantive powerlessness might be thought to generate an indefensible system of expression.

More concretely, the argument goes, the pornography industry is so well financed, and has such power to condition men and women, that it has the effect of silencing the antipornography cause in particular and women in general. The silencing involved is not the kind of silencing associated with totalitarian regimes. Instead, women who would engage in "more speech" to counter pornography are denied credibility, trust, and the opportunity to be heard – the predicates of free expression. The notion that "when she says no, she means yes" – a common theme in pornography – thus affects the social reception of the feminist attack on pornography. Legal intervention is required because of a maldistribution of private power that interferes with a well-functioning political marketplace.

In one sense, this argument, carried to its logical extreme, might be thought to establish a precedent for regulation whenever it is necessary to protect the powerless against the operation of a free expression regime. Such a precedent would be difficult to defend. But a fundamental limitation is that antipornography legislation would apply only to low-value speech. One can accept arguments from substantive powerlessness in the antipornography context without accepting them generally.

The approach that underlies the American Supreme Court's rejection of attempts to promote free expression through the regulation of powerful private actors appears to stem from an amalgam of three factors: (1) the view that disparities in private power do not significantly interfere with a well-functioning system of free expression; (2) the perception that if government is permitted to intervene on behalf of groups deemed powerless, lines will be impossible to draw, and government will be licensed to act for impermissible reasons; and (3) the belief that if some people – even if they have disproportionate power – are not permitted to speak, a genuine impairment of freedom results, even if that impairment is made in the interest of equality.

These concerns raise large and difficult issues that can be addressed only briefly and tentatively here. First, it is fanciful to suggest that disparities in private power do not undermine the operation of a system of free expression. When those disparities are large, the principal goals of free speech will be subverted unless the government intervenes with corrective measures. The guarantee of free speech is designed largely to combat the evils of factional tyranny and self-interested representation, and to ensure that government outcomes are the product of some form of deliberation on the part of the citizenry. If portions of the citizenry are powerless and for that reason unable to participate in deliberative processes, free speech will not serve its goals.

There is, however, a legitimate fear that judicial or legislative decisions about the relative power possessed by various groups are likely to be contingent and unreliable. Especially when freedom of expression is at stake, such contingency may be unacceptable. The best guarantor of freedom, according to this view, is a general rule forbidding the consideration of substantive power – not because this factor does not matter, and not because the disparities are not real, but because the cost of allowing the inquiry might be intolerable. This general rule is based in part on the familiar fear of "slippery slopes." Judgments about who is powerful and who is not must refer to some baseline; they are highly manipulable – because of the lack of consensus or the absence of clearly defined standards on the issue – and they themselves can be affected by power. In light of these considerations, it may be best to avoid the inquiry altogether.

Finally, a decision to silence the views of the powerful may well be regarded as an infringement upon freedom that ought to be weighed in the constitutional balance, even if the goal of equality might be promoted by the infringement. To some degree this argument stems from concerns about the identity of the decision-maker. But it depends as well on the understandable belief that even comparatively well-off people have a right to complain if they are silenced.

These considerations suggest that, as a general rule, inquiries into substantive powerlessness should not be used to defend restrictions on the expression. But the issue is a difficult one, and the tentative character of the conclusion should be emphasized. Pornography, moreover, includes a limited and distinctive content. It operates at a subconscious level. Its influence is hard to match through "more speech." Ideological counterargument cannot easily compete with the process by which pornography communicates its message. Moreover, pornography is far afield from the core of the principle of free speech. I conclude that examining substantive differences in power as a basis for regulation of pornography is appropriate in this context, and helps the case for regulation, even if we ought to avoid such an examination as a general rule.

SLIPPERY SLOPES, VAGUENESS, AND OVERBREADTH

Some of the most powerful objections to antipornography legislation concern vagueness. Even if a definition of pornography identifies the specific class of materials with which one is most concerned, there remains the problem of overinclusion – regulating materials that have some social value and that are unlikely to produce the relevant harm. Three limiting strategies, therefore, might be helpful.

First, it might be desirable to limit antipornography legislation so that at the very least it protects "isolated passages" in longer works. Some materials that have pornographic components may on the whole generate little of the relevant harm. Second, as under current obscenity law, the regulation could be limited to material devoid of serious social value. Matters having serious social value are, by definition, excluded from the category of low-value speech; their regulation is thus to be tested by more stringent standards which, for reasons suggested above, generally preclude regulation.

Third, it may be desirable to limit regulation to motion pictures and photography, and to exclude purely written materials. The evidence suggests that motion pictures and photography do the most to generate sexual violence; the data are more obscure with respect to written material. Moreover, the harm to women participating in the production of pornography is, of course, limited to motion pictures and photography.

Strategies of this sort suggest that it should be possible to draft an antipornography ordinance that is sufficiently definite to withstand challenges of vagueness and overbreadth. But one final objection remains. That objection points to the familiar dangers posed by the "slippery slope" – dangers about which we are rightly concerned in the context of free speech. The lines to which I have referred thus far are not so crisp as to alleviate all fear of misapplication. In light of these considerations, it might be suggested that the disadvantages of suppression are simply too great to justify the acceptance of what has become a relatively elaborate and complex set of doctrinal distinctions.

Whether this argument, like others premised on slippery-slope concerns, is persuasive depends on two factors. The first is whether the problem at issue is a genuine one. If one believes that pornography is a legitimate source of concern, the possibility of misapplication will be relevant but not decisive. If one believes that pornography is not a serious social problem, or that the problem can be solved through "more speech," the dangers of misapplication support rejecting the argument entirely. The case for antipornography legislation thus depends on simultaneous beliefs that pornography produces significant harms and that those harms cannot be alleviated through public debate alone. I have offered arguments suggesting that both of these beliefs are true.

The second factor is the possibility of holding the line. If one believes that pornography is genuinely indistinguishable from forms of speech that merit protection – either because of their value or because of their failure to produce harm – the argument premised on slippery-slope concerns will be quite powerful. But the rationale suggested here is designed to diminish the likelihood of misapplication. Pornography has special characteristics with respect both to its effects and to the harm it produces. With art and literature generally, attempts to regulate would be unlikely to be justifiable by reference either to low-value analysis or to harms, and both justifications are necessary under the approach set out here. The traditional lawyers' facility in identifying the difficult intermediate case, or the seemingly contrary hypothetical, sometimes operates as an obstacle to legislation that is on balance highly desirable. In the free speech setting, fears about difficult intermediate cases and misapplication are generally salutary. But at least in the context of pornography, they have proved a barrier to legislation that would in all likelihood do more good than harm.

CONCLUSION

The conflicts raised by antipornography legislation suggest that there is a tension between freedom of expression and sexual equality. It is possible, however, to defend such legislation without significantly interfering with freedom of speech. Pornography falls within the general class of low-value expression; under any plausible view of what entitles speech to special protection, pornography, as defined here, is likely to rank low on the free speech hierarchy. In light of this conclusion, the harms produced by pornography justify the regulation of that expression. The most troubling issue is that the regulation of speech must be neutral with respect to point of view; but antipornography is based on harm rather than viewpoint. Furthermore, to the extent that antipornography legislation might be deemed to be based on viewpoint, its status as such is less troubling in light of the peculiar character of the method by which the pornographic "message" is communicated.

I conclude that the skepticism about antipornography legislation is based on a simultaneous undervaluation of the harm pornography produces, a misapplication of conventional principles calling for neutrality, and – perhaps most important – an overvaluation of the dangers produced by generating a somewhat different category of regulable speech bound to have some definitional vagueness. At least as the notion is used here, antipornography legislation should produce important social benefits without posing significant threats to a well-functioning system of free expression.

NOTES

1 See A. Dworkin, *Pornography: Men Possessing Women*, (1983) London: The Womens' Press; C. MacKinnon "Pornography, civil rights and free speech," *Harvard Civil Rights – Civil Liberties Law Review* 1 (1984): 20.

2 413 US 15 (1973).

3 See MacKinnon (*supra* note 1): 32–60 (similarly categorizing the harms caused by pornography).

4 Numerous examples of abuse were reported to the US Attorney General Commission on Pornography; see *Final Report of the Attorney General's Commission on Pornography* (1986): 856–69.

5 458 US 747, 761–2 (1982).

6 See D. Zillmand and J. Bryant, "Pornography, sexual callousness, and the trivialization of rape," *Journal of Communication* (autumn 1982): 10, 16–17.

7 See *Final Report* (*supra* note 4) at 979, 1005; E. Donnerstein, "Pornography: its effect on violence against women," in N. Malamuth and E. Donnerstein (eds.) *Pornography and Sexual Aggression* (London, 1984): 78 (test results show that massive exposure to pornography leads students to recommend significantly shorter prison terms for rapists).

8 See D. Copp, "Pornography and censorship: an introductory essay," in D. Copp and S. Wendell (eds), *Pornography and Censorship* (New York, 1983): 12; S.H. Gray, 'Exposure to pornography and aggression toward women: the case of the angry male," *Social Problems* 29 (1982): 387, 394.

9 See L. Baron and M.A. Straus, "Sexual stratification, pornography and rape in the United States," in N. Malamuth and E. Donnerstein (eds.) *Pornography and Sexual Aggression* (London, 1984): 206.

10 See J.H. Court, "Sex and violence: a ripple effect," in *Pornography and Sexual Aggression* (*supra* note 9): 157–67.

11 See *Final Report* (*supra* note 4): 944–6. The experience of Denmark – which legalized pornography in 1967 and 1969, and thereafter saw a decrease in some types of sexual violence – is sometimes cited as support for a "catharsis" theory; see B. Kutchinsky in *Pornography and Sexual Aggression* (*supra* note 9): 171. But the incidence of rape, as opposed to other sexual crimes, did not decrease in Denmark during the relevant period (ibid., at 166), suggesting that the data do not support the catharsis theory. See E.D. Giglio, "Pornography in Denmark: a public policy model for the United States?" *Comparative Social Research* 8 (1985): 281, 297.

12 See C. Champion, "Clinical perspectives on the relationship between pornography and sexual violence," *Law and Inequality* 4 (1986): 22, 25; see also M.H. Silbert and A.M. Pines, "Pornography and sexual abuse of women," *Sex Roles* 10 (1984): 857 (study of street prostitutes suggested relationship between sexual behavior depicted in pornography and sexual abuse of women).

13 *Brandenburg v. Ohio*, 395 US 444 (1969) (*per curiam*) (overturning conviction of Ku Klux Klan leader for advocating violence at Klan gathering).

14 See *New York Times* v. *Sullivan*, 376 US 254, 269 (1964).

15 See *Roth* v. *United States*, 354 US 476, 481 (1957).

16 771 F. 2d 323, 332 (7th Cir. 1985), *aff'd*, 106 S. Ct 1172 (1986).

17 See *City of Renton* v. *Playtime Theatres*, 106 S. Ct 925 (1986).

10

Pornography and free speech: the civil rights approach

Barry Lynn

Many practitioners of "wicca," a pre-Christian nature religion, have engaged in a lengthy public relations campaign against the filming of John Updike's *The Witches of Eastwick* because of the film's allegedly negative stereotyping of "witches" as Devil-worshipping fanatics. Some Arab-Americans and Asian-Americans have orchestrated well-publicized protests against *The Delta Force* and *Year of the Dragon*, respectively, because of those films' depictions of ethnic groups in an allegedly derogatory fashion. Black Americans in some communities continue to object to the use of Mark Twain's *The Adventures of Huckleberry Finn* in public school classrooms because, notwithstanding its author's apparent sympathy with abolitionism, the work contains characters using racial epithets considered demeaning and objectionable. Even Christian fundamentalists have launched objections against television networks in the United States for their supposed systematically unfavorable portrayal of members of the clergy.

In each of these cases, the often rightly indignant group has essentially argued that the imagery in the objectionable books or films would be interpreted by readers or viewers to reflect the general, or perhaps even total, experience of the class: that all "witches" are evil or all Arab nationals are terrorists. In essence, the protesters argue that the depictions "lie" by suggesting universality for the worst attributes of a few members of the group or, even worse, misrepresent the group by fabricating erroneous attributes. All this is of concern because of the belief that speech, written or visual, has the power to alter (or at least reinforce) perceptions and thus to shape attitudes and, in the long run, actions.

Supporters of a free speech principle, guaranteed in the United States Constitution in the First Amendment which warrants that "Congress shall make no law . . . abridging the freedom of speech, or of the press," would resist any effort by any of these groups to use the coercive power of government to prohibit or "correct" the imagery and ideas contained in the offending productions. Nevertheless, few would argue that the chain of reasoning employed was wholly irrelevant, since free speech advocates recognize that one major significance of the principle is that speech may indeed persuade persons to view some issue differently, and perhaps to act in accordance with that worldview. If speech had no impact, there would be little but academic interest in protecting it. The communicative possibility of words and pictures is precisely why they must be so vigorously protected.

In a fashion akin to that of the ethnic and religious groups cited above, some feminist groups have picketed screenings of explicit "pornographic" films which "displayed" women, as well as helped shutter more "mainstream" horror films which depicted grotesque brutality against women.

Some feminists have taken their effort one step further, however. Although claiming to eschew "censorship," they have been promoting so-called "civil rights" laws which could make publishers, film-makers, distributors, and even retail merchants extremely cautious about creating or disseminating certain sexually oriented images and ideas. These laws are to replace existing regulation of sexual material under "obscenity" laws.

Current US Supreme Court jurisprudence does reflect the view that a certain class of sexually explicit material, labeled "obscenity," is devoid of free speech protection, and therefore can be regulated. The court quite erroneously concluded that there were no "ideas" to protect in such material. According to the 1973 decision in *Miller* v. *California*, the essential elements of the legal definition of "obscenity" are:

(a) whether "the average person, applying contemporary community standards" would find that the work, taken as a whole, appeals to the prurient interest . . .; (b) whether the work depicts or describes, in a patently offensive way, sexual conduct specifically defined by the applicable state law; and (c) whether the work, taken as a whole, "lacks serious literary, artistic, political or scientific value."[1]

It is regrettable that the US Supreme Court has created a different standard regarding "speech" – words and pictures – about sex than it has established in regard to any other topic, from politics to automobile mechanics. In other arenas, the court has required a close and demonstrable causal relationship between speech and antisocial conduct before the speech may be penalized. In *Schenck* v. *United States*, the court held that an utterance was unprotected if the words were used "in such circumstances and were of such a nature as to create a clear and present danger that they would bring about the substantive evils that Congress has the right to prevent."[2] Subsequent decisions clarify that even the advocacy of revenge against unnamed public officials by armed Ku Klux Klan members or the threat of student revolutionaries to "take the fucking street" was insufficiently tied to imminent lawlessness to be penalized.[3] This is not the same high standard where "sexual speech" is the predicated.

"Obscenity" regulation, in fact, is a test of community offensiveness, not a test which requires any demonstration of harmful effects caused by the material. The new feminist anti-pornography theoreticians argue that it is precisely this lack of reference to harm which makes existing regulation ultimately useless, except as an acknowledgement that all sexually explicit material is not presumptively protected by the Constitution. They have cast their new "civil rights" laws as regulating certain materials as a form of "sex discrimination" under the theory that they eroticize, and thereby at least covertly legitimatize, male domination over women.

In essence, this approach would permit civil lawsuits against those who create (and in most cases those who distribute) "pornographic" material in which women are coerced to appear, where the material is used to harass women in the workplace, or which is implicated in some act of sexual assault. Most also create liability for "trafficking" in certain forbidden material. The definition of "pornography" in recent county ordinances in Indianapolis, Indiana, and elsewhere, drafted by law professor Catherine MacKinnon and author Andrea Dworkin, was the "graphic sexually-explicit subordination of women, whether in pictures or words" which also include scenarios ranging from those in which women are "presented as sexual objects who enjoy pain or humiliation" to those which depict women in "postures or positions of servility or submission or display."[4]

Whether the rubric for analysis is "obscenity" law or newer "anti-pornography" approaches, the universe of material to be controlled is largely co-extensive. The definition of "pornography" is no more "objective" than that in "obscenity" law, and is therefore no less susceptible to abuse. In fact, the new definition is as subjective and fluid as that created by the *Miller* test, taking within its ambit vast amounts of popular culture, from the writings of Erica Jong and Ernest Hemingway to feminist health-care and sex-education materials. It poses the problems related to any vague statute, including inducing citizens to "steer far wider of the unlawful zone" than if the boundaries of the forbidden areas were clearly marked.[5] This is the so-called "chilling effect" which occurs where the fear of future sanction has the practical effect of influencing whether a product is created or distributed. Moreover, these new statutes generally reflect the mistaken view that the product called pornography is itself what "harms," when in fact it is the action of some who produce or consume it which is what should be regulated.

There is actually nothing which ought to distinguish pornography itself from other constitutionally protected speech. Although *Das Kapital* is indeed different in form from a centerfold in *Hustler* magazine, rational discourse should not be treated as a matter of law as superior to even the rawest of emotional appeals. Producers of communicative material should have the opportunity to speak through whatever medium they choose. If someone wishes to argue the merits of oral sex, he or she should not be accorded lesser constitutional protection if the "argument" is made in a XXX-rated video than in the prose of an academic psychology journal.

It is important to re-emphasize that pornography is indeed "communicative." Religious opponents of the material quite correctly note that it often represents a dazzling assault on the concepts of traditional morality, urging a "pornotopic" vision filled with lack of commitment, abandon, non-procreational goals, and a search for pleasure for its own sake. Feminist opponents also recognize much of it as a powerful advocate for the view that women affirmatively desire domination in sexual relationships. If it were not successful in transmitting these views, no one would bother to find ways to suppress it.

This material is sometimes characterized as "low-value" speech (see Chapter 9), but no effort to separate it from other material is ultimately successful. It is not "false" as in misleading advertising. Certainly, there is clear rhetorical power in the assertion that it "lies about women," but *Penthouse* is no less entitled to constitutional protection even if that is true than *Moby Dick* is regulable because it inaccurately portrays the nature of whales.

That pornography achieves its communication through primarily non-cognitive means should not distinguish it constitutionally, either. Even the Supreme Court, in a famous case in which it upheld the right of a war protester to wear a jacket emblazoned with the words "Fuck the Draft," noted that

> We cannot sanction the view that the Constitution, while solicitous of the cognitive content of individual speech, has little or no regard for that emotive function which, practically speaking, may often be the more important element of the overall message sought to be communicated.[6]

The court also has upheld the claim that live nude dancing was "speech,"[7] and lower courts have accorded First Amendment protection to the "emotive" (and sometimes even "wordless") communication of rock and roll, jazz, bagpiping, and even mime.[8]

Ascribing to certain materials the label "low-value speech" is difficult to sustain historically, particularly since the framers of the Constitution did not think in twentieth-century categories which might make some distinction between, say, "political" and "erotic" speech intellectually viable. Moreover, to allow legislatures to make decisions about the relative "value" of essentially fictional accounts is to allow them to serve as arbiters of taste, a role which is utterly inconsistent with the free expression guarantees of the First Amendment. The US Seventh Circuit Court of Appeals, in holding the Indianapolis anti-pornography ordinance unconstitutional, rejected the claim that the material had "low-value" precisely because the city and its supporters believed "that this speech influences social relations and politics on a grand scale, that it controls attitudes at home and in the legislature."[9] Moreover, they correctly deemed the effort to attack pornography as unconstitutional viewpoint discrimination, since

> speech treating women in the approved way – in sexual encounters "premised on equality" – is lawful no matter how sexually explicit. Speech treating women in the disapproved way – as submissive in matters sexual or enjoying humiliation – is unlawful no matter how significant the literary, artistic, or political qualities of the work taken as a whole. The state may not ordain preferred viewpoints in this way.[10]

Of course, communication does not have value only if it has some role in a political debate. Pornography also has what may be characterized as a "self-actualization" function. Its "message" can be significant to the self-identity of some viewers, particularly to those in sexual minorities. Indeed, now that pornography has transcended its earlier nearly exclusive interest in the breasts of young women, there is a message that 50-year-old grandmothers, pregnant women, and other-abled persons may also be viewed as sexual beings. Perhaps the real tragedy is that it is only in sexually explicit materials that this message is likely to be found. Certainly, the acknowledgement of the sexual diversity of our society can be an important step in the direction of a healthier understanding of overall human sexuality.

Moreover, the material can simply legitimatize the exploration of fantasy, without any impact on conduct. The Feminist Anti-Censorship Taskforce has noted:

> Depictions of ways of living and acting that are radically different from our own can enlarge the range of human possibilities open to us and help us grasp the potentialities of human behavior, both

good and bad. Rich fantasy imagery allows us to experience in imagination ways of being that we may not wish to experience in real life. Such an enlarged vision of possible realities enhances our human potential, and is highly relevant to our decision-making as citizens on a wide range of social and ethical issues.[11]

This "positive" value to sexually explicit material is yet another basis for rejecting the characterization as "low-value" speech.

Clearly, there is no serious basis for treating sexual speech differently than other speech. Moreover, the specific elements of these "civil rights" ordinances illustrate the dangerous fallacies generally utilized to justify the suppression of sexually oriented material.

The first component of such measures is a cause of action for assault "caused" by pornography. There is no question that there are "copycat" actions where people replicate in real life the things they see in a variety of pornographic and non-pornographic material. Children see stunts on television and attempt them with tragic results; Japanese teenagers commit suicide after they learn on the national news of the suicide of a pop music idol; a man who views the television movie *The Burning Bed* burns his sleeping wife to death that night, mirroring the action of the abused wife against her abusive husband in the film; and a boy dies of strangulation with a men's magazine containing an article (albeit critical) about auto-erotic asphyxiation found open near his corpse. Certainly, though, no reasonably open society can permit the suppression of material because of its unintended effect on the most suggestible person who sees it. To do so would be to reduce the populace to sitting in darkened rooms, fearful that some errant image would cross the eye of someone who will react in an anti-social manner. To date, courts have properly rejected claims of publisher or broadcaster liability in such circumstances.[12] Ironically, the more pathological an individual is, the less likely it will be that anyone would be able to determine in advance what would trigger such violent conduct. An infamous British mass-murderer claimed to be "set off" by attending Anglican masses.[13] Collectors of child pornography are often discovered to have not only commercial material, but also hand-designed "creations" consisting of individually captioned children's underwear advertisements from Sunday newspaper supplements.

The argument of causation, of course, usually goes beyond the neat parallelism of anecdotal evidence. However, there is no general scientific evidence to support the view that pornography "causes" men to commit sexual assault. Even researchers whose work was cited in the recent Attorney General's Commission on Pornography *Final Report*, to buttress its conclusion that pornography was harmful, have now publicly repudiated any claim that their data demonstrate such causation.[14] Two commissioners, one a well-known sex offender therapist, writing in partial dissent, noted that "efforts to tease the current data into proof of a causal link between these acts simply cannot be accepted."[15] The most that scientific data can show is some short-term attitude change in some experimental subjects after significant exposure to certain kinds of pornography. That is, some viewers temporarily see women in a more "negative" light, or have a more "positive" attitude toward non-marital sexual activity, and indicate such opinions on attitudinal surveys.[16] This is hardly a surprising finding, since laboratory studies show short-term attitudinal alteration after exposing subjects to almost any "message," from those in anti-smoking films to those in movies portraying other-abled persons in a favorable light.[17] The longevity of these altered impressions is likely to be short, and even laboratory data on the effects of violent "anti-women" films demonstrate only brief alterations in opinions of subjects.[18]

The US Pornography Commission and other pornography critics allege that attitude changes obviously affect behavior. Although it is logically true that attitude change always precedes behavioral change, not every attitude shift results in behavior modification. There are literally thousands of passing thoughts which would get the average person in trouble, if not in jail, every day if governments were allowed to punish "bad thoughts." Luckily, however, this nation regulates acts, not thoughts. In fact, were a demonstration of attitude change itself sufficient to permit the regulation of speech, the First Amendment would lose all significance. Certainly the amendment at least means that persons shall have an unencumbered opportunity to alter the attitudes of others by presenting them with powerful ideas and images.

Measures of association between pornography circulation and rape incidents are also not viable as a justification for regulating this material. One widely publicized study, by Baron and Straus, has been interpreted as a demonstration that sexual assault rates correlate with circulation rates of adult magazines.[19] This study, however, has now been characterized by one of its authors as not indicating that pornography causes rape. Moreover, he has indicated that introducing new factors into the equation statistically invalidates the relationship between circulation and assault rates.[20] In other countries, there remain data supporting correlations between wide availability of "hardcore" material and low rape rates (Japan),[21] as well as decreased or stable rates of sexual assault and other "sex" crimes as material is decriminalized (West Germany and Denmark, respectively).[22]

In other words, there is nothing to demonstrate any measurable increase in the aggregate level of sexual violence in the nation due to the presence of pornography. One commentator argues that "it is highly plausible to believe that the general climate reinforced by pornography contributes to an increased level of sexual violence against women" (see Chapter 9). Such a standard of "plausibility" is not only insufficient to regulate speech; such speculative conclusions would properly preclude even regulation of commodities like food products and medicine. If there was a clear connection between pornography and sexual violence it would be apparent, not "plausible."

It has also become popular to label pornography as a "how-to" manual for sexual assault. In fact, it is at worst a recipe book for masturbatory fantasy. When the federal Pornography Commission examined "victims" of pornography, many were both courageous and articulate, but with the exception of the few who were literally coerced into the making of pornography, most of these individuals were women so mired in abusive relationships steeped in pathology, substance abuse, and family crisis that any central contribution ascribed to pornography for their problems seemed more likely a tangential afterthought. Describing this as "pornography victimization" actually diverts attention away from abusive acts and social pathologies toward the scapegoating of sexual material itself.

The civil rights approach also usually contains a remedy for the "forcing" of pornography on unwilling persons. Public display of this material is hardly a major problem for most Americans. Surveys show that a remarkably high percentage of persons have never seen it at all, as it remains invisible to most non-consumers.[23] Many who are bothered by the material actually see nothing more explicit than the covers of the monthly *Cosmopolitan* or the swimsuit issue of *Sports Illustrated* when they look at the cover of the pornographic item. They are really concerned about the internal contents, which they would view only were they to open the periodical or insert the video cassette into a player.

Unwanted presentation is not a trivial matter, but no tolerant society can impose legal sanctions on the basis of chance encounters with offensive images. The Supreme Court, in a decision regarding nudity occasionally spotted by drivers passing an outdoor movie theater, noted that, absent a showing that substantial privacy interests were being invaded in an "essentially intolerable manner, the burden normally falls upon the viewer to avoid further bombardment of [his] sensibilities by averting [his] eyes."[24] It is in fact possible to walk through the vast majority of streets in America without observing, even by happenstance, a single explicit sexual image.

Where there are truly occurrences of malicious harassment by forced exposure to pornography, tort laws in most states already provide an avenue for redress.[25] In addition, courts are increasingly allowing suits under Title VII of the 1964 Civil Rights Law where employers, for example, display graphic material in the workplace so that a specific woman worker is presented with an essentially intolerable work environment.[26] These legal remedies are often justified, but the mere presence of offensive material inside magazines or the black plastic cases of video cassettes must remain an uncompensated offense, a *damnum absque injuria*, that the law cannot be reasonably expected to redress.

Even the possible perusal by children is an insufficient basis for regulating this material. The protection of children cannot too readily become a catch-all justification for the curtailment of the rights of adults. As Justice Felix Frankfurter wrote in *Butler* v. *Michigan*, in striking down a statute which prohibited the sale of books "tending to the corruption of the morals of youth," the risk it posed was "to reduce the adult population to reading only what is fit for children."[27] The same issue arises today in regard to newer technologies: inappropriate movies may be seen on cable television, and erotic messages can be dialed on the telephone through so-called "dial-a-porn" services. There are ways to help parents control access from their homes to such media through "lock-boxes" and "scramblers," and these can be provided in ways which do not violate First Amendment guarantees. However, efforts to ban such services completely because of their possible accessibility for children clearly runs afoul of Frankfurter's warning.

The third element of most ordinances, "coercion" into pornographic production, should be dealt with primarily as a criminal matter. Even where children are the subjects of coerced sexual activity, focusing attention on the product, pornographic pictures, rather than on the persons who produced, financed, or "created" the pictures through the criminal sexual abuse of children, is a tragic example of law enforcement which is too little and too late. Any unwanted sexual activity (whether photographed or not, and between strangers or spouses) should be treated as sexual assault.

Very few adults testified even during the recent Pornography Commission hearings that they actually entered such productions against their will. William Margold, a "talent" manager in Hollywood who recruits models for adult productions, explained that, in an industry where only 100 to 125 models are needed at a time, there is such an abundance of willing participants that coercion, or even undue encouragement, is unnecessary.[28]

Few would assert however that participation is viewed as the most positive of all employment options. However, to subsume the absence of a full range of employment options and every economic disadvantage as "coercion" is to denigrate the significance of the latter category. Feminist professor Kate Ellis of Rutgers University has argued cogently that "Women may have fewer options than men, and older women fewer than younger women, and poor women fewer than rich women, but this does not mean that they have no control over their lives and their sexuality."[29]

It has also been argued that regulation of pornography is necessary because the significant profits from pornography will make manufacturers continue to take the risks of discovery if only the underlying acts of coercion are actionable. This position assumes the completely unsupportable view that there is widespread coercion in this industry, and implies that the coerced quality of the material is one of its "selling points." In fact, both of these views are wrong. Unlike in the area of child pornography where the creation of the material can be argued to be wholly non-consensual and where the age of the model is the rationale for the product, adult pornography is marketed on other bases.

A final cause of action is the most amorphous of all, creating a remedy against those who "traffic" in pornography. This is an apparent effort to permit any woman who believes that pornography has led to discrimination against her to sue the publisher, distributor, or retailer. This is possibly the baldest effort in such laws simply to frighten people out of the business of sexually explicit material from fear of lawsuits, even by those who have never been coerced into performing, forced to observe it, or assaulted by a viewer. It is predicated, however, on the assumption that pornography plays some major role in sex discrimination, but this, like previous arguments, is untenable. The status of women in places like Saudi Arabia, where there is virtually no pornography, cannot be considered superior to the position of women in the United States, where there is possibly an $8 billion industry in the material. Likewise, measures of the economic status of women in various states correlate positively with the circulation rates of major pornographic magazines. The fact that there is statistical correlation between higher women's status and a large number of sexual magazines is certainly not the result of any causative relationship, but it also tends to disprove the significance of the material in causing social disparity between the sexes.[30]

One other facile argument which has been advanced to justify new restriction is that the First Amendment rights of anti-pornography activists (and, by extension, the women they purport to "represent" in their efforts) have somehow been abridged by the pornographers, and that the government therefore owes some affirmative duty to try to equalize the power of those competing voices.[31] In fact, a vast amount of public attention has been given to the feminist anti-pornography effort in every conceivable popular medium. The underlying critique of the "pornotopic" vision is also present in a large array of scholarly and mass-market books which are readily available. Feminism as a vital social critique can hardly be said to have generated equality, but it has certainly changed both the consciousness and culture of American society. It has always done so by a critique of existing patriarchal doctrine, and not by an effort to silence the patriarchs. There is no constitutional basis for demanding that government scrutinize speech about any subject in order to determine the relative volume expressing particular viewpoints, much less then to effect a balance by curtailing some expressions of the "majoritarian" speakers.

Another variation which infuses the "new" debate over pornography is that there is no "corrective" to the way in which women's sexuality is depicted in the material. However, responsible researchers like Edward Donnerstein have been careful to "debrief" their experimental subjects, who have been "taught" rape myths with certain visual material, by providing them with factual information about the nature of sexual assault. They consistently find significant improvement in the understanding of rape following the debriefings, a demonstration that erroneous viewpoints about sexuality can indeed be successfully combated through the presentation of alternative ideas.[32] "More speech" supplants even "pornographic" speech. There is no magical or mystical ability of this material to alter behavior, notwithstanding its general ability to cause erections. It is no better a conditioner than any other form of expression, and when its viewpoint is offensive it may be effectively rebutted in the same way one can challenge the views of witches, Arabs, Asians, blacks, or Christians with which this chapter began.

Regardless of the name given to the efforts to regulate pornographic images, it is hard to construe them as anything but efforts at governmental censorship. All require enlisting the state, directly or indirectly, in removing certain sexual views from the culture. It is the political or moral ideas expressed therein which are offensive, and therefore deemed dangerous. Although Catherine MacKinnon, the author of the Indianapolis ordinance, repeatedly claims that hers is not a "moral" crusade,[33] she is in fact enlisting the government's courts to support her view of correct sexuality. By frightening "incorrect" expressions from the scene for fear of civil sanction, she is attempting to hurt financially those who promote such attitudes. Ultimately, there is little difference between the goal of her ordinances and the goal of traditional obscenity law.

The treatment by the US Supreme Court of sexual materials as a unique content-circumscribed class clearly has a ripple effect of ominous proportions. The very existence of "obscenity" laws, predicated on the constitutional difference between explicit speech about sex and other speech, has helped legitimatize the premise of these new ordinances that some sexual material is entitled to no First Amendment protection. "Sexual speech" fuels local efforts of others to ban Judy Blume novels from the high-school shelves or to eliminate the feminist works on women's health care from the local library, because these material too are "about" sex. Whether any individual effort succeeds or fails, censorship is no phantom danger. The goal of regulating or suppressing certain sexual viewpoints is, nearly, in turn, indistinguishable in purpose from that noted by Justice William Brennan in his dissent in *Paris Adult Theatres* v. *Slaton*:

> If a state may, in an effort to maintain or create a moral tone, prescribe what its citizens cannot read or cannot see, then it would seem to follow that in pursuit of that same objective a state could decree that its citizens must read certain books or must view certain films.[34]

If the courts may tell us what is wrong or incorrect, why not tell us precisely what is right and correct as well?

The ferocity of the debate among feminists is strong evidence of the complexity and danger of the effort to constrain a correct female sexuality. The Feminist Anti-Censorship Taskforce, in its *amicus* brief challenging the Indianapolis ordinance, notes with irony that the ordinance

> delegitimates and makes socially invisible women who find sexually explicit images of women "in positions of display" or "penetrated by objects" to be erotic, liberating, or educational. These women are told that their perceptions are a product of "false consciousness" and that such images are so inherently degrading that they may be suppressed by the state.[35]

The whole discussion of pornography and the law was substantially polluted in 1986 by the release of the *Final Report* of the Attorney General's Commission on Pornography, a curious mix of moralizing and pseudo-feminist musings which urged a nationwide crackdown on sexually oriented material. Since the commission's method of data-gathering was so intellectually irresponsible, it is regrettable that its data and conclusions have received any acceptance by responsible persons. Indeed, the conclusions of the commission were essentially embodied in the documents which created the body, most notably the serious problem posed by the material and the need for further regulation. When combined with a membership which had, for the most part, staked out an "anti-pornography" position before their appointment, the likelihood of serious inquiry was jeopardized.

Although the Pornography Commission's emphasis on enforcing existing (or slightly "improved") obscenity laws was rejected by feminist anti-pornography advocates, those groups generally endorsed the conclusions of the commission about the "harmfulness" of the material for women, including its implication in acts of sexual violence. Moreover, the commission's recurring conclusion that regulating much of this material had no serious free speech implications was also seen by some feminists as a boon to their analysis, particularly since the commission endorsed legislative examination of the new "civil rights" laws.

In a curiously revealing manner the US government through the Pornography Commission was living proof of the fallacious reasoning of Sunstein and others that if the state finds material to be harmful, the "harms" somehow remove the statute from skepticism about governmental motivation (see Chapter 9). The commission adopted a "harm" rubric, but the *Final Report* is none the less filled with personal statements of commissioners and general conclusions of the body that indicate that, collateral to any real harms, they had discovered "moral" harms to the sanctity of certain religious traditions which they felt duty-bound to protect.[36] Content-based restrictions will be the result of the passage of even "civil rights" laws allegedly premised on "harms."

The new approaches rest on unacceptable analytical principles and a legal philosophy that is antithetical to the civil liberties guarantee of free expression. It would hold speech about sexuality hostage to even the most unique and unintended response of the most susceptible viewer or reader.

NOTES

1 413 US 15, 24 (1973) (citations omitted).

2 249 US 47, 52 (1919).

3 *Brandenburg* v. *Ohio*, 395 US 444 (1969); *Hess* v. *Indiana*, 414 US 105 (1973).

4 Indianapolis, Ind., City–County General Ordinance 35 Sec. 16–3 (q) (6) (11 June 1984).

5 *Grayned* v. *City of Rockford*, 408 US 104, 108–9, quoting *Baggett* v. *Bullitt*, 377 US 360, 372 (1964), quoting *Speiser* v. *Randall*, 357 US 513, 526 (1958).

6 *Cohen* v. *California*, 403 US 15, 26 (1970).

7 *Schad* v. *Borough of Mount Ephraim*, 452 US 61, 65 (1981).

8 See *Cinevision Corp.* v. *City of Burbank*, 745 F. 2d 560, 569 (9th Cir. 1984) (music); *Fact Concerts, Inc.* v. *City of Newport*, 626 F. 2d 1060 (1st Cir. 1980) (jazz); *Davenport* v. *City of Alexandria*, 710 F. 2d 148 (4th Cir. 1983) (bagpiping); *Birkenshaw* v. *Haley*, 409 F. Supp. 13 (E. D. Mich. 1974) (mime).

9 *American Booksellers' Assn* v. *Hudnut*, 771 F. 2d 323, 331 (7th Cir. 1985).

10 771 F. 2d at 325 (citation omitted).

11 *Amicus* brief of the Feminist Anti-Censorship Taskforce at 29, *American Booksellers Assn* v. *Hudnut*, 771 F. 2d 323 (7th Cir. 1985).

12 See e.g. *Herceg* v. *Hustler*, 565 F. Supp. 802 (S. D. Tex. 1983); *DeFillippo* v. *NBC*, 446 A. 2d 1036 (RI 1982).

13 J. Murphey, "The value of pornography," *Wayne Law Review* 10 (1964): 655, 668.

14 *New York Times*, 17 May 1986, at A–1, col. 1.

15 *Attorney General's Commission on Pornography, US Department of Justice, Final Report* (1986) (statement of Ellen Levine and Judith Becker).

16 See e.g. N. Malamuth and J. V. P. Check, "The effects of mass media exposure on acceptance of violence against women: a field experiment," *Journal of Research in Personality* 15 (1981): 436 (acceptance of violence); *Transcript of Proceedings, US Dept of Justice, The Attorney General's Commission on Pornography*, public hearing, Houston, Texas (11 September 1985): 112 (statement of Dr Dolf Zillman, summarizing his research in acceptance of non-marital sexual activity).

17 See e.g. Timothy R. Elliott and E. Keith Byrd, "Attitude change toward disability through television portrayal," *Journal of Applied Rehabilitation Counseling* 14 (1983): 35; "Smoker's luck: can a shocking programme change attitudes to smoking?" *Addictive Behavior* 8 (1983): 43.

18 J. Ceniti and N. Malamuth, "Effects of repeated exposure to sexually violent or sexually non-violent stimuli on sexual arousal to rape and non-rape depictions," *Research and Therapy* (1985).

19 L. Baron and M. Straus, "Sexual stratification, pornography, and rape in the United States," in N. Malamuth and E. Donnerstein (eds.) *Pornography and Sexual Aggression* (London, 1984): 185.

20 *Final Report* (*supra* note 15): 950.

21 P. Abramson and H. Hayashi, 'Pornography in Japan: cross-cultural and theoretical considerations in pornography and sexual aggression," in Malamuth and Donnerstein (*supra* note 19): 173.

22 B. Kutchinsky, "Pornography and its effects in Denmark and the United States: a rejoinder and beyond," in R. F. Tomasson (ed.) *Comparative Social Research* (1985): 8.

23 See Pornography Commission, *Transcript*, Houston hearing (*supra* note 16): 310–E (author's calculations from testimony of Diana Russell indicate that 58 percent of women had never seen pornography, and 56 percent of those who did were not "upset" by it.)

24 *Erznoznik* v. *City of Jacksonville*, 422 US 205, 210 (1985), citing *Cohen* v. *California*, 403 US 15, 21 (1971).

25 See e.g. *Shaffer* v. *National Can Corp.*, 565 F. Supp. 909 (E. D. Pa. 1983) ("pornographic entertainment" offered to female employee by supervisor can be element of claim for intentional infliction of emotional distress).

26 See e.g. *Kyriazi* v. *Western Electric Co.*, 461 Supp. 894 (D. NJ 1978).

27 352 US 380 (1957).

28 Pornography Commission, *Transcript* (*supra* note 16), public hearing, Los Angeles, California (16 Oct. 1985): 397.

29 K. Ellis, "I'm black and blue from the Rolling Stones and I'm not sure how I feel about it: pornography and the feminist imagination," *Socialist Review* 116 (1984): 75–6.

30 Baron and Straus (*supra* note 19).

31 See e.g. A. Dworkin, "Against the male flood: censorship, pornography and equality," *Harvard Women's Law Journal* 8 (1985): 1, 13.

32 See e.g. E. Donnerstein and L. Berkowitz, "Victim reactions in aggressive erotic films as a factor in violence against women," *Journal of Personality and Social*

Psychology 41 (1981): 710.

33 See e.g. C. MacKinnon, "Not a moral issue," *Yale Law and Policy Review* 2 (1984): 321.

34 413 US 110.

35 *Amicus* (*supra* note 11): 42.

36 See e.g. *Final Report* (*supra* note 15): 89 (statement of Fr Bruce Ritter): 303 (statement of Dr James Dobson) (harm to moral environment).

11
National security and freedom of information
Sarah McCabe

The acquisition, analysis, and prudent disposition of knowledge sometimes is and always should be the prime objective of every individual and of every state. For the former, the pursuit of knowledge is an end in itself; it is the path to a selfhood which is independent of powerful institutions or engrossing states. For the latter, the notion of knowledge as an enhancement of living, an aid to rectitude, has less appeal. In its restricted sense of 'information', however, it is clearly seen as a powerful instrument of control over destructive forces within and without state boundaries. The conflict between the two purposes has, today, become a tug-of-war in which the citizen struggles to obtain from the state as much information as possible, not only for his* own personal enrichment but also so that he may understand and make a responsible contribution to the government's decisions. For these decisions, whatever claims they may have to be beneficial, may sometimes seem to numbers of citizens to be to their disadvantage. After all, there are discrepant views about benefit, in the preservation of the environment, for example, or in the priorities in government spending, for defence, for programmes of nuclear energy, for health care, for education, or for social provision for poverty and disablement. Governments, however, even democratic governments, today assert their right to deny to enquiring citizens such knowledge and information as would jeopardize the pursuit of their policies. This claim is made in the name of the state, with whose justifying mantle successive governments clothe themselves, for they know that citizens may more

---

* The author wishes to avail herself of the elegant justification of the Committee on Fraud Trials: 'Throughout our report we follow convention in using the masculine rather than the more cumbersome he/she, him or her, his or her, but it should not be inferred that we have chosen to ignore half the population' (Roskill Report, c. 1.10).

readily identify themselves with their state than with their government.

Another reason for the struggle between government and citizen over the management of information is the desire for privacy of most ordinary people. When they observe that the state, for its own legitimate purposes, collects information about their income,[1] their medical history, their education, and their occupation, they expect all these data to be protected from unauthorized use or disclosure.[2] They would also oppose such linkage of information that a full portfolio of facts about the life and activities of every individual could be ready for the use of governments or accessible to anyone with the wit and the will to reach the data store.[3] This latter aspect of the citizen's concern was, at one time, related chiefly to his protection from other citizens. It is now, however, commonly believed that the threat to individual privacy comes from the state itself, which, in addition to legitimate data, may acquire information about political affiliations or anti-social tendencies by tapping telephones, intercepting mail, and talking to the associates of the subjects of their enquiry. Most governments have become sensitive to the first of these concerns, the storage of data and its protection from pillage by unauthorized persons; they are less nice about their own use of information collected about their own citizens or those of other states.

Of these two issues – the privacy of the individual, on the one hand, and the concentration of vital knowledge in the hands of the state, on the other – there is now little doubt about which is the more important.

Highly centralized governments all over the world, even those which claim to be representative democracies, have become, like despotic monarchs, distant from their electorates. One reason for this is that the family of nations has become so close that, on important issues, government talks to government, assuming (sometimes honestly, sometimes with cynicism) a popular consent which they may not have. The dangerous reality of this aspect of modern politics is disguised by talk of 'summit' meetings arranged to solve the problems of peoples by private communication between heads of state. More important may be the fact that for any government decision a sea of information must be processed, diluted, and interpreted by technological, economic, and political experts whose advice is influential in the decisions of government about who should know what.

Future historians, observing the present conflicts of interest, may account for them thus or thus. We ourselves can catch glimpses of earlier attitudes to the control of information in the significant development of political ideas in Europe and America – particularly during the revolutionary period of the eighteenth century. And we may reasonably conclude that the dispositions made then are being worked out today in the politics and in the jurisprudence of state security and individual liberty.

THE HISTORICAL DEVELOPMENT OF SECURITY SERVICES

For centuries the search for information by legitimate monarchs or usurpers did not disturb the relationships between state and people. It was taken for granted that Queen Elizabeth I of England should send abroad not only her ambassadors but a whole procession of courtiers, poets, and soldiers to bring home news of what was happening in the courts of her continental rivals. Her enemies at home were contained by a different network of spies and informers whose existence was acknowledged and countered where possible. These enemies, however, were normally close to the throne, involved in intrigues with friends and sympathizers at home or with foreign powers. This system of espionage, which was understood, accepted, and countered by noblemen, did not usually touch the private lives of merchants, shopkeepers, journeymen, or labourers, for the distance between powerful rulers and these humbler segments of the population allowed little opportunity for significant dissidence at the base of the pyramid of power. There was, therefore, little point in surveillance on the one side or demands for privacy on the other; that rulers should share with the mass of their subjects the information upon which decisions of state were made was never contemplated.

The changes in political thinking that marked the Enlightenment in Europe sowed the seeds of the conflict between the citizen and the state in many things. After all, in declaring the self-evident truth that life, liberty, and the pursuit of happiness were the right of all free men, the American revolutionaries gave the most elegant expression to the felicific calculus of the Utilitarians; but they made no general statement about the relationship between the liberties of free men and the powers of the state. The French revolutionaries, with greater realism, introduced into their manifesto the restraining concept of fraternity, which must be taken to be the community power to set limits to individual freedom in the matter of information as well as anything else (Arendt 1963, Palmer 1964). English pragmatists, with no domestic revolution on their hands, acknowledged the conflict between self-interest and the state but accepted state supremacy, declaring that the happiness of the greatest number should be the determinant of state action. Arguably it is the whole-hearted adherence to this theory which has been effective in imposing stricter limits upon individual freedom in the United Kingdom than in most other western European states.

These new notions of the place of the individual in political arithmetic were slow to work out in every state practice even after two successful revolutions. George Washington, an honourable man with a firm belief in the power of knowledge, had an army of spies (some of whom he had to pay out of his own pocket) who gathered information not only about British troops but also about colonists who were alarmed at the enormity of the steps which were being taken to break away from England. French revolutionaries, too, spied upon their fellows and, by setting up the Committee of Public Safety, brought to the guillotine aristocrats and fallen revolutionaries alike. No one was safe, and citizens eyed each other with suspicion and dread. At a later date, when the American state was threatened with secession, the government used a private detective agency to infiltrate the encampments of the southern states and report upon their dispositions and their morale.[4] A member of this agency later (1873), in a spectacular piece of citizen surveillance, lived for two years among the Molly Maguires in Pennsylvania.[5] His evidence was used to secure the arrest, trial, and execution or imprisonment of a number of members of the society.

The general acceptance, or perhaps ignorance, of government methods of surveillance and information-gathering in Europe and the United States showed little sign of change throughout most of the nineteenth century. This long complaisance in the face of grave injustice to a minority of citizens or citizen-aspirants could be explained partly by the limited scale of the intrusion into the private lives of most men and women, and partly by the unwillingness of the majority of all classes to have any truck with ideas of anarchism which might threaten the stability of their lives (Roberts 1973: 185, Lydston 1904: 235 ff.). For anarchism, a direct ideological descendant of the theories of individual freedom, had found allies among revolutionary working-class movements which advocated the overthrow of the free enterprise system. It was, therefore, the principal target of state repression, a repression which was well supported by ordinary citizens. The disenfranchised Irish were a different case. Forcibly yoked to England, many considered themselves to be at war. The surveillance to which they were subject was understood as a defensive measure on the part of their enemy. That it might be questioned as an unjustifiable use of state power was to them of little relevance, for they rejected that state *in toto*.

By the beginning of the twentieth century the threat to governments of anarchist doctrines had been reduced, in Anglo-Saxon countries at least, not so much by the heavy penalties exacted from those who preached them[6] as by the growth of a different, revolutionary, working-class radicalism which annexed the territory of the anarchists and in so doing provided new targets for state surveillance. Although the campaigns for women's suffrage and the development of a strong labour movement in most countries of Western Europe and the United States effected some slight shift in the balance of interest between the individual and the state, this failed to bring about effective questioning of the state acquisition and use of information. The threat of a European war had changed the order of priorities, and in Britain measures for ensuring national safety were taken without dissent. Thus in 1909 the Committee of Imperial Defence agreed to the setting up of a new Secret Service Bureau which would have a home section and a foreign section.[7] The home section later became MI5, which from its inception formed strong links with the Special Branch,[8] sharing with it the protection of domestic security. A further security measure was the extension to all citizens of penalties originally directed at civil servants who disclosed or received official information and were unable to prove an innocent intent.[9]

The activities of suspect citizens, immigrants, and aliens were kept under constant watch by means of physical surveillance, the use of paid informers, and the interception of mail and telegraphic communication. This last means of information-gathering raised no constitutional eyebrows at the time, for, as the later Birkett Report (1957) pointed out, control of the mail was a matter of Crown privilege. It required no legislative sanction, and none had ever been sought. The administrative arrangements for authorizing interception, namely by warrant of the Secretary of State, seemed at that time satisfactory.

The United States, not yet under threat of war, had its own reasons for setting up, in 1908, a national Bureau of Investigation as the investigative arm of the Department of Justice for the enforcement of all federal criminal statutes. In its early years it had no specific security function; nor had its agents any power of arrest. But the drive and power of J. Edgar Hoover, its director from 1924, brought about an increase in the scope of its activities until it became responsible for all internal security; its officers acquired a licence to carry guns (from 1934) and were given the power of arrest. Thus, in the United States and in Britain, formal responsibility for internal security was, in the first instance, put in the hands of an organization whose primary duty was the enforcement of the criminal law. European states, particularly Germany and the Soviet Union, established between the wars large, specialist, civilian organizations for internal security which practically eliminated dissent. In doing so they contributed to the post-war disillusionment of many citizens with the undisputed control by the state of measures intended to safeguard national security.

In the immediate post-war period there were different kinds of pressure upon governments. The division of Europe and fear of Soviet power increased, for every European state and for the United States, the importance of internal and external security services. The Pearl Harbor débâcle had revealed to the American people the weaknesses of uncoordinated military and naval intelligence. Close co-operation with British intelligence during the Second World War was thought to show that a single security service of civilian character could provide the tight control and drive that was needed. President Truman had therefore no difficulty in persuading Congress to legislate for a permanent civilian intelligence agency for the acquisition and analysis of foreign intelligence and for the provision and training of agents who would operate abroad under the general protection of the foreign service (the National Security Act of 1947). The Federal Bureau of Investigation would, however, remain in control of internal security and, as before, of the enforcement of federal criminal statutes.

The line of demarcation between the work of the CIA and that of the FBI would seem to be clear, but there has been considerable intervention in the internal affairs of the United States by the CIA[10] and the resistance to control over its activities is legendary. In the United Kingdom also there was a tidying-up of the wartime arrangements for the protection of the realm. MI5 was hived off from the War Department and came under the control of the Home Office, while the division which deals with foreign intelligence became the responsibility of the Foreign Office. Like their counterparts in the United States and elsewhere, British secret service agents abroad may be located in embassies and consulates,[11] although their sources of information are frequently agents recruited from the local population or United Kingdom specialist business men or journalists who have access to particular areas of information. At home, the humdrum work of surveillance at ports and airports, the vetting of potential immigrants, and the acquisition of information about dissident groups in the country falls to the police Special Branch. Intelligence officers in MI5, who have no power of arrest, may initiate and carry out the investigation of sensitive cases, but the Special Branch must take over when arrest and prosecution are thought to be necessary. There is no legislative support for the British security services nor any obvious means of calling them to account.[12] Parliamentary committees inquire from time to time what is going on;[13] but, like most others, the United Kingdom government manages to evade the most sensitive questions on the ground of public interest.

In the United States, the protection of the Fourth Amendment[14] is offered to those who are threatened with invasion of their persons or their property. But interpretation of the meaning of this amendment has noted its limitations in certain cases. A passage in the judgment in *Katz* is illuminating:

> Those who wrote the Fourth Amendment knew from experience that searches and seizures were too valuable to law enforcement to prohibit them entirely, but they also knew that they should be slowed down and warrants should be issued only after studied caution.[15]

But neither the US Constitution nor its interpretations was able to contain the violence and the fear of the public mood during the McCarthy period. Through the use of informers and the misuse of private information it became possible to thrust from public life anyone who could be proved to sympathize with or to have sympathized with the Communist movement. It was neither the law nor the Constitution but a journalist (Edward R. Murrow) and a television programme which brought the American people to its senses.[16] The shame of this episode may go some way to explain the strength of the sustained civil rights movement in the United States, which has achieved more solid and lasting gains than civil rights movements elsewhere.

THE DEFINITION OF NATIONAL SECURITY: A CASE STUDY

Most states, in the dangerous post-war world, have set up or developed security systems organized for the twofold purpose of obtaining information about their enemies abroad and maintaining surveillance over their enemies within. The policies and activities of these systems are generally defended on grounds of 'public interest', or 'national security', phrases capable of a number of interpretations. These are, from time to time, subjected to critical examination as the citizen's interest in privacy and freedom of information is frustrated by the state's concern for security. In the United Kingdom, for example, there has been a sustained attempt to find a satisfactory definition through the courts and parliamentary committees. It has had little success as we shall see.

The use of information obtained by telephone tapping was one of the first post-war challenges to the UK government which provoked an official inquiry. The circumstances were that a warrant for the interception of telephone communication between a barrister and his client was authorized by the Home Secretary. The information obtained by this interception was conveyed to the chairman of the

Bar Council, which was considering disciplinary proceedings against the barrister. When this became known there was serious concern about such an abuse of private communication, and a Committee of the Privy Council (Birkett 1957) was set up to review the exercise of this Crown prerogative. The report of the committee was brief, for the evidence put before it was not published. The behaviour of the Home Secretary in releasing information from an authorized wire-tapping received a mild reproof, but there was no recommendation for fundamental change in the existing practice. The committee advised against publishing figures for the number of warrants issued but recommended that they should be reviewed at least once a month. A curious note of reservation by P. C. Gordon Walker anticipated *Katz* v. *United States* (see note 15) in saying that the warrants of interception were themselves legitimate but the purpose for which they were issued should be judged by new and stricter standards, particularly in regard to the detection of crime (Birkett 1957: 174). (Mr Hill, whose phone had been tapped, was a crooked bookmaker and gambler, not a violent criminal.)

Turning to security service interceptions, Gordon Walker argued that these should have two principal objectives: direct counter-espionage and the protection of high secrets of state. He then descended in the scale of priorities and suggested that interceptions should be warranted for 'the prevention of the employment of Fascists and Communists in connection with work the nature of which is vital to the State' (Birkett 1957: 177). The reference to this sinister form of 'positive vetting' may indicate that it was already in use as a result of the Burgess–Maclean scandal and that it should be publicly vindicated.[17] But it may not be too fanciful to suggest that McCarthyism cast a long shadow, which fell on the British establishment, too.

The Birkett Committee caused no storms. By the same token it made little progress towards establishing a reasonable framework for state intrusion into the lives of private citizens. The next decade, however, saw the definition of national interest and national security discussed in the courts as groups of citizens joined in vigorous protest against the nuclear policies of the government. One case in particular was thought to be decisive. It is worth considering in some detail since it became a legal precedent for use in judges' instructions to the jury and is still the judicial view of governmental power (Thomas 1986). During the anti-nuclear protests of the early 1960s a number of people attempted to enter the Wethersfield air base. They were arrested, charged, and prosecuted under section 1 of the Official Secrets Act 1911 on the ground that they had attempted to enter a prohibited place. Convicted of this charge at the Central Criminal Court, they appealed. The appeal was turned down (2 All E. R. 142 [1962]), but a further appeal to the House of Lords was encouraged so that the phrase 'purpose prejudicial to the safety or interest to the state' could be construed. The appeal failed, but the discussion of 'state interests' is highly relevant to the continuing argument about individual liberties and the priorities of government. Raising the question of the divergence between these two interests, Lord Devlin argued that expressions such as these were, in general discussion, used loosely, whereas the meaning in the Official Secrets Act must be in the interests of the state as they are and not as citizens thought that they ought to be. It was argued further that the state meant the organs of government of a national community. It was not, therefore, for the court to debate nor for jury to determine what these interests should be (3 All E. R. 314 [1962]).

Readers of this judgment today might be forgiven for thinking that such interpretations are too simple, and that individual, community, or group interest has won a measurable place in the structure of national interest. In the trial of Clive Ponting,[18] for example, McCowan J. followed the narrow interpretation of 'national interest' suggested by the Law Lords in 1962. He told the jury that, in the light of that decision, the defendant must be guilty. The jury rejected this advice, and Ponting was acquitted.

Although, in the 1960s, the debate about the meaning of 'national interest' was brought to the courts and forced on public attention by demands for the right of protest, developing claims for freedom of information and for the protection of individual privacy were measured by the same point of reference. Both, it seemed, could be denied if the 'national interest' or 'national security' were prayed in aid by politicians or government departments. For this reason, the Committee of Justice (1970)[19] suggested and drafted the legislative framework for a system of checks to be imposed on those who held and those who disposed of information about private citizens. The government of the day was unsympathetic to immediate legislation, announcing instead the setting up of a committee of inquiry (Younger 1972) 'to consider whether legislation is needed to give further protection to the individual citizen . . . against intrusions into privacy by private persons and organisations'. By these terms of reference the administration neatly avoided the trap which might have ensnared it. Public breach of individual privacy did not fall to be considered. The report of the Younger Committee concluded that there was no need for a general law of privacy, although minor adjustments in the criminal and civil law might stop up a few holes. There were few implications for the central government in this anodyne report, and the issue of privacy died for the time being.

The second concern of the private citizen, the right to know what was being done in his name, was subject to more searching examination by the departmental committee, under the chairman-ship of Lord Franks, whose remit was the operation of section 2 of the Official Secrets Act 1911. Unlike the Younger Committee (1972), the committee under Lord Franks (1972) was asked to consider the nature and extent of the claims of 'national security' and the areas in which it might conflict with the citizen's wish for a share in governmental thinking. The four volumes of evidence and the conclusions published by the committee are a rich mine of infor-mation about the attitudes and thought processes of government servants, state security officers, police chiefs, and journalists. The clearest statement of the need for reform of the catch-all provisions of section 2 was made in the evidence of Professor Wade, who declared that 'It is extraordinary that a piece of panic legislation of this kind which is fundamentally inconsistent with a free and civilised democracy should have survived for sixty years' (Franks 1972: (4) 162). This was by no means the feeling of some civil servants and members of the security services. Those who represented the departments of the Foreign and Home Secretaries were reasonably content with the present situation. If changes were to be made they would wish that unchallengeable security classifica-tions should be left in the hands of the ministers responsible for the information to be protected. The Director of MI5 and his legal advisers who, innominate,[20] stressed the importance of section 2 as one of the corner-stones of the country's security, recommended retention of the system. This was the view also of the representatives of the Association of Chief Police Officers.

More interesting, however, than these views and counter-views was the half-expressed and only vaguely appreciated sense that there had been a shift in the popular view of the state's prerogative in defining the area of public interest or national security which citizens must accept. One or two of the Civil Service testimonies referred to the feeling that protest against government policies by disclosure of official information might be more frequent than it had been before. The Foreign Office witness, for example, noted that 'people in the present social atmosphere are much more likely to make information available for ideological reasons than they used to' (Franks 1972: (4) 137). In these exchanges the spectre of minority interests making undesirable changes in the policies of a democratically elected majority, first conjured up by Lord Reid in the Chandler case,[21] was incoherently reintroduced by a witness from the Association of Chief Police Officers: 'It cannot be over-emphasized too much to say that the interests of many people have to be balanced against the interests and security of the country and the community' (Franks 1972:(2) 215). The chief police officer knew what he was afraid of, although he was unsure of how to express his fear.

The Franks Report, like that from the Younger Committee, was laid to rest. It was the turn, once more, of the issue of privacy to dominate the continuing battle between the citizen and the state about control of the acquisition and dissemination of knowledge. Yet another committee (Lindop 1978) was appointed to advise the government on the protection from unauthorized disclosure of data accumulated by government and other services. This committee took a tough line, basing its thinking on Article 8 of the European Convention on Human Rights: 'Everyone has a right to respect for his private and family life, his home and his correspondence.' Commenting acidly upon the unwillingness of the security services to co-operate with it, the committee accepted, nevertheless, their need for secrecy but went on to point out the dangers of this secrecy to the services themselves:

> The proper discharge of the duties of the Security Services entails a dilemma. If the job is to be done properly, it must necessarily be done in secret. If that is so, it can never come under public scrutiny. . . . This leaves the Security Services in a hermetic compartment where they can never discuss their problems with anyone outside their own tight community; thus they are not open to the healthy and often constructive criticism and debate which assures for many other public servants that they will not stray beyond their allotted function. (Lindop 1978: 222)

This analysis of the isolation of the security services of any state should be carved in stone. It gives a clear warning of the vicious circle in which most governments find themselves. For it is they who define the limits of state security and, in making this definition, are guided and advised by an organization whose habits and modes of thought are not subject to healthy criticism. Unfortunately, the Lindop Committee did not take this argument to its conclusion but accepted a notion of national security at its complacent face value.

Before the recommendations of the committee were brought, however incompletely, into legislative effect, the battle between the United Kingdom citizen and his government entered another stage. The case of *Malone* v. *Commissioner of the Metropolitan Police* (No 2) (1979) involved the authorized phone-tap of a suspected criminal who later sought remedy for this intrusion on his privacy by suit against the police force which had carried out the interception. Sir Robert Megarry, who denied the plaintiff's application, contributed, nevertheless, to the development of the case for legislation to control the interception of communications, about which there was increasing unease. He said:

This case seems to me to make it plain that telephone-tapping is a subject which cries out for legislation. In any civilized system of law the claims of liberty and justice would require that telephone users should have effective and independent safeguards against possible abuses.

The government paid only lip-service to this firm statement. In a White Paper, *The Interception of Communications in Great Britain* (Cmnd 7873, 1980), it considered the circumstances of most telephone interceptions and concluded that safeguards against abuse were sufficient. Legislation would not be introduced. The persistent Mr Malone took his case (app. no. 8691/79) to the European Court of Human Rights at Strasbourg, which ruled in August 1984 that Great Britain had failed to satisfy with 'sufficient clarity and precision the scope and manner in which the power to authorise telephone interception was exercised'. For this and other reasons, the government introduced legislation in 1985 to remedy the defects complained of. The scope of the legislation was, however, described as an act of 'dumb insolence' to the European Court (*The Times*, 6 March 1985). It contained no provisions for the control of surveillance, including bugging devices, nor was judicial approval to be sought before a warrant for interception would be issued. Unlawful interception (i.e. without the warranty of the Secretary of State) would become a criminal offence.

In the course of parliamentary discussion of this measure an attempt was made to define the phrase 'national security', so as to make it more clearly a notion of 'defence'. In the House of Lords, however, Lord Denning repeated the judicial opinion that the expression was not capable of legal definition (Hansard, HL vol. 464, col. 869). It was a matter for the Secretary of State and not for judges. In the House of Commons, argument came to an end when it was pointed out that the expression 'national security' appears in Article 8 of the European Convention on Human Rights as a restriction upon individual claims of privacy.

After several years of dispute between the United Kingdom's citizens and their government, there are on the statute book two pieces of legislation which, weak though they are, have brought the nation a little nearer to the laws of the United States and of Western European countries.[22] But all legislation of this sort fails to solve the problem of equality between the citizen and the state in the area covered by 'national security'. In Britain the courts have refused to have a part in framing a definition, maintaining variously that it is a matter for the Secretary of State or for organized government or, in the matter of telephone interception, for legislation. Such a vacuum encourages the secrecy of governments and sustains the disquiet of citizens. For, in the absence of guiding principles, the security services of most countries have been able to evade the kind of supervision and control to which all other organizations of the state must submit. As we shall see, this unnatural freedom has put at risk the liberty and even the lives of citizens in many states.

WARMONGERING AT SECOND REMOVE

The unlawful behaviour of some secret services which undertake operations *outside* the country of their origin is sometimes supported by those who see in these activities a kind of substitute for, or a contribution to, a justifiable war. There are, for example, stories (and often there can be no convincing evidence) about the British secret service plot to assassinate Nasser at the time of the Suez crisis. The tortured politics of the time allowed many to accept this as a justifiable act of war. The Central Intelligence Agency was forced to admit that it had been actively engaged in trying to overthrow the government of Chile. The suggestion that it had also been indirectly involved in the assassination of the commander of the Chilean armed forces embarrassed the American administration and made continued oversight of secret service activities necessary. Congressional committees try to do this, calling the director of the CIA to account when illegal or aggressive action is brought to public attention. The agency has, however, been successful in mounting a number of projects, close to war, in countries whose loyalty was deemed necessary to United States policy. The disastrous episode at the Bay of Pigs began as a covert CIA-backed plan to train Cuban refugees for resistance to Castro. It ended with the unwilling involvement of the United States administration which compelled the resignation of Allen Dulles, Director of the CIA, and Richard Bissell, who had planned and executed the project. During the Vietnam war, the CIA was deeply involved in tracking down and disposing of dissidents (Vietcong sympathizers), in stimulating support for the South Vietnamese in neighbouring states, and in manufacturing information for consumption at home. Little of this activity was manifestly illegal or unpopular, certainly not as long as the Vietnam war enjoyed the support of the majority of the population. Criticism came in the anxious dissection of United States policy when the war came to an end.

Again, in another area of American interest, assistance both open and covert was given to the opponents of the Sandinistan government of Nicaragua. American funds and American advisers supported rebel troops in waging incessant war against government forces. This policy of advice and assistance had the firm support of

President Reagan and of many United States citizens. Trading on this support, United States agents became involved in the mining of Nicaraguan harbours – a degree of zealotry which alarmed Congress and induced it to ban the use of congressional funds for support to the rebels. During the course of this freeze on financial aid, millions of dollars were found for the pursuit of the Central American intervention by selling arms to Iran. The whole exploit was totally illegal and utterly secret until it came to light by revelations in the Middle East. The scandal brought about the resignation of two officials of the National Security Council and cast a shadow over the reputation of the Chief of Staff at the White House and the Secretary of State. Even the President, whose policies were being furthered by the illegal transactions, could not escape suspicion of involvement or at least foreknowledge of the arms deal.

It is not usual for European countries to mount, in time of peace, a full-scale security operation in the territory of an ally. The French action against a Greenpeace ship anchored in a New Zealand port did just this. In an explosion which caused the ship to sink, a member of the Greenpeace team was killed. The involvement of the French military intelligence service was discovered by the New Zealand police, who arrested and secured the conviction of two men and a woman, all of whom held commissions in the French service. Information at a later date indicated that the incident was not a minor matter, but a full-scale operation undertaken to protect the nuclear tests which were about to be made in the area. Negotiations between the French and New Zealand governments (involving, it is suggested, the threat by the French to block New Zealand dairy exports by EEC action) ended in the release to French custody of the convicted officers – a consummation of the affair that shocked New Zealanders and raised a few cynical eyebrows elsewhere. Even in France the defence minister was forced to resign; and some commentators (Derogy and Pontaut 1986) suggest that the French head of state was aware of what was afoot, even if he did not actually promote it.

In the chaotic policies of the Middle East there is plenty of evidence that the secret services of almost every country are aggressively active in areas outside their own jurisdiction. The powerful Israeli security organizations whose activities move in step with their military colleagues normally have the whole-hearted support of their own people. Even this faltered, however, when, after criminal action was alleged against the internal security service (Shin Bet), the administration provided an amnesty for all who were involved, thus avoiding a public trial and possible untoward revelations.[23] Although there appeared to be public support for the amnesty, some felt that neither the state nor its security service emerged well from the incident.

The security and information services of the United Kingdom have, whether they operate in conditions of war or peace, the unique advantage of legislation which can be used to muzzle the disclosures of civil servants or the public discussion of matters thought to affect national security as it is defined by the government of the day. Two cases illustrate the impressive advantages given to the administration in this conflict of interest between the citizen and the state. First, an ex-member of the secret service MI5 attempted, in Australia, to publish his memoirs. These revealed that the interception of communications by MI5 extended to the offices of the Prime Minister in a Labour government. Other innocent citizens, such as trade union leaders and members of CND, were also kept under surveillance as 'subversives'. The UK government sought to prevent publication of these memoirs by action in the Australian courts.[24] The ground upon which this move was justified was not that national security was directly endangered, but that it would be, if members of the security service were to be allowed freedom of disclosure after they left the service.

Justifiable defence measures against a potential enemy were, in another case, the ground for preventing the broadcast of a film by the British Broadcasting Corporation about a new communications satellite.[25] Action by the Special Branch to find out who had leaked information about the project resulted in the seizure of large amounts of documentary and film material from the BBC, the *New Statesman*, and Duncan Campbell.

THE ORGANIZATION AND INFLUENCE OF STATE SECURITY IN THE MODERN WORLD

The strength of security service organizations within the political framework of each state is itself a by-product of the cold war and of the structure of international relations in a world of two-power dominance. The system of alliances and vassalages formed around these two great powers inhibits the use of old-style diplomatic manoeuvres. Consequently departments of state which deal with foreign affairs have lost some of their power and influence. Similarly, departments of defence – certainly in countries sheltered, and indeed neutralized, by the superpowers – will have little independent function unless the superpower partnership breaks down. The principal beneficiary of these declensions in influence has been in all states, security service organizations, whose mastery of the sources of information drawn from within and without state boundaries seems to give them a strong claim to advise governments on their foreign and defence policies. It may also be true that the shift in the balance of power between the old and the new departments of state has had the effect of increasing the power and influence of heads of government, who are themselves, in most states, not only the users but the ultimate controllers of secret service activities.

This can be most clearly seen in the establishment in the United States of a National Security Council which reports directly to and advises the President on security matters. This organization is not, in the real sense, a department of state. But its location and overt function give it strong leverage in the internal battles of the administration. In a similar relationship to the Chief Executive are officers of the Central Intelligence Agency, whose operations are intended to further the defence and foreign policies of the government. On several occasions, however, this remit was taken too literally and had to be restrained by Executive Order. President Ford, President Carter, and President Reagan were all compelled to sign such orders forbidding the involvement of the CIA in assassination plots.

Members of the legislature who are excluded from this circle of security advisers and operatives have made several efforts to control their activities. The Hughes–Ryan Amendment (to the Foreign Assistance Act) and the Intelligence Oversight Act, for example, require the President to keep congressional committees 'fully and currently informed of all intelligence operations'. If that were not possible, 'timely' information should be given of the progress of events. But secrecy is the trade mark, as it is the tool, of security operations. Congress can force full disclosure only when there is some hint that security services have been overzealous or mistaken.

The parallel governmental construction of security institutions in the United Kingdom is the Joint Intelligence Committee of the Cabinet, chaired by the Secretary to the Cabinet. This committee briefs the Ministerial Committee on Intelligence (again a Cabinet committee), which is chaired by the Prime Minister. Theoretically, therefore, Parliament has ultimate control of intelligence operations. Bipartisan agreement has, however, for many years made it impossible for the House of Commons to scrutinize these operations or to establish their cost. The Public Accounts Committee, which could be used to monitor their finances, has in practice been excluded from this area of supervision.

Clearly, then, neither the United States nor the United Kingdom has been able to put to full use, as an effective check upon the operations of its security organizations, a constitutional framework and control by the legislature, on the one hand, or ministerial control with parliamentary accountability, on the other. The increase in the influence of security organizations is, however, not entirely due to the weakening of formerly powerful departments of state. It owes something to the exponential increase in the amount of information now readily available, particularly to the superpowers, through the use of satellites, high-flying observer planes, and sophisticated electronic gadgetry which has made the simple bugging device redundant.[26] The mass of information acquired in this way and analysed and interpreted by security officers has several direct and indirect state benefits. It is of great value in framing external policies and it can be used as a bargaining counter to bring intransigent allies into line.[27]

Such Orwellian structures of information-gathering and control do not help individual citizens to take their place, as the American revolutionaries of two hundred years ago intended that they should, alongside their government in the management of their social and political activities. For the most part the citizen is kept in the dark. Only when mistakes or malfeasance leak out may he have the opportunity to comment or protest about what is happening (although the secrecy surrounding security measures, even when they go wrong, may effectively prevent the open discussion of important political decisions).[28] For the depressing truth may well be that Max Weber's analysis of the weakness of political systems in the face of bureaucratic pressure is correct and that the secrecy of state security systems will be defended *à l'outrance* by elected governments because the very bureaucratic organizations whose interests may be threatened advise not only that continued secrecy is necessary in the national interest but also that the limits of that interest are such-and-such.[29] A grim passage in Weber describes what modern experience has shown to be true:

> They [bureaucratic organizations] acquire through the conduct of office a special knowledge of facts and have available a store of documentary material peculiar to themselves. While not peculiar to bureaucratic organizations, the concept of 'official secrets' is certainly typical of them . . . it is a product of the striving for power.
> (Weber 1968:339)

MAXIMIZING THE POWER OF THE CITIZENRY

So what can the individual citizen do to protect himself from 'arbitrary interference with . . . privacy . . . family, home or correspondence'[30] and to assert his right to freedom of information?

Unquestionably these rights are most powerfully protected if they are set out in constitutional or legislative provisions as they are in the United States and in a number of other countries. But even here there are limits to the citizen's access to information. Foreign relations, defence, and intelligence are in the United States held to be encompassed in the notion of 'national security' which is inaccessible to the body of citizens. Their elected representatives, however, have the right to be briefed, in private if necessary, about security operations. This right has, of late, been vigorously asserted both during the Watergate affair and after the disclosure of the arms deals with Iran. Yet the possibility of public disclosure in an open system of this sort may have the effect of even greater measures of concealment on the part of those who direct or engage in covert operations which are claimed to be in the national interest.[31] Corrupted by deviousness, the institutions of the state have, as we have seen, defied both constitutions and legislative prescriptions.

Yet, where there is no acknowledged right of access and therefore no legislative definition of the matters to be protected, the citizen is in much worse case. The long and yet unfinished battle in the United Kingdom to set down some benchmarks to outline those areas of national interest to be protected from citizen enquiry has failed in its objective largely because there is no legislative expression of rights to information which can be interpreted by courts or claimed by public and parliamentary protest. Indeed, the only legislation which deals with the citizen in relation to the 'public interest' is wholly protective of the state and its organs of government, penalizing the citizen for obtaining or receiving information which is not intended to be in the public domain.

Clearly the citizen's right to know is frustrated both in open and in protective political systems by the determined concealment of operations which governments or their servants do not wish to be subject to enquiry. Such concealment makes recourse to the courts (in open systems) and to the protest of elected representatives (in protective ones) difficult and sometimes impossible.

To penetrate the veil of secrecy and dissimulation which sometimes shrouds the operations of the state in security matters, the citizen must turn to the Fourth Estate. This powerful agent of information-gathering and dissemination has been responsible for a number of reviews of policy which some administrations have been forced to make. In this connection we should note that security organizations and the secrecy of government are best protected in those states where the freedom of the press is severely restricted. That is why the covert operations of the Soviet security services, among others, remain hidden. In the United States, on the other hand, the constitutional support for a free press would make censorship difficult. There is little protection, however, against deliberate disinformation. In the United Kingdom there is an effective informal system (the D-notice system) which may dictate the timing or forbid the publication of news and stories whose disclosure may be contrary to the public interest.[32] The definition of public interest might, of course, include the discomfiture of the government. Only a particularly vigorous and courageous press would bring this to light. But it is not only a high-principled editorial policy which will come to the assistance of the citizen. Investigative journalism of persistence and independence is also important. This, however, can only be facilitated, not provided, by constitutional means.

In the end we may reach the conclusion that, in the battle between the citizen and the state for the control of information, laws and constitutions may be subverted or evaded; judicial redress is limited by definitions of public interest which judges are frequently unwilling to make; financial control of security services may be effective as far as it goes but it, too, is neither comprehensive nor enforceable. Only the vigilance of the citizen and the integrity of the press will prevent the definition by government of the interests of the state that coincide with *their* purposes rather than the rights of citizens. In other words, the Enlightenment notion that individual liberties and desires are at one with and could be realized by representative government may be difficult to attain in the area of national security. Yet this is an area of citizen interest which it is manifestly right to defend.

NOTES

1 In Sweden, possibly the most open of western democracies, income tax returns are published.
2 Social scientists learned a salutary lesson from what become known as the Camelot Project, a research scheme funded by the United States Army. Enquiry was originally to be carried out in Latin American states, though much wider application was envisaged. Its aim was to identify, from various social data, the pre-conditions for internal conflict and to construct the most effective methods of dealing with this. One of the countries suggested as a possible base for the enquiry was Chile. The Chilean government was not told of the plan. When it ultimately became known, there was considerable annoyance. The whole project was cancelled by the US Secretary of Defense, and social scientists were taught to ask questions about the sponsorship of their projects and the use to which social data should be put (Barnes 1979: 46 ff.).
3 See the account of the huge array of information available in computerized form to the UK government in Campbell and Corner (1986).
4 Pinkerton's Detective Agency was in some sense the forerunner of the Federal Bureau of Investigation. Its founder, Allan Pinkerton, foiled an attempt to assassinate Abraham Lincoln in 1861. He was not so successful on the next occasion.
5 The Molly Maguires were organized groups within an Irish brotherhood – the Ancient Order of Hibernians – which undertook the task of 'disciplining' coal-miners in and around Pennsylvania who resisted attempts to unionize them.
6 The key case in the United States is the Haymarket massacre in Chicago. In 1886

a meeting of working men met in Haymarket Square. The police, alleging that the crowd was made up of revolutionary anarchists, arrived in considerable numbers to break up the crowd. A bomb was thrown from a corner of the square, no one knows by whom. There were a number of fatal casualties. A few men of known anarchist views were arrested and tried. Four were convicted and hanged, one killed himself in his cell, and two were imprisoned for life. No one of these was proved to have been implicated in the bomb-throwing (Lydston 1904: 235 ff.).

In Britain the seige of Sidney Street, where two known anarchists, suspected of shooting three police officers, were found to be living, ended in a shoot-out with the police in which the anarchists were killed (Allason 1983: 19–20, Bunyan 1977: 150).

7 The ostensible and indeed one of the real functions of this new organization was to counter the activities of German naval officers on leave or ashore in Britain. They were known to be keeping their eyes and ears open for evidence of British naval preparations for war.

8 This branch of the Metropolitan Police, originally called the Special Irish Branch, was set up in 1883 to counter the threat of Fenian bombings. As this threat diminished, the branch was used as a general secret service. Theoretically responsible to the Metropolitan Police Commissioner, it had strong links, through him, with the Home Secretary, whose concern with a possible anarchist threat determined the next target for the new police department (Allason 1983, Bunyan 1977).

9 The Official Secrets Act of 1889 was brought into being to prevent the leakage of information by civil servants, one of whom had been tried and acquitted of any offence because he had not stolen official papers but simply memorized their contents. In the pre-war hysteria of 1911, section 2 of the Act, which applied the previous penalties to any receipt, transfer, or use of official information by anyone at all, passed quickly through the House of Commons. But it is inaccurate to say that the measures themselves had been hurriedly thought up. They had been cooking in the government pot for some time (Franks 1972).

10 A report in the *New York Times* of 22 December 1974 claimed that there had for many years been an illegal domestic intelligence operation conducted by the CIA. A congressional committee (the Church Committee) investigated the allegations and handed its findings to the Department of Justice, which found itself unable to prosecute in view of the difficulties in proving guilt beyond a reasonable doubt. Operation Chaos, which attempted to find the source of anti-Vietnam activities in American universities was undertaken by the CIA when the FBI was reluctant to be involved.

11 The agents of many countries are attached to their foreign service establishments, sometimes as passport control officers (which keeps them in touch with the local population), as information officers, or simply as third secretaries with an unspecified area of responsibility (Philby 1967: 124).

12 Special Branch officers are, officially, accountable to their Chief Constables, but lack of information about their activities makes public complaint difficult and action by Chief Constables unlikely. Officers of MI5 are civil servants, recruited in the normal way. They are, therefore, responsible for their day-to-day activities to the head of their department and, through him, to the head of the Civil Service. Policy decisions, however, are theoretically a matter for the Intelligence Committee of the Cabinet, which is chaired by the Prime Minister. The distinctions between policy decisions and the methods of their implementation is often unclear.

13 The most recent inquiry was by the Select Committee on Home Affairs, which explained the duties and responsibilities of the Special Branch. Its report (HC 71, 1985) did not clarify the central question of who controls the information-gatherers.

14 Citizens have a right 'to be secure in their persons, houses, papers and effects against unreasonable search and seizure'.

15 *Katz* v. *United States*, 389 US 347 (1967).

16 The CBS television programme *See It Now*, in an edition of March 1954, showed American citizens what was really happening in their country.

17 The unhealed wound in the secret services of the United Kingdom is the fact that members of a group of young men who studied at the University of Cambridge in the 1930s became committed communists and voluntarily gave their services to the security forces of the USSR. The most prominent of these, Guy Burgess, Donald Maclean, Kim Philby, Anthony Blunt, and perhaps others were in key positions in the government services of the United Kingdom. Burgess, Philby, and Blunt held influential positions in British security, while Maclean held an important Foreign Office post. In 1951, after the revelations of Krivitsky, a Russian defector, Burgess and Maclean were warned by their contacts that discovery of their real position was imminent. Both fled to Moscow. Philby survived for another decade but he too fetched up there in 1963. Blunt managed to continue living in the United Kingdom, although his treasonable activities were known.

18 Clive Ponting, a senior civil servant in the Ministry of Defence, passed to a Member of Parliament documents concerning the sinking of the Argentine cruiser *General Belgrano*. He was charged under section 2 of the Official Secrets Act. The trial lasted from 28 January to 11 February 1985 and was reported in *The Times* throughout.

19 Justice is the name given to the British section of the International Commission of Jurists.

20 The foolish obsession with the protection of the identity of members of the security services in the United Kingdom (which persists to this day) contrasts with the openness, in superficial matters at least, of the security services in the United States. Openly displayed in a children's bookshop in the UK is a very workmanlike account of the activities of the CIA, naming names and providing the dates and locations of important doings and decisions.

21 In the House of Lords judgment, Lord Reid made the interesting comment that 'the interests of the State did not necessarily mean the interests of the majority'.

22 It is ironic that while this stately *pas de deux* in the courts and parliamentary committees was going on, the security services in Britain are alleged to have been engaged in the grubby business of surveillance of the government itself, on the ground that it might be too readily influenced by foreign propaganda of a subversive kind. Trade unionists and officers of the Campaign for Nuclear Disarmament were then and allegedly still are subject to the constant attention of MI5.

23 Two Arabs, suspected of placing explosives in a bus after they had hijacked it, were handed over to Shin Bet by the military. The lawful procedure would have been to prosecute the Arabs if, after questioning, there was reason to believe they were involved. Instead, they were shot out of hand.

24 Peter Wright defended his claim for justifiable disclosure in a case before the Australian courts in late 1986. At the time of writing final judgment has not yet been given.

25 Duncan Campbell of the *New Statesman* produced a programme for the BBC which revealed the existence of a spy satellite being built in the United Kingdom for surveillance of Soviet communications.

26 See the analysis (R. Cecil, 26 September 1986, p. 1076) in *The Times Literary Supplement* of two opposing views of intelligence gathering. One (West 1986) stresses the predominance of electronic surveillance ('SIGINT') in present-day and future spying. The other (Laqueur 1986) takes the view that the activities of spies and informers ('HUMINT') will remain crucial to the information services and to all governments.

27 The New Zealand government recently brought such discipline upon itself after it had refused to receive United States warships into New Zealand ports unless they were guaranteed to be free of nuclear motive power and nuclear weapons.

28 The defence of 'national security' is used to conceal incompetence and political chicanery perhaps as often as it preserves the safety of the state.

29 'Generally speaking the trained permanent official is more likely to get his way in the long run than his nominal superior the Cabinet minister who is not a specialist' (Weber 1968: 338).

30 Article 17, United Nations Covenant on Human Rights.

31 There are, from time to time, suggestions that something akin to the United Kingdom official secrets legislation might reduce the temptation to deviousness by protecting the secrecy of matters confided to United States government servants in the course of their duties. Experience in the UK does not support this view.

32 A committee, ultimately responsible to the Cabinet, called the Services, Press, and Broadcasting Committee, has the power to issue to the press and broadcasting services a direction (a D-notice) that the publication of such-and-such information should be delayed or suppressed. This instruction is normally obeyed, although there is no legal sanction for ignoring it. The most recent acknowledged example of a notice of this kind was during the court case in Australia which concerned the memoirs of Peter Wright. British journalists were prevented from giving the name of the legal adviser to MI5, although it had already been revealed in the Australian press.

REFERENCES

Allason, R. (West, N.) (1983) *The Branch 1883–1983*, London: Secker & Warburg.

Andrew, C. (1985) *The Secret Service*, London: Heinemann.

Arendt, H. (1963) *On Revolution*, London: Faber & Faber.

Barnes, J. A. (1979) *Who Should Know What*, Harmondsworth: Penguin Books.

Birkett Committee (1957) *Report of the Privy Council on the Interception of Communications*, (Cmnd 283), London: HMSO.

Bryce, J. (1890) *The American Commonwealth*, London: Macmillan.

Bunyan, T. (1977) *The History and Practice of the Political Police in Britain*, London: Quartet Books.

Campbell, D. and Corner, S. (1986) *On the Record: Surveillance, Computers and Privacy*, London: Michael Joseph.

Derogy, J. and Pontaut, J. M. (1986) *Enquête sur trois secrets d'etat*, Paris.

Encyclopaedia Britannica (1910–11) Kropotkin on 'Anarchism', vol. I, 11th edn, Cambridge.

—— (1910–11) McDonald on 'George Washington', vol. XXVIII, 11th edn, Cambridge.

Franks Committee (1972) *Report of the Departmental Committee on section 2 of the Official Secrets Act* (Cmnd 5704), London: HMSO.

Justice (British section of International Commission of Jurists) (1970) *Privacy and the Law*, London: Justice.

Laqueur, W. (1986) *The World of Secrets*, London: Weidenfeld & Nicolson.

Lindop Committee (1978) *Report of the Committee on Data Protection*, (Cmnd 7341 esp. c8), London: HMSO.

Lydston, G. F. (1904) *The Diseases of Society*, Philadelphia.

Moore Jr, B. (1967) *The Social Origins of Dictatorship and Democracy*, London: Allen Lane.

Ording, A. (1931) 'Le Bureau de Police du Comité de Salut Public' in *Skrifter der Norske Videnskpas Akademi* (2) 3.

Palmer, R. R. (1964) *The Age of the Democratic Revolution*, Princeton: Princeton University Press.

Philby, K. (1967) *My Silent War*, London: Panther Books.

Roberts, R. (1973) *The Classic Slum*, Harmondsworth: Penguin Books.

Thomas, R. M. (1986) 'The British Official Secrets Act and the Ponting case', *Criminal Law Review*, August: 491–510.

Weber, M. (1968), in T. Parsons (ed.) *Theory of Social and Economic Administration*, New York: The Free Press.

West, N. (1986) *GCHQ. The Secret Wireless War*, London: Weidenfeld & Nicolson.

Younger Committee (1972) *Report of the Committee on Privacy*, (Cmnd 5012), London: HMSO.

Index